A SOCIETY FIT FOR

HUMAN BEINGS

D0933185

SUNY Series in
Constructive Postmodern Thought

David Ray Griffin, editor

A SOCIETY FIT

FOR HUMAN

BEINGS

E. M. Adams

STATE UNIVERSITY OF NEW YORK PRESS

Published by
State University of New York Press, Albany

For information, address the State University of New York Press,
State University Plaza, Albany, NY 12246

Production design by David Ford
Marketing by Anne M. Valentine

Library of Congress Cataloging-in-Publication Data

Adams, E. M. (Elie Maynard), 1919–
    A society fit for human beings / E. M. Adams.
        p.   cm. — (SUNY series in constructive postmodern thought)
    Includes bibliographical references and index.
    ISBN 0-7914-3523-7 (hc : alk. paper). — ISBN 0-7914-3524-5
(pb. : alk. paper)
    1. Humanistic ethics.   2. Civilization, Modern—1950–   I. Title.
II. Series.
BJ1360.A33   1997
144 — dc21   96-52316
                                                CIP

10 9 8 7 6 5 4 3 2 1

For Crawford Logan Taylor, Jr.

friend and champion of philosophy and human values

Of the progress of the souls of men and women
　　Along the grand roads of the universe, all other
　　Progress is the needed emblem and sustenance.

– *Walt Whitman, "Song of the Open Road"*

contents

introduction to SUNY series

CONSTRUCTIVE

POSTMODERN

THOUGHT

The rapid spread of the term *postmodern* in recent years witnesses to a growing dissatisfaction with modernity and to an increasing sense that the modern age not only had a beginning but can have an end as well. Whereas the word *modern* was almost always used until quite recently as a word of praise and as a synonym for *contemporary*, a growing sense is now evidenced that we can and should leave modernity behind—in fact, that we *must* if we are to avoid destroying ourselves and most of the life on our planet.

Modernity, rather than being regarded as the norm for human society toward which all history has been aiming and into which all societies should be ushered—forcibly if necessary—is instead increasingly seen as an aberration. A new respect for the wisdom of traditional societies is growing as we realize that they have endured for thousands of years and that, by contrast, the existence of modern society for even another century seems doubtful. Likewise, *modernism* as a world view is less and less seen as The Final Truth, in comparison with which all divergent world views are automatically regarded as "superstitious." The modern world view is increasingly relativized to the status of one among many, useful for some purposes, inadequate for others.

Although there have been antimodern movements before, beginning perhaps near the outset of the nineteenth century with the Romanticists and the Luddites, the rapidity with which the term *postmodern* has become widespread in our time suggests that the antimodern sentiment is more extensive and intense than before, and also that it includes the sense that modernity can be successfully overcome only by going beyond it, not by attempting to return to a premodern form of existence. Insofar as a common element is found in the various ways in which the term is used, *postmodernism* refers to a diffuse sentiment rather than to any common set of doctrines—the sentiment that humanity can and must go beyond the modern.

Beyond connoting this sentiment, the term *postmodern* is used in a confusing variety of ways, some of them contradictory to others. In artistic and literary circles, for example, postmodernism shares in this general sentiment but also involves a specific reaction against "modernism" in the narrow sense of a movement in artistic-literary circles in the late nineteenth and early twentieth centuries. Postmodern architecture is very different from postmodern literary criticism. In some circles, the term *postmodern* is used in reference to that potpourri of ideas and systems sometimes called *new age metaphysics,* although many of these ideas and systems are more premodern than postmodern. Even in philosophical and theological circles, the term *postmodern* refers to two quite different positions, one of which is reflected in this series. Each position seeks to transcend both *modernism* in the sense of the world view that has developed out of the seventeenth-century Galilean-Cartesian-Baconian-Newtonian science, and *modernity* in the sense of the world order that both conditioned and was conditioned by this world view. But the two positions seek to transcend the modern in different ways.

Closely related to literary–artistic postmodernism is a philosophical postmodernism inspired variously by pragmatism, physicalism, Ludwig Wittgenstein, Martin Heidegger, and Jacques Derrida and other recent French thinkers. By the use of terms that arise out of particular segments of this movement, it can be called *deconstructive* or *eliminative postmodernism.* It overcomes the modern world view through an anti-world view: it deconstructs or eliminates the ingredients necessary for a world view, such as God, self, purpose, meaning, a real world, and truth as correspondence. While motivated in some cases by the ethical concern to forestall totalitarian systems, this type of postmodern thought issues in relativism, even nihilism. It could also be called *ultramodernism,* in that its eliminations result from carrying modern premises to their logical conclusions.

The postmodernism of this series can, by contrast, be called *constructive* or *revisionary.* It seeks to overcome the modern world view not by eliminating the possibility of world views as such, but by constructing a postmodern world view through a revision of modern premises and traditional concepts. This constructive or revisionary postmodernism involves a new unity of scientific, ethical, aesthetic, and religious intuitions. It rejects not science as such but only that scientism in which the data of the modern natural sciences are alone allowed to contribute to the construction of our world view.

The constructive activity of this type of postmodern thought is not limited to a revised world view; it is equally concerned with a postmodern world that will support and be supported by the new world view. A postmodern world will involve postmodern persons, with a postmodern spirituality, on the one hand, and a postmodern society, ultimately a postmodern global order, on the other. Going beyond the modern world will involve transcending its individualism, anthropocentrism, patriarchy, mechanization, economism, consumerism, nationalism, and militarism. Constructive postmodern thought provides support for the ecology, peace, feminist, and other emancipatory movements of our time, while stressing that the inclusive emancipation must be from modernity itself. The term *postmodern,* however, by contrast with *premodern,* emphasizes that the modern world has produced unparalleled advances that must not be lost in a general revulsion against its negative features.

From the point of view of deconstructive postmodernists, this constructive postmodernism is still hopelessly wedded to outdated concepts, because it wishes to salvage a positive meaning not only for the notions of the human self, historical meaning, and truth as correspondence, which were central to modernity, but also for premodern notions of a divine reality, cosmic meaning, and an enchanted nature. From the point of view of its advocates, however, this revisionary postmodernism is not only more adequate to our experience but also more genuinely postmodern. It does not simply carry the premises of modernity through to their logical conclusions, but criticizes and revises those premises. Through its return to organicism and its acceptance of nonsensory perception, it opens itself to the recovery of truths and values from various forms of premodern thought and practice that had been dogmatically rejected by modernity. This constructive, revisionary postmodernism involves a creative synthesis of modern and premodern truths and values.

This series does not seek to create a movement so much as to help shape and support an already existing movement convinced that modernity can and must be transcended. But those antimodern movements which arose in the past failed to deflect or even retard the onslaught of modernity. What reasons can we have to expect the current movement to be more successful? First, the previous antimodern movements were primarily calls to return to a premodern form of life and thought rather than calls to advance, and the human spirit does not rally to calls to turn back. Second, the previous antimodern movements either rejected modern science, reduced it to a description of mere appearances, or assumed its adequacy in principle; therefore, they could base their calls only on the negative social and spiritual effects of modernity. The current movement draws on natural science itself as a witness against the adequacy of the modern world view. In the third place, the present movement has even more evidence than did previous movements of the ways in which modernity and its world view *are* socially and spiritually destructive. The fourth and probably most decisive difference is that the present movement is based on the awareness that *the continuation of modernity threatens the very survival of life on our planet.* This awareness, combined with the growing knowledge of the interdependence of the modern world view and the militarism, nuclearism, and ecological devastation of the modern world, is providing an unprecedented impetus for people to see the evidence for a postmodern world view and to envisage postmodern ways of relating to each other, the rest of nature, and the cosmos as a whole. For these reasons, the failure of the previous antimodern movements says little about the possible success of the current movement.

Advocates of this movement do not hold the naively utopian belief that the success of this movement would bring about a global society of universal and lasting peace, harmony, and happiness, in which all spiritual problems, social conflicts, ecological destruction, and hard choices would vanish. There is, after all, surely a deep truth in the testimony of the world's religions to the presence of a transcultural proclivity to evil deep within the human heart, which no new paradigm, combined with a new economic order, new child-rearing practices, or any other social arrangements, will suddenly eliminate. Furthermore, it has correctly been said that "life is robbery": a strong element of competition is inherent within finite existence, which no social-political-economic-ecological order can overcome. These two truths, especially when contemplated together, should caution us against unrealistic hopes.

However, no such appeal to "universal constants" should reconcile us to the present order, as if this order were thereby uniquely legitimated. The human proclivity to evil in general, and to conflictual competition and ecological destruction in particular, can be greatly exacerbated or greatly mitigated by a world order and its world view. Modernity exacerbates it about as much as imaginable. We can therefore envision, without being naively utopian, a far better world order, with a far less dangerous trajectory, than the one we now have.

This series, making no pretense of neutrality, is dedicated to the success of this movement toward a postmodern world.

David Ray Griffin
Series Editor

preface

We often take a self-congratulatory view of our society and culture. Indeed, America has thought of itself from the beginning as a shining light on a hill and a model for the whole world. There is a lot in the American way of life that is good and right, a lot that is better than ever before or anywhere else. Yet the American people recognize that we have deep problems, but we are confused about what to do because we have no clear understanding of our cultural and social condition. This is not surprising, for our intractable problems and our greatest successes arise from the same source.

The greatest success of modern Western civilization has been in the pursuit of wealth and power. With the rise of the middle class in the early modern period, the culture was transformed by the increasing emphasis on materialistic values. Our culture-generating stance toward the world shifted in the early modern period from a dominant concern with what reality requires of us (what we ought to be and ought to do) to a governing concern with what we want and how to get it. First, there was the Great Reformation. As intellectuals sought to understand the world in a way that would give us power to impose our will on nature, they wrought a reformation in our way of understanding the world. Value and other humanistic categories were eliminated from the scientific descriptive/explanatory conceptual system. The world was disenchanted. No longer did we recognize any inherent ends or normative laws in nature. Reality was understood as imposing only factual limits on our will, limits that could be progressively pushed back by advances in science and technology. Human identity, values, morals, and religion have been problematic ever since. As Ernest Gellner says, "Our identities, freedom, norms are no longer underwritten by our vision and comprehension of things" (*Legitimation of Belief* 1974, p. 207). Nietzsche referred to this intellectual development as "the death of God." C. S. Lewis spoke of it as "the abolition of man."

Second, there was the Great Transformation. In all societies prior to the nineteenth century, as Karl Polanyi points out (*The Great Transformation* 1944), the social order was dominant, with the economic order ancillary to it, but during the past two centuries the economic order became dominant, forcing the social order into a subordinate, diminished, and transformed role, increasingly dominated by the rationality of the marketplace.

Until the latter part of the nineteenth century, education focused on the moral, civic, cultural, and religious enterprises, which we may call simply the "humanistic" enterprise, for short, but ever since the economic order became dominant, education has become increasingly geared to the needs of the economy. Liberal education has been replaced by career education, with general or core education designed as the common denominator of various career-education programs. The culture in general is shaped by materialistic values and economic concerns.

With the humanistic culture (i.e., the moral, civic, artistic, and religious culture) intellectually undermined and with the dominance of the economic order driven by the rationality of individual self-interest maximizers, the social infrastructure that nourishes the human spirit and supports the civic enterprise has progressively disintegrated. There is little wonder that many families are dysfunctional, that the crime level is high, that psychotherapy is a thriving business, and that antidepressant drugs are big money-makers.

The modern regulative and welfare state arose to protect human beings, the social order, and the environment from the ravages of the economic juggernaut as well as to service the economy itself and to keep it thriving. The modern state has had its successes. It has been a major player in our economic success and it has put something of a human face on what otherwise would be a satanic mill. But like the economy, its successes generate new problems.

The regulative and welfare state has become weighted down with a bureaucracy that operates more by rules and regulations than by informed practical judgment; furthermore, in our civilization, the bureaucracy lacks the kind of civic culture, commitment, and public confidence and support that would make it work well. And consider the evils of welfare dependency, especially under the conditions of poverty. But in spite of all its weaknesses and failures, the regulative and welfare state is essential to the economy and the society under capitalism. With the weakening of the humanistic culture and the impairment of the social order, it is the only effective moral counterweight we have to the economic order, with its morally blind, ruthless rationality. A big capitalistic economy makes big government inevitable.

Our problems are deep. There is no real solution in an unleashed economy or increased governmental action. The culture, our human identity, the social order, and our major institutions need serious rethinking. This is not a job the government can do; only a change in our dominant culture-generating values and ways of thought would bring about the cultural and institutional reforms we need. The government, however, can encourage and facilitate the broad-based critical self-examination and the creative thinking necessary for cultural and social renewal.

In this book, I contend that the modern Western mind is deranged, that the values of our culture are inverted, that the virtues required for the success of our economic and military systems are morally corrupting, that our dominant intellectual vision of humankind and the world generates a profound human identity crisis and undercuts the humanistic dimension of the culture that supports the human enterprise, and that our civilization is on a self-destructive course. The only real corrective, I contend, is a radical transformation of our culture and social order by shifting our priorities from materialistic to humanistic values (those indigenous in the moral, civic, artistic, and religious enterprises), by giving the framework of thought in lived experience and the humanistic culture priority over that of the sciences in shaping our intellectual life, by subordinating the economic enterprise to the humanistic enterprise, and by replacing capitalism as we know it with a humanistic economy.

In the first chapter, I give a brief philosophical diagnosis of our cultural condition and social ills and make a summary case for realistic humanism (i.e., the objective validity of the basic humanistic categories, especially the categories of value and meaning) and the need for a humanistic cultural reformation. These are matters I have argued in detail over the past forty years in professional journals and in a trilogy of books (*Ethical Naturalism and the Modern World-View* 1960, 1973, 1985; *Philosophy and the Modern Mind: A Philosophical Critique of Modern Western Civilization* 1975, 1985; and *The Metaphysics of Self and World: Toward a Humanistic Philosophy* 1991). Readers who would like a fuller philosophical argument, in dialectical debate with alternative views, for my diagnosis of our cultural condition and for realistic humanism should consult these works. I would recommend also *Mind, Value, and Culture,* edited by David Weissbord (1989), in which sixteen philosophers critically examine these theses in my work.

At a time when philosophy is accused of being a highly technical discipline devoted to in-house problems of little concern to the public, the burden of this book is to remind the philosophical community and to show the educated public the importance of the philosophical problems in our culture and the relevance of the technical work of philosophers for our civilization; and, specifically, to explore the import of realistic humanism for our human identity, the framework for a successful life, and the structure of society. I discuss in particular a humanistic way of thinking about and reforming the family, education, the economy, government, the military, and religion. The concluding chapter is about steps we can take toward such a humanistic turn and the development of a constructive postmodern civilization.

There is no going back to an earlier stage of our history as some would have us do. We must work our way through our modern culture, preserving what is good and right in our way of life, to some new stage of civilization that will make for human growth and the flourishing of the human spirit.

This work offers my vision, however cloudy, of what a new humanistic stage of civilization might be, but it is not merely a personal vision. It is a vision from the perspective of realistic humanism. It is the product of years of philosophical criticism of our culture and efforts to reconstruct the foundations of modern Western civilization in a way that would solve long-standing philosophical problems in our culture and make sense of the human enterprise. It is a vision backed by arguments that challenge deep-seated commitments of the modern mind — arguments about our knowledge-yielding and critical powers and how the culture reveals or obscures the structure of the world. It is a rationally accountable vision of an integrated culture and a social order that would support the human spirit by reopening the wells of meaning.

The book is not a manifesto for political action, but a call for serious in-depth cultural criticism and an invitation for culturally aware people to join with concerned citizens in all walks of life in thinking deeply about the human enterprise and the kind of society that would make for human growth and well-being. It is important to bring our critical powers to bear on fundamental problems in our culture and to bring about a corrective change in our organizing and governing values and ideas. There can be no radical social change without deep cultural change. It is my hope that a humanistic understanding of the culture and the world will emerge, with intellectual respectability, from research centers for philosophy and cultural criticism; that this understanding will reform education and religion; that a humanistic cultural reformation will occur through heightened cultural awareness at all levels of the population; and that the cultural transformation will give rise to a society fit for human beings.

Although I have tried to make the text as reader-friendly as I can, the first three chapters of the book are more abstract and perhaps more demanding for some readers than the later chapters. This is because they focus on and attempt to reconstruct our thinking about fundamental matters about which our civilization seems to have gone wrong. We cannot, or so I contend, come to grips with the widely recognized personal and social problems in our way of life without dealing with these basic philosophical issues. Yet, for the most part, our culture and educational system do not prepare us to think effectively at this level. Nevertheless, I invite, indeed I urge, serious readers to learn to think deeply on these matters, for only in that way can we bring these controlling issues under our critical review and mastery. In the later chapters, I hope readers, at least for the sake of understanding the text, will approach the material from the perspective of realistic humanism and the humanistic understanding of the human enterprise, even if they are not prepared to embrace this perspective.

Given the popular conception of humanism as an atheistic philosophy opposed to religion, perhaps I should make it clear in the beginning that humanism, as I am using the term, is opposed to scientific naturalism, not theism. Indeed, the humanistic perspective, as I have already indicated, is the perspective of life, morality, art, religion, and the humanities. It is contrasted with the technological/scientific approach in which we try to understand the world in a way that will enable us to control the conditions of our existence and to impose our will upon the world. Humanism defines the world in terms of categories of thought grounded in selfhood and the full spectrum of lived experience. Naturalism defines the world in terms of the categories of scientific thought grounded in sensory experience. Naturalism, not humanism, is an atheistic philosophy opposed to religion. It is a contention of this work that an integrated culture and a unified world view are possible only from within the humanistic perspective and framework of thought.

One further caution. Many people seem to think that any one who believes in value truths and an objective morality is a social and cultural conservative. But quite the contrary. If there is a normative dimension of reality and if we have the capacity for moral knowledge, then we have an objective ground for criticizing and reforming the culture and the social structure. Conservatives typically do not have faith in our ability to correct and to make advances in morality and to make social reforms accordingly. They tend to think that we have no guide other than the historically evolved morality and social structure. They typically want people to fit into the society as it is rather than trying to reform society to make it fit for people.

I have made use of some ideas and material from several previously published papers, most of which were developed from this project while it was in progress. They include "The Moral Dilemmas of the Military Profession," *Public Affairs Quarterly*, vol. 3, no. 2 (April 1989): pp. 1–14; "Rationality and Morality," *The Review of Metaphysics*, vol. 46, no. 4 (June 1993): pp. 683–97; "Character: The Framework for a Successful Life," *The Southern Journal of Philosophy*, vol. 33 (1995), no. 1: pp. 1–17; "Art, Culture and Humanism: Religion for Our Times," *Religious Studies and Theology*, vols. 13–14, nos. 2 and 3 (December 1995): pp. 17–30; and with Warren Nord, "Continuing Liberal Education," *National Forum* 1988 (Winter): pp 44–45. I am indebted to these journals for permission to draw on these articles in the present book. I am also indebted to Temple University Press for permission to use several sentences from my *Religion and Cultural Freedom* (1993) and *The Metaphysics of Self and World*, as indicated in notes 3 and 7 for chapter 10.

I am grateful to Thomas Alexander, Paul Betz, Harry Jones, Seth Holtzman, Warren Nord, and the readers for the SUNY Press for correction of a number of errors and many helpful suggestions for the clarification of ideas and improvements in the text. I am also greatly indebted to David Griffin, editor of this series, and Clay Morgan, David Ford, and the editorial staff of the Press. And I owe a special debt of thanks to my students in Philosophy 37 at the University of North Carolina at Chapel Hill in the fall term in 1994 and in 1995. Their excitement and enthusiasm for the point of view and ideas in this book were most encouraging and rewarding.

xxii   •   A SOCIETY FIT FOR HUMAN BEINGS

It is with great pleasure that I dedicate this work to my former student and good friend Crawford Logan Taylor, Jr. His humanistic vision and unwavering commitment to the cause we share gladdens my heart and gives me hope in the evening of my life.

1

Culture and the Human Enterprise

The term "culture" is often used broadly to include all the ways and products of human work, expression, and creativity. In this broad field, we may distinguish among the material, the social, and the semantic cultures. The material culture consists of all the physical tools, buildings, equipment, and things we produce for our use and enjoyment. The social culture consists of all the social instruments, structures, and systems we generate or create to meet human needs and to satisfy human aspirations. The semantic culture consists of our language and symbols, our ways and products of semantically appropriating and organizing reality and possibility, the wisdom acquired for guiding and directing our lives and institutions, and the ways and products of artistic comprehension and expression. It is the semantic culture with which we are concerned here. For simplicity, I shall speak of it simply as the "culture."

1

DEVELOPMENT OF THE CULTURE

The culture of a people is their most important product and pos-
session. It is what most distinguishes human beings from all other
creatures. Our culture determines, in broad outline, what we become and how we live as individuals and function as societies. It provides the concepts in terms of which we define ourselves and the
world, and the framework of beliefs and commitments by which we
live and run our institutions, including the norms in terms of which
we judge truth and falsity, perfection and defect, well-being and sickness, right and wrong, success and failure. But the culture itself
may go awry as the genome of a species does sometimes. (Think of
the saber tooth tiger and the Irish elk; they developed efficient sin-
gle-purpose but ultimately self-destructive physical features.) Reality
may not be any more tolerant in the long run of mistakes deep in
the culture of a people than in the genetic constitution of a species.

The genetic structure of a biological species is an "expression"
of the "wisdom" of nature. The culture of a people, although the
product of human powers, is also a product of "nature" in a sense.
At least early cultures must have been largely the product of unconscious processes and operations that involved little thought of
the end being realized. Human beings had to have a measure of
cultural capital before they could take a rational, critical role in the
correction, reconstruction, and advancement of the culture.

Early in human history, generations, finding a culture in place,
took it to have been given along with nature by some higher power,
for they did not understand how it, or at least the most important
aspects of it, could have been generated by human beings. And
when some individuals dared to amend or to change the received
culture, the proposed amendments or changes were either rejected or accepted as revealed or inspired by a higher being. Historically,
cultural institutions concentrated, for the most part, on the preservation and transmission of the culture. It took a long time for
human beings to realize that the culture was a human product and
that critical intelligence could be brought into the reconstruction

and ongoing development of the culture. This insight was the defining mark of the Enlightenment. Although the ancient Greek Enlightenment anticipated this development, only in modern times have societies developed and supported institutions with the mission to examine, correct, and advance the culture on all fronts. Even now the public frequently demands that our graduate/research universities concentrate on their teaching mission. The idea that the culture is our most important product and that the whole human enterprise depends on it is still incomprehensible to those who are unconscious of their culture and its role in forming their identity and defining their lives and their world. And there are those who, even at this late date, insist that the moral and religious dimensions of the culture come from a higher source and are immune to human criticism and improvement. This of course tends to stagnate the whole culture. The culture is logically webbed in such a way that protection of one part of it from critical reconstruction and advancement restrains developments in other sectors that would present a logical challenge to the protected area.

The culture is both an extension and product of our native semantic powers. We share with other animals the power to hold our bodily and environmental conditions *present to* ourselves in sensory experience. And no doubt many animals share with us, at least in a rudimentary form, the power to hold things present to themselves in memory and imagination.

We need to be careful, however, about what we mean by "present to *themselves*" in speaking of animals. We are not warranted in attributing to culture-free animals the kind of selfhood that culture-bred human beings have. Indeed, we are not warranted in attributing to them the same kind of sensory experiences, to say nothing of the same kind of memory and imagination. Neither are we warranted in attributing to pre-cultural "human beings" anything like the selfhood and modes of experience, memory, and imagination that we find in ourselves. But clearly animals, including pre-cultural "human beings," have rudimentary semantic powers. Some bodily and environmental conditions are present to such beings in ways that evoke behavioral responses. No doubt some constitutive memory (the power to integrate and to hold together in experience a complex happening that takes time to occur) and imagination are involved in any form of awareness that can evoke a behavioral response, but recall memory and pure imagination (imagination without immediate sensory stimulation) seem to require more integration of subjective states and acts than simple sensory awareness. Behavioral memory (the capacity to respond to a new situation in ways learned from similar situations in the past) comes earlier than memory as a purely internal rerun of an earlier experience. The capacity for this kind of memory seems to be required for imagination as the capacity for pre-run or feigned sensory experiences of actual or possible situations. Memory and imagination that can function with some independence of sensory stimulation and behavior require a budding self — some internal organization of subjective states and acts that can function as a system without engaging the whole organism behaviorally.

It is often said that human beings differ from other animals primarily in that we develop and use physical tools to extend our bodily power over our environment, but our most important tools are semantic — language and symbols. They enhance our semantic power to appropriate things, to hold them present to ourselves, and to relate to them on the basis of their semantic presence to us. Indeed, language and symbols have opened to us the past, the future, the distant present, the depths, the heights, the wholeness, and the order of the world, even the possible, the contrary to fact, what ought to be, and what must be. Hence, language and symbols not only greatly expand our power over our physical environment, but also make possible our selfhood, our semantic world, and the cultural/social structures in which we dwell. Without language and symbols we would not be human beings. We would have neither sufficient semantic power nor a sufficiently integrated subjective center for rational thought, for higher emotions and aspirations, for a rational will, or for a human life.

Of course our selfhood, our mental powers, and our culture had to develop together; they are interdependent. But somehow our early ancestors, with their native semantic powers, were able to develop a protolanguage; and with the added powers this rudimentary language made possible, they were able to improve their semantic tools. This has been, and still is, an ongoing process. But at some point in the long history of culture and self-development there was a sufficiently enlarged and empowered self and sufficient cultural capital for the culture to takeoff. We are now at the point in human history where we are more consciously committed to, and involved in, self development and the advancement of the culture than ever before. But many are pulling back from efforts over the past century to bring critical intelligence into the development of the society. Yet developments in the culture play themselves out in the society, even though there is usually a social lag.

In early societies, as previously remarked, the culture developed more or less unconsciously and uncritically. This does not mean that there were no restraints or requirements on the culture. Cultural developments that met needs of the society tended to survive and those that did not perished. Cultural criticism, however, was rudimentary and lax. The contents of most experiences, even the contents of some fantasies and dreams, were taken to obtain in the world. This resulted in a very rich but chaotic world. The history of cultural development has been a progressive tightening of the principles of logical and epistemic criticism and a correlative shrinking of the world in some respects and enlargement of it in others, with increasing orderliness. As we turn the pages of history from antiquity toward modern times, as David Hume remarked in the eighteenth century, it is amazing how much more orderly the world becomes.

THE INVERSION OF MODERN
WESTERN CULTURE

Of course cultural development, whether by unconscious or critical processes, can go awry, even at very basic levels. The most fundamental requirement on the culture is that it be fruitful in the human enterprise. How this requirement works, however, depends on the way the human enterprise is understood, and, of course how the human enterprise is defined is itself a cultural matter.

A culture defines the human enterprise by its dominant values — what the people count most important and give top priority. The values of a culture are shown by the kinds of institutions that are dominant in the society, the kinds of people who are most admired and those who are looked down on — those who are given the top rewards and benefits or the most prestigious awards, and the kind of people who are considered villains, undesirables, or simply failures.

It is a commonplace to say that our modern Western culture is materialistic. Obviously for-profit institutions are dominant in our society and the primary marks of personal success are wealth and power. We count poverty and powerlessness the major indications of failure. In America everything has to be organized around, or yield to, economic growth and military supremacy, including even the family, community, education, and our intellectual life. We organize our private lives, for the most part, for the pursuit of ever greater material gain or power or both. So the fundamental demand made on our culture is that it provide us, individually and collectively, with the knowledge and understanding, the virtues, the skills, and the social organization for success in the pursuit of these goals. We count our culture superior to others because of its greater success by these standards.

Moslem fundamentalists, however, call America, the recognized vanguard and leader of Western civilization, "the Great Satan." They are afraid that their people will succumb to the Western way of life, with a radical transformation of their historic civilization for the worse. They are joined in their judgment on our modern way of life by many Christian fundamentalists in our own society. Yet both the Moslem and Christian fundamentalists seem prepared to embrace our commitment to wealth and power without realizing that this is the underlying cause of all that they find most abhorrent and threatening in our civilization.

When a culture is organized around, and the dominant restraints and requirements on it are, the twin objectives of wealth and power, it naturally develops in a way that is fruitful in terms of these objectives. This means that knowledge must be conceived in a way that, at least in principle, provides human beings with the understanding needed for remaking or controlling the conditions of their existence. In short, the world must be understood in such a way that it lends itself to human domination and exploitation. For these reasons, our civilization has generated the modern scientific conception of knowledge and the naturalistic world view presupposed in our technologically oriented science.

All the great classical civilizations were based on humanistic values and were largely defined by them, at least in their intellectual vision of humankind and the world and in their artistic and religious life, if not in their practical endeavors. Humanistic values are grounded in the needs or normative requirements of selfhood and society — the needs the satisfaction of which is essential, not so much for bodily well-being and comfort, but for the moral well-being and enrichment of the spirit of persons, families, communities, institutions, and states. We all need self-respect and the respect of others; we need to love and to be loved; we need meaningful experiences and relationships; we need meaningful activities and work that involves self-expression and self-fulfillment; we need a stable social order in which we feel at home; we need justice and beauty in our lives; we need the call of the universal and the transcendent to lift us out of the perversions of self-centeredness and to orient us toward higher values; we need roots in a historical and metaphysical context that makes sense of our existence and sustains the human spirit. These are only some of the more important humanistic values.

Social institutions and the society as a whole are sources of humanistic values in their own right; they have their own normative requirements. An institution or a society may be well-formed or deformed, healthy or sick. But the normative structure of society, as the next chapter will explain, is grounded in, and derivative from, the normative structure of persons. Human beings need and normatively require a healthy family, a healthy community, healthy specialized institutions, and a healthy society. And by extension human beings require what the family, the community, the specialized institutions, and the society require.

Of course we cannot separate human beings and their society. They do not form two realities. Without a cultural community there would be no human beings; and without human beings there would be no cultural community. Yet it seems obvious that the ground of the whole complex lies in the constitution and needs of human beings as persons. We advance the culture and the cultural society for the benefit of human beings and the environment in which human beings dwell. Indeed, we have a responsibility for ourselves and for our corner of the universe. Although this responsibility may be more deeply grounded in the structure of the universe, we find it inherent in our constitution as human beings. Whatever transcending imperatives there may be, they do not override those inherent in our own constitution by which we define and live our lives and participate in organizing and running our society.

Within the humanistic perspective, we may raise questions about whether the deep or holistic structure of the universe normatively requires or needs human beings. In other words, is the universe coming to a higher level of fulfillment or perfection in human existence? It might be contended that the universe is coming into self-knowledge in human culture and that the processes of nature reach a new level in the knowledge-based creativity of human beings. Furthermore, it might be said that a level of freedom is achieved in human rationality that is not known to exist elsewhere. All of these developments may be regarded as fulfillments or perfections of being. If there are normative requirements of the universe being fulfilled in humankind, then such requirements are humanistic in the sense that the concept of them falls within our humanistic conceptual framework.[1]

The revolution in Western civilization in the early modern period that gave rise to our modern culture was occasioned by a shift in the organizing and governing interests of the civilization, a shift in priorities from humanisitic to materialistic concerns. Of course people have always tried to satisfy their materialistic needs, but in the modern period in the West the quest for wealth and power over the conditions of our existence became the overriding concern. Unlike humanistic values that have to do with our identity and inner well-being, we have an external relationship with materialistic goods and so they are replaceable; they may be bought or exchanged. Hence the dominance of the market economy and its mode of rationality in the modern world.

This shift in dominant values not only gave rise to the hegemony of the market economy, but also a transformation of the culture. It led us to look to our sensory encounters with our physical environment for the data with which to construct an intellectual account of the world that would, at least in principle, make possible mastery of nature in a way that would enable us to exploit it for our materialistic purposes. It is not surprising that the world we know from this approach is one that imposes only factual limits on our will — limits that may be progressively pushed back by advances in science and technology. Such a world is factually constituted through and through without inherent ends, totally devoid of inherent structures of meaning and normativity; it is a world that imposes no normative limits and no normative requirements on us. Natural change, according to this view, is not value oriented; that is, causality engages only present or antecedent elemental or environmental factual conditions. It is a world made to order for us to impose our will upon it.

A major difficulty, however, is that this is a world in which we ourselves cannot dwell; it is no longer our home. Indeed, the impact of the modern intellectual revolution on the culture in terms of which we define ourselves, live our lives, and organize and run our institutions has been devastating. It has cut the grounds from under our humanistic culture — our human, social, moral, political, aesthetic, and religious concepts and ways of thought. The dominant philosophical issue in our culture for the past three hundred years has been how to understand the humanistic dimension of selfhood and the culture (especially subjectivity, normativity, knowledge, rationality, agency, freedom, morality, art, and religion) in light of the modern theory of knowledge based on sensory experience for data-gathering and theory confirmation, and the resulting naturalistic world view presupposed in modern science. It is widely held that, regardless of the human consequences, some interpretation or explanation of the humanistic dimension of the culture must be found that protects the scientific view that reality is only factually constituted through and through, without either a value or a meaning dimension. Consequently, it is not uncommon for religious beliefs to be regarded as superstition, art as subjectivistic expression, and moral and political beliefs as ideology (that is, as not part of the cognitive enterprise but only expressions of the preferences and choices of the power structure of the particular historical community, without any claim to objective truth). Even some defenders of religion and morality contend that neither religion nor morality is a part of the cognitive enterprise. Some conservatives claim that religion is a matter of unreasoned faith that is immune to criticism and that moral judgments are grounded in faith-based assumptions or beliefs, with no cognitive ground.

With our increasing emphasis on wealth and power, growing dependence on science and technology, and rising levels of education geared to economic growth and military power, the scientific/technological way of thought dominates our practical endeavors, our intellectual life, and our educational system, and, even though we complain about the lack of scientific literacy, the broad outlines of the naturalistic world view of science is widely accepted. The result is that the humanistic dimension of the culture has become problematic, gone soft, and lost much of its power in our lives and in our institutions.

Our identity, our rationality, our norms and values, and our social institutions are no longer underwritten by our intellectual vision of humankind and the world. In disenchanting the world in our effort to gain mastery of it, we evicted ourselves. It is a world in which we as knower-agents have no place. Our selfhood, indeed the whole human phenomenon, is rendered a dangler without a context that makes our lives meaningful and our existence intelligible. Faced with this absurdity, the dominant response has been to reprocess ourselves conceptually in such a way that we and the whole human phenomenon will fit into the world as scientifically defined. But in doing so, we deny our humanity.

This is not just a matter of belief; it disturbs our selfhood, for we are knowledge-based beings. Each person is constituted by one's normative self-concept as a human being and as the individual one is. We define and live our lives in terms of our understanding of ourselves and our world; and our life attitudes and inner strength depend on how we comprehend ourselves as human-beings-in-the-world. So we mutilate ourselves and thwart our lives by intellectually reprocessing ourselves so that we will fit into the scientifically defined world. The ways of thought that disenchanted the world and reduced the idea of God to a superstition by eliminating structures of meaning, normative laws, and teleological causality from our view of things, when turned upon ourselves, render personhood a superstitious idea and dehumanize us; they reduce us to complex physical systems, without a subjective or normative dimension (without freedom and dignity), subject to the same naturalistic causal laws and pointless processes of change as everything else.

One major response to this development at the present time is skepticism about the whole intellectual enterprise or outright rejection of any foundation in knowledge or the structure of reality for any part of the culture, not even for modern science itself. This is often proclaimed as "postmodernism," but it is not so much a counter response to modern naturalism as a logical consequence of it, for modern naturalism, fully developed, eviscerates the cognitive enterprise, including science itself.

Such a culture fails most fundamentally. It undercuts and defeats the human enterprise, however it is conceived. The modern conception of knowledge and the world view generated by our dominant cultural perspective undermine the humanistic foundations of human identity, society, and the whole culture, even science and the technological enterprise on which our wealth and power depend. Clearly something is radically wrong. We can conclude only that modern Western civilization is misdirected and self-defeating. It is only within the humanistic perspective and its conceptual system that we can achieve a coherent culture and a unified world view. Indeed, it is only within the humanistic perspective and a humanistic culture that we can live as human beings and run our institutions.

THE NEED FOR A
HUMANISTIC RENAISSANCE

The human plight in our age cries out for a humanistic renaissance, one that would be nothing less than a major cultural revolution. The humanities, philosophy and the disciplines that study life and culture in terms of a conceptual system that is grounded in selfhood and lived experience, should play a major role in preparing the way for cultural renewal. They constitute our primary disciplinary approach to cultural criticism and reconstruction. But unfortunately the humanities are ill prepared for the task, for they themselves have become perverted in their search for intellectual respectability in our scientific/technological age. In their study of the culture and its ways of understanding the world, the humanities, for the most part, concentrate on facts and accept modern science as the paradigm of knowledge and intelligibility. The first order of business for the humanities is to examine themselves. They must regain their own proper perspective, their authentic framework of thought, and their own methodology; and, then, they should assume their proper role in the study and criticism of life and culture.

The humanistic culture is primarily the culture that is grounded in, forms, and expresses selfhood, lived experience, and social reality. It is the culture in terms of which we define and live our lives and organize and run our institutions and society. The dominant humanistic categories are those of meaning, subjectivity, the mental, spirit, value, normativity, selfhood, personhood, agency, acts, rationality, freedom, lives, cultural objects, social entities and structures, human history, teleological causality, and the like. These categories are extended to ultimate reality in religion and theology. The humanistic culture contrasts with the modern scientific culture, which is defined by our concern to know and to understand the world in a way that would, in principle, give us power to manipulate and to control the conditions of our existence and to impose our will upon the world. The scientific categories are grounded in, form, and express only sensory observation of, and thought about, objects in a way that guides action on things. In modern times, the scientific descriptive/explanatory conceptual system has been cleansed of all humanistic concepts. Its dominant categories are existence, factuality, energy, physical objects, events, quantity, and nonteleological causality that engages only elemental or antecedent existential and factual structures.

The modern scientific world view gives us a world devoid of an inner realm of subjectivity, inherent structures of meaning, normativity, values, rationality, and teleological causality. Modern naturalism takes this world picture to be true of the world as it is. Human beings and their cultural and social products are intellectually reprocessed to fit them into the world understood in this manner. So it has to give either a subjectivistic or a reductionistic interpretation of the humanistic culture, especially the language of value and meaning. Realistic humanism, on the other hand, is the position that the humanistic culture is objective, that the correct world view must be based on an integrated culture that is grounded in and expresses the whole range of human experience and thought, and that it must be such that it makes sense of and reinforces the human enterprise as we know it in lived experience.

Realistic humanism is based on the knowledge-yielding character of both our emotive (affective and conative) experience in which the value dimension of the culture is grounded and the modes of experience in which the language of meaning is grounded, namely, reflection on our own subjectivity and behavior and perceptual understanding of the expressions and behavior of others. If these modes of experience do not give us knowledge-yielding access to dimensions of value and inherent structures of meaning in the relevant subject matter, we must interpret the language of value and meaning in purely factual or physicalistic terms or as not part of the language of knowledge. While some philosophers have taken the latter alternative for value language, it is difficult to see how it could be an option for the language of meaning. The realistic humanist, however, takes emotive experience, reflection on our own subjective states and acts, and experience of the expressions and acts of others as capable of yielding perceptual knowledge of their subject matter, thus opening to us dimensions of reality not available through sensory observation alone. (For a summary argument for these claims, see "The Case for Realistic Humanism" in Appendix A.)

The basic humanistic categories are value and meaning. The realistic value theory assumed in this work (but argued for in appendix A and in earlier books) takes *ought* to be the basic value concept. Accordingly, something is good if it ought to be or if it is more or less the way it ought to be; and something is bad if it ought not be, if it is not the way it ought to be, or if it is a way that it ought not to be. An "ought" sentence indicates a normative requiredness in its subject matter. It indicates that a given situation normatively requires a being of a certain kind (e.g., the work load in the office requires another secretary); or it indicates that a given individual ought to have certain features (e.g., James's job requires that he learn how to use a computer). These are social situations, but anything that may be by its own inner dynamics well-formed or deformed, healthy or sick, or mature or immature not only possesses certain features and properties, but also has an inherent normative structure. It ought to have or ought to come to have a certain form or it ought to function in a certain way. In other words, some subject matters have things, features, or structures *normatively in* them as well as existentially or factually in them. Normativity, like factuality, is a mode of constitution; it is a way in which various kinds of elements or features are bound together to form identifiable wholes. To describe this kind of subject matter factually (i.e., in terms of its elements and their factual relationships or the features and properties exemplified in it) is to leave out an important dimension of it, namely, its normative or value dimension. And surely such normative structures in some things or situations make a causal difference; they must be caught up in the causal dynamics inherent in the subject matter. This is teleological causality — the causal constraint or pull of what ought to be in its own realization. In other words, contrary to a widely held dogma in modern thought, value concepts must have a descriptive/explanatory role in our intellectual efforts to know and understand some subject matters, especially in the biological and behavioral fields.

Meaning is the other most distinctive humanistic category. Subject matter with an inherent structure of meaning has a logical form and a semantic (or intentional) content (e.g., a sensory experience, memory, desire, feeling, thought, intention, act, image, picture, symbol, text, or anything of the kind). We may say that any such subject matter has something *semantically in* it, as distinct from having something existentially or normatively in it. In other words, meaning or intentionality is another mode, along with factuality and normativity, by which some things are constituted. Something with an inherent structure of meaning has its identity and unity in terms of its logical form and what is semantically in it, even though it may have a factual and normative dimension as well. Subjective (or mental) states and acts are the primary inherent structures of meaning, but all cultural and social entities and structures have a meaning dimension. And surely inherent structures of meaning are involved causally in behavioral and social dynamics, if no where else.

If philosophers, humanities scholars, and other cultural critics should regain confidence in the foundations of the humanistic culture along the lines of realistic humanism, they could play a powerful role in bringing about the humanistic renaissance we seek.

HUMANISTIC CRITICISM AND

SOCIAL REFORM

In critical studies of the culture, we need to distinguish among the social character, the structure of feeling, and the mind of a culture.

The social character of a culture is constituted by the human identities, institutions, offices, and roles that the culture generates and legitimizes. With respect to human identities, a culture may be tribal, nationalistic, or cosmopolitan; aristocratic, class-based, or meritocratic; racist, sexist, or egalitarian. With respect to institutions and offices, a culture may be humanistic or materialistic, according to whether the dominant institutions and offices serve primarily humanistic or materialistic needs. Of course there is overlapping. The family, for example, is primarily a humanistic institution, but it serves many materialistic needs as well. It serves fewer materialistic needs in advanced technological/industrial/service societies than in earlier times when people depended less on the market economy and the government. On the other hand, a bank, which is primarily a materialistic institution, may provide career opportunities for people that may be integrated into their identities and their lives in a way that enhances their sense of self-worth and makes their lives more meaningful.

Of course materialistic needs must not be neglected. They include the need for food and drink, conditions for bodily health and comfort, physical security, and the like; they also include the need for the necessary material or economic means of satisfying the humanistic needs of individuals, institutions, and the society as a whole, for ends without means are only dreams. The danger to be avoided, however, is the cultural conversion of material means into ends themselves — the pursuit of wealth and power as a means to more wealth and power, or, what is as bad, a cultural emphasis on the accumulation of material wealth or power, leaving the ends to be achieved by means of it to uncultivated or even harmful and dehumanizing desires, passions, and whims.

Everyone understands and seeks materialistic values; they are objects of universal concern. All of us want food and drink, bodily health and comfort, security of body and property, and the material means for doing what we like and having what we want. So it is not surprising that materialistic values become dominant. Unlike higher values, they appeal to all without regard to moral character or the level of education and refinement.

Talk about higher values and the cultivation and refinement of affective sensibilities sounds like elitism in a culture that has expunged value concepts from its descriptive/explanatory language. Cut loose from its grounding in reality, value language is tied to and defined in terms of desires and affective experiences, with no recognized value reality or conceptual system in terms of which desires and affective experiences can be educated or judged and ranked. Any effort to cultivate, refine, and instruct our value experiences and attitudes that goes beyond attending to or instructing about their factual conditions is taken to be cultural imperialism — the effort to impose the likes, desires, and preferences of an individual, class, or ethnic group on others.

However, if realistic humanism is true, and the case for it is convincing, then attitudes, feelings, desires, and aspirations can be appraised, cultivated, and educated. People may be prepared educationally to attend to and to feel the pull of higher values and normative requirements. Indeed, higher values move people more powerfully than materialistic values. Wars, for instance, are always fought in the name of higher values, for it is difficult to get people to make major sacrifices for purely materialistic reasons.

The social character of a culture is judged, in part, by the structure of feeling of the people. The emotive quality of, and the basic attitudes generated by, lived experience within the personal identities and social forms of the society constitute an experiential judgment on the social infrastructure of the society and on the culture embodied in it. People who are formed by and live within a culture and its social structures have some sense of the judgment of their own experience and the experience of those with whom they live in close relationships. But perhaps the most reliable access to the structure of feeling of a society is through its expression in the art and the psychopathologies the society produces. Although the art and the reports of counselors and psychotherapists constitute a reservoir of emotive data, they stand in need of interpretation and assessment by humanistic scholars and critics.

The artistic culture and the reports of psychological counselors, however, will reveal only the general judgment of lived experience on the social character of the culture or some aspect of it; it will only indicate whether the society is more or less healthy or suffering from some serious disorder. If there are social pathologies, neither the art nor the psychotherapist's reports on the malaise of individuals will be of much help in diagnosing what is specifically wrong. Social scientists can provide empirical data and theories that will help social critics locate particular social disorders, and philosophers can locate deep troubles in the culture that underlie some kinds of personal and social disorders.

It is the task of philosophers to examine the cultural mind of a civilization — that is, the basic organizing and governing interests, ideas, and beliefs that shape how the people think and act. The governing interests define the people's culture-generating stance toward the world; they shape, or at least influence, the basic ideas and beliefs in terms of which the people order their experience, define the world, live their lives, and organize their society. Even if the dominant interests that shape the culture and the society are being more or less satisfied, the verdict of lived experience may be that the culture and the social structure are thwarting or distorting the identity and the lives of the people. Philosophers, sensitive to logical difficulties in the deep structure of the culture, may find that the basic ideas and beliefs that govern the way the people organize their experience and define the world are inconsistent with the unavoidable presuppositions of human experience, thought, and action. And they may find that the false ideas and assumptions in the culture about the knowledge-yielding powers of the human mind and the basic structure of the world were generated by the society's culture-generating stance toward the world. The fact that the organizing and governing interests generate a distorted, life-destructive culture and social structure is sufficient reason to call them into question. And a philosophical exploration of the nature of selfhood and society may reveal what the culture-generating stance of human beings should be.

There is general agreement that materialistic interests define the culture-generating stance of modern Western civilization and many critics agree that we are suffering from cultural inversion. It is a thesis of this work that, if we are going to have a culture and a social order oriented toward growing and nurturing human beings, we must restore humanistic values to their proper governing role in our lives, in our culture, and in our social order. This is a big order; it is the greatest challenge of our age.

Philosophers need to expose the basic faults in the foundations of our culture by an examination of the philosophical perplexities that the culture generates; and they should propose and debate in the intellectual community ways of achieving coherence in the foundations of the culture that would preserve its life-supporting functions. There could emerge from such debates a vision of humankind and the world that would underwrite the human enterprise properly defined in humanistic terms. This will not be easy, however. Philosophers, being products of the culture, usually try even desperate measures to validate the prevailing cultural mind before they will consider alternatives. Philosophy was said to be the handmaiden of theology in the Middle Ages; and it is, for the most part, the handmaiden of science in our age. Nevertheless, philosophy proved itself to be a powerful revolutionary force in the transition from Christian feudalism to modern Western civilization, both in dismantling the old and in building the new culture. And it can be such a force again for a humanistic cultural revolution in our time.

In order for the intellectual vision and conceptual resources of a humanistic philosophy to grip the imagination of the age and conceptually inform and structure the whole range of human experience, thought, and behavior, and thus effect a cultural revolution, there would have to be a responsive cultural climate. The people, especially the trend-setters and opinion-makers, would have to come to realize that our dominant way of life is failing us and that the trouble lies with our governing values and ways of thought. The big problem is how the people, in living their lives and running their institutions, can shift from our reigning materialistic values and naturalistic ways of thought to humanistic values and a humanistic vision of humankind and the world.

Philosophers, humanities scholars and critics, and students of society should work together on how our society can heal itself; but the healing is something that the society must do itself, for healing can come only from within. A deranged culture and a disordered society, if left to blind historical forces, are likely to grow worse. Like the damaged self, a pathological society needs probing self-examination and reeducation; it needs to reconstitute its value system by turning toward humanistic values and to rethink its ways of thought and behavior in light of its new orientation.

In a humanistic culture under a realistic interpretation, human beings, morality, and society would be understood in quite different categories than in our present scientifically oriented culture; the human enterprise and success in life would be conceived in radically different ways, with the emphasis on human growth and inner well-being rather than economic growth and military power; education would be a very different process; and the major institutions would be revolutionized. In the following chapters, we shall explore what these transformations would be like. In the concluding chapter, we shall consider some steps we can take to bring about such a society.

2

HUMAN BEINGS AND

SOCIETY

A Humanistic View

Our human identity and the norms by which we live and govern society are no longer underwritten by our comprehension of things. As we bring ourselves and society under the categories of scientific thought, we deny our humanity, morality loses it objectivity, and authority collapses into a power structure. Our purpose here is to reformulate and validate a humanistic view of persons, morality, and society.

Human beings are peculiar beings. Ancients regarded them as an anomaly, neither gods nor mere creatures of nature. The gods were said to be jealous, threatened by the rational and creative powers of human beings and determined to keep them in their place. According to a Greek myth,[1] at the creation of animals, Epimetheus was given the task of distributing talents among them for their self-preservation. When Prometheus inspected the work of Epimetheus, he found that human beings, unlike the other animals, had been left naked and defenseless. Feeling sorry for the helpless creatures, Prometheus stole fire and the mechanical arts from the workshop of the gods and gave them to the humans. Zeus was upset about divine powers being given to creatures, but he knew that human beings would not survive without further divine attributes. So he sent Hermes to bestow a sense of justice and reverence on each of them so that they could organize and live peacefully in society and engage in cooperative endeavors.

The biblical creation myth says that human beings were created in the image of God and given dominion over all other creatures on earth. But it also contains the Garden of Eden story according to which it was not God's plan for human beings to have knowledge-yielding powers. When Eve and then Adam ate the forbidden fruit from the tree of knowledge of good and evil, they had to bear the consequences as divine punishment. They became subject to shame and guilt feelings, they had to live with awareness of their pending death, Eve had to suffer greater pain in childbearing and be subject to her husband, and Adam had to work hard to make a living from the earth. The whole biblical story is one of God's continual struggle with human beings in their knowledge-based striving for power in the service of their own ends.

What is unique about human beings, as these ancient cultures recognized, is that they are knower-agents. I use this description to differentiate human beings from purely behavioral agents who act in response to stimuli under impulse or instinct. As knower-agents, human beings may act sometimes in response to sensory stimuli under impulse or instinct, but more characteristically they do not accept instinct, impulse, or stimuli at face value. They operate with a normative self-concept (one that imposes internal restraints and requirements on themselves) and with knowledge, principles, plans, and critical judgment. They are engaged in defining and living a life under the guidance of their own knowledge-yielding and critical powers, a life that has its identity and unity in terms of a life plan that holds it together like the plot of a novel.

Being culturally generated and having knowledge-yielding, reflective, and critical powers, a somewhat normal and more or less mature human being is a self integrated under a normative self-concept and has a world unified under a descriptive/ explanatory conceptual system. These are not just facts about human beings. If a human being is not a self more or less integrated under a governing self-concept and does not have a world more or less unified under a descriptive-explanatory conceptual system, then that human being is either not normal or not mature. This indicates that human beings have an inherent normative structure such that, if they do not develop their knowledge-yielding and critical powers and become a more or less integrated self under a normative self-concept and have a world more or less unified under a descriptive/explanatory conceptual system, something will have gone wrong; they will be defective as human beings; they will not be able to live a human life.

Furthermore, more or less normal and somewhat mature human beings are, by their inherent normative structure, under an inner imperative for their self-concept and their world view to be correct. Any inconsistency or other indication of error in either is disturbing and motivates one to try to correct the matter. We all want, not only our experiences, beliefs, and actions to stand justified under critical examination, but our identities, lives, and general world view as well. This is no ordinary want; it bears on us from within as a categorical imperative. No one can sacrifice or seriously compromise it without doing damage to one's identity and self-respect, for it damages the integrity of one's selfhood and one's life.

THE THINKING SELF

We do not have to convince people that they ought to be logical. Logical appraisals of our experiences and beliefs tap into the organizing and governing principles of our minds. Everyone with somewhat normal and mature human powers finds oneself already operating under inner logical imperatives, for one is committed to the consistency and correctness of one's perceptions and beliefs in being a thinking self. A thought is one's own, not so much by being a member of a set of thoughts occurring in one's mind, but only when one's mind (one's total mental complex) as a functioning whole endorses or embraces it. As long as one is of two minds on a subject, one has not made up one's mind and is not prepared to put forth a specific thought or belief about the matter in question, for he or she has none. Making a truth-claim or taking something to be the case requires the unity of one's mind; the unity of one's mind involves logical integrity. Thus, the very nature of a mind normatively requires that one be consistent and correct in one's thoughts — that one's truth-claims, perceptual takings, and beliefs stand justified under logical criticism. If one is not already committed to being logical, no one can teach him or her anything.

This is not all. As thinking beings, we require that what we take to be the case make sense, that it be intelligible. This is a matter of our being able to fit whatever we take to be real into a context; ultimately this means fitting it into our view of the world order. A unified mind requires a unified world view. If we take the content of a perception or belief to be real but cannot fit it into a place in the world, the world order as we know it is threatened, and a challenge to our view of the world threatens the integrity of our minds, for it challenges the consistency and correctness of our fundamental assumptions and beliefs. Hence, as thinking beings, we are under an inherent imperative to render intelligible whatever we take to be real; that is, the normative structure of our minds requires an explanation for whatever we take to obtain in the world and it requires a world view that makes such explanations possible. The human mind cannot be content with things or events that do not make sense.

THE MORAL SELF

Neither do we have to convince people that they ought to be moral, but this needs more showing. Just as thinking beings are committed to the unity and integrity of their minds (and thus to the consistency and correctness of their perceptions and beliefs, to the intelligibility of the real, and to the unity and correctness of their world view), rational agents are committed to the unity and in-

tegrity of their lives and thus to the justification and meaningfulness of their actions, for otherwise their lives would not be their
own — they would be a hodgepodge of impulsive actions or hap-
penings; they would be, at best, like a tale told by an idiot. Furthermore, rational agents are committed to the intelligibility, and
thus to the meaningfulness, of their lives in their commitment to
the intelligibility of whatever they count as real. This requires a
world view in which meaningful and worthwhile lives are possible. We are compelled in these commitments by inner imperatives
grounded in our nature as thinking selves and rational agents.

One's self-concept is the organizing and governing principle and
driving force of one's life. It is involved in and governs what one
counts as options among possible actions; it determines one's feelings of insult, embarrassment, shame, guilt, disappointment, failure, self-reproach; and the opposite feelings: ambition, drive, satisfaction, pride, self-respect, self-approval, and the like. In other
words, one's self-concept defines the parameters of one's life, charts
one's course, and drives, pulls, and steers one along life's way. One's
deepest and strongest emotions and motivations are tied to it. The
principles and criteria of self-criticism are found in it. Indeed, one's
core self-concept, one's concept of oneself *as a human being,* shapes
one's moral feelings and appraisals not only of oneself but of other
human beings as well. Moral emotions and appraisals would be
too weak to govern one's life unless the moral point of view were
anchored in one's normative self-concept and understood as grounded in one's self-hood.

We have to distinguish different levels or dimensions of one's
normative self-concept. The most obvious distinction is between
one's concept of oneself as a human being and one's concept of
oneself as the particular individual one is. Regardless of one's upbringing and circumstances, everyone is a human being; and everyone's self-concept must include what one ought to be or ought to
become as a human being in one's particular circumstances. Moral
appraisals of the behavior of an individual reflect on him or her as
a person in much the same way as medical appraisal of a physician's work reflects on him or her as a physician. In other words,
one's moral appraisals of one's own behavior or that of another

normative requirements, or fails to give them appropriate consideration. In short, one is rational in action to the extent one's acts are guided and justified by responsible beliefs and value judgments about oneself and the situation one is in. We demand of ourselves that our actions stand justified under rational appraisal — that they be right or at least all right.

Of course rational appraisals operate within a culture. We have no chance of reaching a consensus on rational appraisals without reaching a consensus in beliefs and other value judgments about the relevant situation. Even if this is possible in principle, it is often *practically* impossible. But the relativistic thesis about rational appraisals claims that a consensus in rational appraisals is impossible in principle. The position is based on either a subjectivistic view of value judgments or a relativistic view of basic conceptual systems or both. Realistic humanism rejects both theses.[3]

We may conclude that the rational thing to do is what the situation normatively requires or allows one to do. In other words, the rational thing to do, objectively speaking, is to act in accordance with reality, or at least in accordance with the best available beliefs about reality. This may sound like a widely accepted current view, but the view of reality operating here goes against the grain of modern thought.

According to the typical modern view, there is no objective normative structure and so reality imposes no normative limits and requirements on rational agents. But according to our version of value realism, each human being has an inherent normative structure. And with somewhat normal, mature human powers, one is under an inner imperative, one grounded in both one's human nature and in one's well-formed self-concept, to define and to live a life of one's own that would be worthy of one as a human being and as the individual one is. This means that one is under an imperative, an imperative that is a responsibility, to define and to live a life that would pass muster under rational criticism. Correlative with this inherent imperative are certain rights: what one must be free to do and have the means to do if one is to be able to fulfill this human responsibility. These rights impose normative limits and requirements on other human beings. Other human beings have the same inherent normative structure as oneself, the same defining responsibility and correlative rights. Anyone who defines and lives a life that is not responsive to the normative limits and requirements imposed on him or her by the normative structure of other human beings or any other aspect of the environment is living a life unworthy of a human being. Such a life is not a moral life; it will not stand approved by moral appraisal. Furthermore such a life is not a rational life; it will not pass muster under rational criticism; it is not a life lived in accordance with reality. Here we find that moral appraisals and rational appraisals overlap. Indeed, moral appraisals just are rational appraisals that take into account the moral dimension of the situation. It can never be rational to ignore moral limits and requirements.

THE NORMATIVE STRUCTURE OF SOCIETY

We live and have our being in social space, and that space is occupied by a variety of social entities and structures. Persons are the basic or elemental social entities. Indeed, personhood is the basic social office; it is a natural office in contrast with conventional ones. As previously observed, the defining responsibility, enabling powers, and correlative rights of personhood are inherent in the normative nature of human beings — what they by their natural constitution ought to become and the kind of life they ought to live. Nevertheless, human beings have their more specific identity as individuals, largely in terms of their relationships to other persons and the offices they hold and the roles they play in social structures. Thus, persons are not only in society and occupy offices, play roles, and stand in relationships in it, but the social structure is internalized in them. We are who we are largely in terms of our relationships, offices, and roles. We are sons or daughters of particular parents and have a set of relatives and a line of ancestors; we come from a particular cultural community and speak its language and participate in its ways. Even if we adopt a new community and learn its language and its ways, our origin will remain with us, even if in an adulterated form. We are husbands or wives or single persons; we are fathers or mothers or childless; we are engaged in some enterprise or hold some office or position, and so forth. We cannot be divorced from all such relationships and positions; indeed, we cannot give up any of them without affecting our identity. We are not independent social atoms and society is not simply a collection of independent persons in complex external relationships.

A society is a complex, integrated, more or less self-sustaining and self-governing organization of social entities, offices, roles, and structures. In addition to persons as the most elemental, the class of social entities includes families, businesses, schools, hospitals, religious institutions, and states — whatever social organization that deliberates and acts as an agent. All of these may be thought of as social structures; but we may include under the concept "social structure" our institutional ways of relating and behaving as well as such things as the managing, purchasing, and marketing structures of corporations; the faculty and administrative structures of universities; the economic, health-care, educational, governmental structures of societies; and so forth.

Of course without people there would be no society, but the society is no more a collection of individual people than the human body is a collection of cells. A society can maintain its essential identity over time with all the individual members replaced; and it can undergo considerable change while maintaining most of its members. If all the members of a society should suddenly perish from some toxic gas that enveloped the territory, the society would become a reality of the past except as an abstraction, for it is a social structure embodied in its members; they give it substance and vitality.

In addition to the people and the social structure, there is another important factor that must be taken into account, namely, the semantic culture. It is not only expressed in the society's linguistic products, artistic works, and material culture, but it is embodied in the subjectivity and behavior of the people and in the institutional ways and social structures of the society. We are more accustomed to thinking about the way the culture structures and informs the subjectivity and behavior of people than with how it is embodied in institutions and social structures. But clearly the assumptions, beliefs, and general value judgments of a culture are to be found in the institutional ways and social structures of the society. Every institution has its functions, the offices of an institution are structured to serve the ends of the institution, and each office is constituted by a set of responsibilities and rights. A complex set of assumptions, beliefs, and value judgments are embodied in the whole institutional structure. In addition, racial and gender judgments may be built into the employment practices of the institution; and the ways of treating, and the demands made on, the employees may show assumptions about human beings and the governing values of the institution.

Individuals are bonded to their society by virtue of embodying in their subjectivity and behavior the same culture that is embodied in the institutions and social structures of the society. But when individuals do not internalize the culture embodied in the social structures of the society or find the institutional assumptions, governing values, and ways of the society grating on their intellectual and moral consciences, they may become alienated or even angry and hostile. Acculturation of individuals and social reform must be continuing processes in a free society where the culture is dynamic and progressive.

Stable societies tend to generate individual members who will more or less fit into and emotionally embrace the existing social order. This is accomplished for most individuals largely by the process of growing up in the society and absorbing and being taught the culture embodied in the social structures and prevailing institutional ways. Some think that there is no other way to go in growing people, that we have no other guidelines. But obviously this does not work for societies that are unstable or in rapid transition, regardless of why they are undergoing change. Nor does it work in societies with a free culture that is open to ongoing criticism and rational development, especially with science-based technological innovations. A free society committed to cultural and technological progress can achieve stability only by the institutionalization of social reform. And the institutionalization of social reform must be guided rationally. This means that we must be able to judge the existing social order and to reform it according to the way it ought to be. Hence, the social structures that have evolved historically cannot be the source of our norms.

I have spoken of how a social structure embodies a structure of meaning — the culture of the society. This inherent structure of meaning includes the culture's dominant beliefs and judgments. A society's embodied value judgments may be at variance with its own inherent normative structure. This is parallel with the way in which individuals may embrace in their self-concept normative assumptions and judgments about what they ought to be or ought to become that are not in line with their inherent normative structure as human beings or as the individuals they are.

Each more or less self-directing human being, as previously observed, lives under the guidance of a normative self-concept. This concept may be more or less correct or adequate. If incorrect or inadequate, it will thwart or pervert one's selfhood and one's life. In like manner, a more or less self-governing society has at least implicitly a self-concept that defines how it ought to be structured and how it ought to function. And, as in the case of an individual, an incorrect or inadequate self-concept will thwart or pervert the society.

As each individual's self-concept contains a concept of what one ought to be and how one ought to act both as a human being and as the individual one is, the normative self-concept of a society contains a concept of how any society ought to be structured and how it ought to function as well as a concept of itself as the particular society it is and how it ought to function in its particular historical circumstances. The generic self-concept of a society is correct or incorrect according to how well it captures the inherent normative structure of a society as a society, without regard for the exigencies of its historical situation. The specific self-concept of a society is correct or incorrect according to whether it embraces the correct generic concept of a society and fleshes it out correctly with regard to the traditions and historical contingencies of the particular society.

The generic normative structure of a society is derivative from, and grounded in, the generic normative structure of human beings. As previously observed, human beings, with more or less adequate knowledge-yielding and critical powers for living a life, are, by virtue of their inherent constitution, under an inner imperative to define and to live a life worthy of their humanity and their individuality. In other words, human beings, with at least the minimum competence for living a life, have the responsibility, as persons, to define and to live a life of their own that would stand up under moral and rational criticism — a life that would be a responsible rendition of what it is to be human with their particular abilities and disabilities in the circumstances of their existence. This defining responsibility of personhood, the primary and most elemental office in any social structure or society, entails certain rights and further responsibilities. The rights that pertain to the office of personhood, as previously indicated, are the areas of freedom and the conditions one must enjoy and the means one must have at one's disposal in order to have an opportunity to fulfill the primary responsibility of the office. The further responsibilities include respecting the rights of others and coming to their assistance when their rights are in jeopardy, provided one's assistance is needed and one is in a position to help without putting oneself in greater jeopardy. This personal responsibility extends to cooperating with others, when the situation requires or warrants it, in providing societal ways of protecting and supporting the basic rights of all members of the society.

The basic freedom right of a person is the right to define and to live a life of one's own so long as one does it in a responsible manner — that is, with proper respect for the rights and needs of others and regard for the normative limits and requirements that impinge on one in one's concrete situation. This is simply the freedom to strive to fulfill the defining responsibility of personhood. It includes the freedom of access to, or the freedom to acquire, the relevant knowledge and to form responsible judgments about whatever bears on one's life and activities; this includes the freedom to express one's views and judgments, to have access to the views and judgments of others, and to debate these matters openly. The basic freedom right includes also the freedom to participate in, or to be heard on, decisions that obligate or make demands on oneself, or even, in many cases, decisions that would affect (especially adversely) one's interests. Of course the effects of many decisions of others are simply part of the environment with which we have to cope. For example, the specific decision of others to produce and to market a product or service that would put me out of business is not necessarily a decision that I would have a right to participate in or to be heard on. But I do have a right to participate in the more general decision of my society that people be allowed to compete in this manner. Furthermore, the basic freedom right includes the right of individuals to acquire, in a responsible way, the necessary means for living lives worthy of them; this includes specifically the right to productive work and the right to benefit from one's labors.

Human beings are normatively persons from conception (that is, they have an inherent normative constitution that, in an appropriate cultural and social environment, will bring them in time to full personhood, unless something goes awry), but they are not functionally full persons and thus do not have the full freedom rights of a person until they acquire the requisite powers for responsible self-direction. Nevertheless, they have certain welfare rights in their immaturity, specifically, the right to the conditions that make possible overall healthy development to the point that they can take on the full responsibilities of personhood. These rights in immaturity impose normative limits and requirements on others, especially on parents or other guardians and on the society at large.

The family is generated and sustained by natural needs, emotions, and relationships, but it is also a societal institution, one in which society has a compelling interest and one that society has a responsibility to support and to regulate. In the rearing of children and even in the primary care for and support of adults, the family functions in *loco societatis;* it functions for, or in place of, the society. When a family fails or there is no family at all, society has a responsibility to take over, to the extent it is able, the basic responsibilities of the family for children and for disabled adults who cannot take care of themselves.

Furthermore, the society has a responsibility, within the limits of its ability, to provide protective and support systems for the well-being of its members that extend far beyond the capacity of families. This includes support for advancement of the culture, education for the major human enterprises, a health-care system available to all, an economic system that provides opportunities and support for all, a political system in which all competent citizens can (and are encouraged to) participate that protects the rights of all and works for a healthy, well-functioning, just, and peaceful society in which all the people have the opportunity to flourish according to their individual potential.

Contrary to cultural relativism, there is a universal normative constitution for society, or so I argue, because there is a universal normative constitution of human beings and human beings are common to, and have a basic common office in, all societies. As individuals should embrace the universal human constitution in their self-concepts and life plans, societies should embrace the universal normative societal constitution in their societal identities (or self-concepts) and societal plans. There are universal moral judgments to be made on individuals and their behavior in terms of the universal human constitution, and there are universal judgments to be made on societies in terms of the universal societal constitution. It is with respect to this constitution that every society is subject to being judged as underdeveloped or more or less developed, as deformed or well formed, as healthy or pathological.

The primary office in any society or institution is the office of personhood and persons are the primary holders of all other offices. The primary moral judgment to be made on any secondary office is whether the person who holds it can fulfill the responsibilities of the office without having to sacrifice or compromise one's primary responsibilities as a person. Of course, if the responsibilities of an office can be embraced within the responsibilities of the officeholder as a person, so much the better, for then the duties of the office are integrated directly into the life plan of the officeholder so that in fulfilling the duties of the office one is fulfilling one's selfhood. A further moral judgment to be made on an office is whether the holder of the office can perform well in it without thwarting or in some way damaging oneself as a person. Of course offices are judged also according to how the fulfillment of their duties bear on the rights and welfare of others and on the public good.

The overall judgment on a society pertains, not to its gross economic product or its military power, but to how well it generates human beings with worthy identities and life plans and with inner strength; how well the people are provided with the opportunity to, and are supported in, defining and living worthy lives of their own; how well the society embraces the lives of the people so that, in living their own lives, the people serve society and, in serving society, they live their own lives successfully; and how well the culture provides a way of integrating the human enterprise into the universe in a way that preserves and reinforces the meaningfulness and worthwhileness of the lives of the people.

3

CHARACTER

The Framework for a Successful Life

The most important information we can have about people, especially those with whom we have dealings, pertains to their character. This is so because character is the constitution by which people order and structure their experience, thought, and behavior. We often distinguish between intellectual and moral character. The former is the framework that guides and shapes the way people organize and employ their experience and thought in search of truth about and understanding of the world; the latter is the framework in terms of which people organize and structure their experience, thought, and behavior in living their lives and in participating in society. A good intellectual character is one that makes for success in the search for truth and understanding. In a similar manner, a good moral character is one that makes for success in defining and living a worthy life and in being a good member of society.

Although intellectual and moral character are distinguishable, they should not be separated. Divorcing them as we do in our modern culture leads to the distortion of both. As a consequence, we have a world view that puts in jeopardy our human identity and the norms and values in terms of which we live our lives and run our institutions. Realistic humanism, which holds that there is an objective normative structure to which our value judgments are accountable, offers a solid foundation for our human identity and moral character, for it recognizes an inherent cognitive content to our self-concept and to the whole domain of value experience and judgment.

The basics for success in life, I suggest, are a well-formed self-concept, a life plan that is appropriate to one's humanity and individuality, and an understanding of the context of one's existence in a way that is commensurate with one's powers and constructive in one's life.

THE RIGHT SELF-CONCEPT AND LIFE PLAN

We develop a self-concept in growing up in a society; and we criticize and modify it in the thick of life with urgent problems pressing. Our first image of who we are is forged by the circumstances of our existence, the culture we absorb, the example of role models and heroes, the tutelage of guardians, the expectations, demands, and criticisms of others, and encounters with the hard edges of reality. Only later, with a self-concept already formed, do we have the cultural capital, the critical powers, and the self-transcendence to gain a critical mastery of our own self-concept and to make it authentically our own. Too many remain simply creatures of their time and place, governed by an unexamined self-concept, and thus enslaved by their provincial culture and local situation.

In the dominant culture of our age, those who become critical of their self-concept that was generated in growing up have nothing to which to appeal but their own feelings and desires and those of some group with which they identify, with no conceptual framework in terms of which these feelings and desires can be validated or reconstructed. This drives self-critical and enlightened people toward a subjectivistic individualism or an ethnic or peer-group relativism, leaving society dependent on contractual relationships based on self- or group-interest and legalisms generated by bargained political agreements among powerful individuals or interest groups. Too often those who look for an alternative to this kind of individualistic or interest-group contractual utilitarianism turn to some form of authoritarianism, religious or otherwise. Communitarians try to shore up the social foundations of morality by emphasizing family, community, and common interests, without an effort to examine the intellectual foundations of morality.[1]

Human beings constitute a break with nature. We are not merely beings with knowledge-yielding powers; we are knowledge-based beings. In a more or less mature state, we are constituted by our self-concept and the way we understand our place in the order of things. In a sense, we are a human "invention" or "creation," for our self-concept and our understanding of our place have been developed by human powers; indeed, existentialists say that we should individually invent or create ourselves. But contrary to the existentialists, this is not the whole story. In forming one's self-concept and sense of one's place as a human being and even as the individual one happens to be, there is, as indicated in chapter 2, something in one's nature, relationships, and circumstances to which one is responsible. This is why we need to draw on the experience and thought and criticism of others; we need their help to get these matters right. If we go wrong in forming our self-concept, in understanding our place in the scheme of things, or in the values that we take to be worthy of pursuit, we will pervert or distort our identity and wreck our lives.

Contrary to many who think of human beings as simply on one end of a biological continuum, differing from other animals or even plants only in degree, human beings are, indeed, unique in a very special way. While many animals share some of our psychological powers, we are the only beings on this planet who live by rational knowledge and critical judgment under a self-concept and world view. Furthermore, only human beings live in a society organized by, and governed under, a moral constitution. In other words, among the beings we know, only human beings are persons and only persons are knowledge-based in their identity, form knowledge-based and morally regulated societies, and have religious anxieties and attitudes toward themselves as beings in the world.

Those who talk about animal rights do so because of the way they understand both personhood and human society. According to realistic humanism, only persons or person-like agents (e.g., corporations, states) who are defined by responsibilities have rights, and only human societies embody, and are self-regulated by, a moral constitution. Tigers, for example, live the life of the tiger; they live from instinct, impulse, sensory awareness, and no doubt a measure of memory, imagination, and cunning. They neither live under or from a normative concept of themselves as tigers or have an understanding of, and feelings and attitudes toward themselves as beings in society or in the world, nor do they have a life story built around a plot or plan that integrates their lives and gives them their identity and unity. Their lives are more or less a series of behavioral episodes that are united largely by connection with the same biological tiger. Human beings, on the other hand, have lives to define and to live under the imperative force of their inherent normative constitution as formulated in their self-concept, lives to live under the guidance of rational knowledge and critical reflection. The imperative to define and to live a life worthy of oneself as a human being and as the individual one is bears on one as a categorical responsibility. There is no escaping it for one with the requisite powers. It is this responsibility that constitutes the natural (nonconventional) office of personhood and generates the natural rights that are inherent in it. No other animals have such a responsibility; no other animals are persons; no other animals have rights.

This is the point where we break with nature. The tiger is a tiger by the natural order. Our identity, like that of a computer, is knowledge-based; but, unlike artifacts, our normative human constitution, even though it has to be known in order to be actualized, is present in an unactualized state in our natural being. Contrary to the existentialist, we do not really *invent* what it is to be a human being; we discover it. The defining form of an artifact, the form specified in the functional concept of it, is imposed upon material for which the form is unnatural. Our self-concept as a human being is a correct or incorrect grasp of what we by our nature ought to be and ought to become.

Our individual identity is more of an invention; but even in forming our self-concept as an individual, we not only have to take account of the facts and design a life that can be lived well as far as the facts are concerned, but also there are normative requirements and limits that we must embrace and respect. We are required, as revealed by rational appraisal language, to render in our lives an appropriate interpretation of what it is to be human in our circumstances. Although there may be acceptable alternatives in many cases, in an important sense one discovers whom to marry, whether to have children, what one's life's work should be, and so forth. Many couples feel that their relationship is so beautifully fitting that it was meant to be; that their marriage and their individual lives would be incomplete without children; and many people feel that their profession is really a calling, that it was imperative for them, that any other would have been a mistake. Obviously some self-concepts for one as the individual one is may be better than others, some may be bad, and some may be simply wrong. Such evaluations presuppose that there is a normative structure of one as an individual in one's context with respect to which one's self-concept is corrigible.

Human lives can fail in ways in which artifacts cannot. Each individual life is unique; it has its own life plan. The plan of an airplane can have multiple instantiations. The plan of an individual life is embodied, not instantiated; it is a particular structure of inherent meaning. Although it is abstract in that it is not fully detailed, the life plan of a person can have only one embodiment, for it embraces within itself particular events, circumstances, relationships, and objectives, and the normative requirements grounded in them. For instance, my life plan includes not only the general requirements and purposes inherent in being a human being but also the responsibilities, entitlements, and purposes grounded in being the son of my parents, the brother of two particular men, the husband of a particular woman, the father of two particular children, a member of several particular institutions, a citizen of several particular polities, and a philosopher and educator by profession. All of this is embraced in my self-concept and helps define for me what my options are and what I ought to do. No one else could live the life defined by my life plan as an individual.

My self-concept as an individual may be correct or incorrect in ways in which the design for an artifact cannot be. It may be false with respect to my inherent normative structure as a human being, as indicated above; it may be false with respect to the objective normative structure grounded in relevant enduring facts and relationships that pertain to me as an individual; it may fail to provide for the normative requirements that impinge on me by virtue of the circumstances of my time and place; and it may embrace false or unworthy goals. No design concept of an artifact is accountable to its subject matter in this manner.

Although one's self-concept and one's success in life may be brought under review at times, especially in crises, they are not the focus in a good life. One's self-concept is more presupposed, especially in self-criticism and the consideration of options. And success comes not by pursuit of success as such but by pursuit of worthy ends the achievement of which constitutes success. The focus in living a life is primarily on what one loves, what one is devoted to, what one feels needs to be done, what one works to bring about or to realize.

The measure of one and of one's life is not merely a matter of how well one meets the ordinary responsibilities and normative requirements that impinge on one, but largely a matter of the values that engage one in a way that organizes and energizes one's life, what one lives for. These values must be worthy of one as a human being and as the individual one is in the circumstances of one's existence. They should be such that they elevate the level of one's life and empower one to become all that one ought to be and is capable of becoming. We are, in an important sense, a creature of what we know and what we love — what we attend to and what we are devoted to, what we are occupied with and value most highly. Great human beings feel the pull of self-transcendent normative requirements and the lure of higher values.

One can be an excellent person without being a great person, just as one can be an excellent artist without being a great artist. Excellence in a work of art has do with perfection of skill, mastery of material, and the fittingness of form and material for the meaning expressed in it. But greatness in art has do with the depth and significance of the meaning expressed in an excellent work. The same can be said about a human life. Any human being may be an excellent person; anyone may live a life befitting his or her humanity and individuality. The greatness of a person, however, goes beyond moral goodness; it is a matter of the greatness of the requirements that impinge on one or the greatness of the values that lay hold of and command one, and how well one responds to these requirements and values in defining and living one's life. Both of these factors of greatness depend on the abilities of the person involved. Great normative requirements and values do not impinge on or engage people with low ability or little knowledge.

Every great value has its greatness in the normative requirements that are or would be satisfied by that which has the value. But normative requirements that invest something with great value may not impinge on just any individual. There may be, for example, a great need for a cure for a dreaded disease. A college student may take on the challenge and organize her life around the goal of finding such a cure. We would not say that the need for such a cure imposed a normative requirement on that particular individual in such a way that she would have been at fault and blameworthy if she had not committed herself to this particular pursuit, but we would praise her for devoting her life to the task. We would say, however, that one should pursue values for which one is especially suited, values that are worthy of one and of which one is worthy. One is at fault if one does not commit to some value or complex of values that is worthy of one; and one is at fault if one commits to values of which one is unworthy. Only the first kind of fault is a moral fault; the second is more a matter of inadequate knowledge of either oneself or the requirements for realization of the goal in question.

Some people in our culture, committed to the doctrine of equality, shy away from talking about higher and lower or greater and lesser human beings. They think this commits us to elitism. Our modern doctrine of equality was forged originally against a feudalistic aristocracy, according to which people had unequal status and unequal rights according to the social class into which they were born. What the equality doctrine proclaims is that every human being is a person and that, as a person with somewhat normal and mature human powers, each one has the responsibility to be the executive of one's own life, with all the rights grounded in this responsibility. The doctrine is correct in that we all hold, or are destined to, the office of personhood as rational agents and thus, in somewhat normal maturity, have the responsibility to define and to live our own lives and thus the set of rights grounded in this responsibility. It means that no one as a person, with one's rational powers developed and intact, is subject to the will of another human being as such. Of course this does not mean that a society cannot generate offices by a division of responsibilities so that some officeholders have the responsibility and thus the right to make certain kinds of decisions that obligate others. What is required is that these special offices be open so that anyone with the qualifications may enter the competition for them.

There is nothing in the doctrine of moral equality that militates against our evaluation of people as greater or lesser human beings. We evaluate presidents of the United States as greater or lesser presidents, physicians as greater or lesser physicians, novelists as greater or lesser novelists, and on and on. And of course we evaluate human beings all the time as greater or lesser human beings. Nothing is more important in the evaluation of the greatness of human beings than the depth, expanse, and power of their minds, the responsibilities they feel and take on, the steadfast loves that lift and move them, and the extent to which their lives embody and express their knowledge and understanding and are governed by their responsibilities and the higher values to which they are committed.

So the most important measure of success for anyone is the extent to which one develops a correct and appropriate self-concept, one that defines for one, in light of one's humanity, individuality, and circumstances, a worthy life — a life that encompasses what one ought to become and ought to do, given one's inherent nature, abilities, and the set of more or less enduring facts and relationships that enter into one's identity. Of course there are in one's life many facts and relationships with normative requirements and restraints grounded in them that are not embraced in one's normative self-concept or life plan, but one's life plan should embrace strategies for assessing and accommodating them.

A false or inappropriate self-concept would close off what should be options and open roads that should be closed. It would lead one to pursue false goals and to ignore the ways to real success; and it might permit unallowable means in one's pursuits. Only with a correct and appropriate governing self-concept can one's life be a success. Thus, without some measure of success in forming one's self-concept and general life plan one is doomed to an unsuccessful life, regardless of success in achieving set goals. If one is wrong at the basic level of one's self-concept, one will be systematically wrong in one's judgments and decisions about most issues. But if one is right in the foundations of one's self-concept, one has the leverage to correct errors and inadequacies at more superficial levels. Indeed, the distorted self can correct itself so long as his or her natural normative constitution on which one's self-concept is based is not deranged.

There are those who say that self-perversion can be so fundamental that it is beyond self-correction, for it corrupts one's values and moral judgments through and through. This is the so-called wicked person, who, according to some religious thinkers, has to be transformed, if at all, by grace — by some external power such as divine or human love. Certainly a person with a long-standing, deeply distorted self-concept is a hard case. But one's natural constitution as a knower-agent is presupposed by all the acts of the self, even acts of misconception of one's self. It is this logical tension within oneself between one's misformulated self-concept and one's natural constitution that makes possible self-correction. Only if the distortion in one's self-concept were pathologically caused in a way that rendered it immune to criticism or if it reflected an actual derangement in one's natural constitution would it be entirely beyond the powers of self-correction.

The point is that a more or less mature, normal human being is responsible for one's own identity and life. Of course without proper education and training in critical self-examination and self-development one may have a justifiable excuse for failure to correct distortions in one's self-concept that was forged in one's upbringing. But excuses only mitigate one's blameworthiness. As long as it is within one's power to correct one's errors, even in one's self-concept, one is responsible for them.

VIEW OF SOCIETY

A further condition for a successful life, it will be recalled, is understanding the context of our existence in a way that is constructive in our lives. This includes understanding society and the wider world in which we exist. It is obvious to all that we need to understand the contingent features and circumstances of our environment with which we have to cope in living our lives, but the point I want to emphasize is the logical interplay between our understanding of the basic structure of society and the world on one hand and our self-concept and our idea of what would be a worthy life for us on the other.

We all have our being and live our lives in a society. Human beings require a supportive cultural/social context somewhat in the way in which biological organisms require an ecological system. One's defining self-concept, as previously remarked, embraces one's important social positions and enduring relationships. We are not atomic beings; we internalize much of the social structure within which we live. We cannot divorce ourselves from our society without affecting our identity. Indeed, we may best think of ourselves as nodes in a dynamic cultural/social matrix. We may be largely passive nodes, letting the cultural and social forces around us surge and pulsate through us, or we may be active nodes by critically processing and approving or reconstructing the cultural and social forces operating in and through us. The extent to which we are aware, constructively critical, and master of our own lives is a measure of our freedom.

In the development of one's self-concept and in living one's life, one inescapably develops a normative concept of society and of one's place in it. One cannot, for example, consistently think of oneself as under an inherent imperative, by virtue of one's nature as a human being, to define and to live a worthy life of one's own and at the same time subscribe to a feudalistic view of society, with peasants as servants of a lord or an aristocracy with the masses subjects of a ruling class. One's concept of oneself as a person entails a normative concept of society to the effect that any office or position in it should be compatible with the office of personhood — that is, any office or position should be so constituted that a human being could occupy it and fulfill its responsibilities without having to compromise his or her responsibilities as a person. Indeed, one's self-concept as a person requires a correlative concept of society to the effect that any society ought to be free from domination and exploitation, with the rights of all secure. In fact, personhood and citizenship are interdependent concepts. One cannot be a good person without being a good citizen or vice versa. Of course being a good citizen does not mean that one must accept and participate in all the established ways of one's society; on the contrary, it may require one to challenge the status quo.

Just as one's concept of oneself as a human being entails a normative concept of society, one's normative concept of society entails a concept of oneself as a human being; indeed, one's concept of society may entail a concept of oneself as a man, as a woman, as a husband, as a wife, as a father, as a mother, as a member of this or that race, as a business person, as a manager, as a laborer, or whatever. Often the normative concept of society controls the normative concept of human beings and of classes of human beings. Obviously a society can, and often does, misconceive, or develop in a way that is contrary to, its own natural constitution and the values to which it should be committed, and, if so, the society will become misshapen or pathological. And a distorted or pathological society, especially in its governing self-conception, will distort and pervert the members of the society; it will corrupt their regulative self-concepts and life plans.

Given the logical interdependence between one's idea of one's normative constitution as a human being and as the individual one is and one's idea of the normative constitution of society, where is the testing ground for correctness? This is the issue that divides those who believe that the ground of moral judgment lies in society and those who believe that it lies in the nature of human beings. It is also what divides those who believe that human beings should be developed to fit society and those who believe that society should be reformed to fit human beings. I contend that we can get our concept of society right only by first getting our concept of human beings right. We have to appeal to the natural normative constitution of human beings to test both our concept of ourselves as human beings and our concept of society. Ideally we should have a society fit for human beings before we try to develop human beings who will fit into the society. In reality, however, these two processes are interactive. While developing human beings to fit society, we try to reform society to fit human beings. But we must not forget that the whole process is grounded in, and accountable to, the natural normative constitution of human beings. The test of any society is how well human beings flourish in it, and how well they prepare the way for future generations.

WORLD VIEW

The focus here, as in the case with society, is on the bearing of one's views about the subject matter in question on one's self-concept and life plan, not the more mundane matter of how one's comprehension of or beliefs about the facts of one's situation bears on one's ordinary plans and actions in living one's life.

No one can have a successful life, regardless of one's self-concept and life plan, without being undergirded with positive life attitudes, without an operating faith in the meaningfulness and worthwhileness of life, without some measure of life morale. High life morale may be one's awareness of success in living a good life; or it may be hope for, or expectation of, success in life, or simply faith that success in life is possible. The first form is more characteristic of life morale in later life; the other forms are more prominent in youth. Life despair is life-crippling, life-defeating at any point in life.

Life morale is much like job morale. Job morale requires doing well in getting the job done; but that is not enough. Regardless of the pay and benefits, one has to believe that there is a real job, not just make-work. Furthermore, one has to believe that it is an important job, that it is worthy of one's best efforts, and that one is worthy of the job. And one needs confirmation of these things by the respect and appreciation of others.

Living a life is something most of us want to be engaged in, even though much of the times it is a struggle with a lot of disappointment and heartache. But the sheer value we experience in being alive is not enough to make a life worthwhile any more so than the sheer value one experiences in singing is enough to make one's career as a professional singer worthwhile. The joy in being alive may be no more than awareness of the well-functioning of one's body or the well-functioning of one's mind in solving a crossword puzzle. The career of a professional singer or ballplayer requires an appropriate context to make it meaningful and worthwhile. The activity must have a significant place in the lives of others and in the culture. In like manner, a human life, regardless of the value one may experience in being alive or in one's activities, requires an appropriate context to make it really meaningful and worthwhile.

Some contend that the family, friends, community, country, and certainly human history provide all the context we need for meaningful and worthwhile lives and thus for high life morale. And certainly our social context, however limited or extended it may be, helps in meeting this need. Nevertheless, countless human beings have found that the social context of their lives, however extended, is not sufficient to endow their lives with the full measure of meaning and worth that our peculiar nature seems to require;

they feel that any meaning-endowing context short of the total universe or what is ultimate is fragmentary and incomplete. Although those who subscribe to the limited-context view charge those who insist on the ultimate context for a fully meaningful and worthwhile human life with suffering from a pathological ego-anxiety, a case can be made for the latter claim.

Inherent in a positive life attitude is the feeling that one is a being of worth, that in defining and living one's life one is about something important, that one must find worthy goals in life and pursue them in an appropriate manner, that great risks are involved because something of momentous value is at stake, and that success in life depends as much or more on the kind of person one becomes and how one defines and lives one's life as on the actual achievement of the ends sought.

These assumptions or beliefs about oneself are embedded in or entail assumptions or beliefs about the world. A successful life requires a world view, and especially a view of oneself as a human-being-in-the-world, that makes sense of human existence, the life one is living, and the values and normative requirements that define one's life.

We may be mistaken about the world at different levels. We may be mistaken about such matters as the cause of lung cancer, the effects of the national debt, the age of the earth, the origin of life, the laws and constants of physics, and the like. A certain amount of knowledge of the factual and causal structure of the world is essential for successful action of any kind. The primary concern here, however, is with the fundamentals of one's world view — one's philosophical world view. This has to do with the basic ways in which reality is constituted and the nature of change and causality. Although we give little attention in our educational system to such metaphysical questions, a correct philosophical view of the world is important for a successful life, for it is an important factor in one's basic life attitudes.

A human life and its historical/social context, whatever the scope of the historical/social context, must be placed in some wider context that makes sense of the whole complex, for otherwise the historical/social context remains an ontological dangler; it does not have a context that makes it intelligible. The central question concerns the kind of world view that is required to make sense of human lives and their historical social context.

One may understand the world in such a way that one takes oneself, as in the biblical tradition, to be in the image of God with a divine mission or calling; or, as in the Hindu tradition, one may take oneself to be a piece of the divine engaged in the fulfillment of ultimate being; or, as in Buddhism, one may take oneself to be engaged in a karmic process that may require many reincarnations for one to bring oneself to completion in moral perfection. On the other hand, with an image of oneself and others as knower-agents with freedom, responsibility, and dignity in an otherwise physicalistic universe that is devoid of value and meaning, one may see oneself and one's companions, paraphrasing Albert Camus, as absurd actors playing their role without a stage; or one may understand human beings in the manner of scientific behaviorism so that they fit into a physicalistic world in such a way that belief in human freedom and dignity is regarded as a folk superstition that will be jettisoned as a more fully scientific culture develops.

In other words, one's world view may be such that one relates to and resonates with the forces at work in the world in a way that elevates one's sense of self, enhances one's sense of the importance of defining and living a worthy life, and provides spiritual support and inner resources for a life well defined and well lived in response to comprehensive normative requirements and in pursuit of higher values. On the other hand, one may have a world view such that one's life and the whole human scene appear meaningless in an indifferent world in which nothing really matters. One's world view may nullify ideas and beliefs about the normative and meaning dimensions of human selfhood and of human life in general. It may even call into question or invalidate the belief that one can define or live a life at all. Such a world view, when really taken to heart, is numbing, paralyzing, destructive. So one's world view, especially the world view of a culture, bears heavily upon not only success in living a human life, but even on the possibility of a human life at all. Hence, having the right world view is as important in living a life as having the right self-concept.

We cannot explain subject matter with inherent structures of meaning and normativity in a world that is otherwise devoid of such inherent structures, or so I have argued in other works. The emergent thesis only names the mystery; it explains nothing. This is why physicalists feel compelled to reject the view that there are inherent structures of meaning and normativity in human selfhood and society. If we admit meaning and normativity in the human sphere, which I think we must, then we must acknowledge that they reflect something similar in the deep structure of reality.

Indeed, human selfhood, human lives, and social structures cannot be made intelligible by showing that they are necessary conditions of, or even normatively required for, our biological survival as individuals or as a species. Such an explanation would trivialize our selfhood and human culture and society; it would not render intelligible the value and meaning we find in human existence. We are compelled, by the demands of intelligibility, to think of our biological existence as a required condition for our selfhood and the lives we live rather than the other way around.

But we find no normative structures in local situations that would provide an adequate teleological explanation for the existence of human selfhood and the whole human phenomenon. If there is a teleological explanation for what is most distinctive about human beings, as the anthropic principle suggests,[2] it must be in terms of normative requirements that transcend the local environment in which human beings exist. Such transcendent normative requirements, it would seem, must be grounded in the ultimate reality that is being developed in the universe or somehow inherent in the wholeness of things. And a universe that in its development fulfills such inherent or holistic normative requirements exhibits "wisdom" in the process in much the way in which we speak of the "wisdom" of the human body. The "wisdom" of nature is shown in the proper ordering of things to keep the process on course in fulfilling inherent or holistic normative requirements. Only such a universe, it seems to many, would make the existence of human lives and human history intelligible. And without a world view that makes the human phenomenon intelligible, we can only regard human life as we know it in lived experience as absurd; we remain actors without a setting that would make our lives meaningful.

Some may think that I am guilty of an ambiguity in the use of the word "meaningful" - ambiguity between something's being meaningful in the sense of being intelligible or making sense, which is an intellectual matter, and a life's being meaningful in a way that connects with its being worthwhile and generates a positive life attitude. The point I wish to make is that when the subject matter in question is that of a human life, with its inherent intentional and normative structure, these two senses of "meaningful" coincide. There is no way, or so I contend, in which the phenomenon of human life can be made intelligible other than by showing that its normative and intentional structures fit into a context that involves normative and intentional structures. Seeing ourselves and human history in such a context enhances the meaningfulness and worthwhileness of the human struggle in a way that boosts life morale. For instance, if we think of human existence as partial fulfillment of a holistic or transcendent imperative that is being realized in the developing universe, we may think of the imperative inherent in our own normative constitution to define and to live a worthy life as a manifestation in our own being of the cosmic imperative in the normative constitution of the universe. Something like this is no doubt what religious people have in mind when they talk about the moral imperative as the will of God.

The fundamental point is that a successful life requires not only a correct or appropriate self-concept that embraces a plan for a worthy life and a correct normative concept of society, but it also requires a world view that makes human selfhood and the phenomenon of human lives and human history intelligible in a way that integrates one's self and the life one is living and human history into the universe in a way that is life affirming and reinforcing. This requires that the higher imperatives (the ones that override others, not by sheer force but with justification) that we find inherent in our own selfhood and in society have a grounding or backing in our world view.

Of course many people seem to have successful lives without such a supportive world view. But many people, no doubt, have a tacit world view in their lived experience that is contrary to their intellectual world view. One may, for example, be brought up with, or somehow acquire, a supportive world view that remains lodged in, or presupposed by, one's deep emotions and life attitudes while operating with, or openly espousing, a non-supportive world view in one's intellectual life. Such people may live in a supportive social context without taking to heart how they and their social context fit into the world according to their intellectual world view. Indeed, some well established emotional structures may remain stout and resist a threatening intellectual vision consciously held. But such emotional security is always at risk. It is vulnerable to one's self-transcending reflective and critical powers and may collapse into depression in some crisis or reflective moment.

SPRINGS OF ACTION

Some may protest that emphasis on the role of one's governing self-concept, normative concept of society, and world view in living successfully is too intellectualistic. First of all, as previously observed, we do not develop these ideas in an intellectualistic way; they are developed in growing up in the thick of life, although they need critical examination, intellectual validation, and often reconstruction. Furthermore, it is commonplace in our age to think of the rational and the intellectual only in the forms they have taken in our scientific/technological culture; and so those who want to cultivate and to bring some order into the inner working of the human spirit are inclined to think only in terms of the emotions, the imagination, and their various modes of expression. Realistic humanism, however, rejects this restricted view of the rational and the intellectual. It holds that the proper intellectual perspective is grounded in and draws its data from the full spectrum of human experience, and that reason has a role to play in validating and bringing order to all realms of experience and activity.

Our self-concept, concept of society, and world view are not inert ideas; they have a powerful bearing on the "habits of the heart," to use Robert Bellah's felicitous expression;[3] indeed, they are the organizing and governing ideas of our emotive and volitional life. One's self-concept is expressed in one's conscience, but it is more. Where one's conscience, usually understood as a moral immune system, speaks only in the negative, one's normative self-concept speaks in both positive and negative terms; it is embedded in and shapes one's felt responsibilities, aspirations, pride, happiness, self-disappointment, self-reproach, community feelings, jealousies, felt insults, felt injustices, alienation, and so forth. Likewise one's normative concept of society lays hold on one's emotive life; it engages one's feelings of loyalty, alienation, civic responsibility, political obligation, sense of social justice, and so forth. One's world view enters into one's life attitudes and either grounds or tends to undermine one's organizing and governing emotions and commitments to higher values. In other words, in getting our self-concept, concept of society, and our world view more or less right, we rightly order our feelings, emotions, desires, actions, and lives, provided that the unity of the self is maintained. And the inner dynamics of the self, under a clear and strong self-concept that is supported by coherent humanistic views of society and the world, work for the integrity of the self. If we get any of these matters wrong, we are likely to be thwarted, perhaps fail, as individuals and as a society.

Of course a correct self-concept that embraces an appropriate life plan, a sound normative concept of society, and a world view that makes sense of and supports the human enterprise do not assure a successful life. Everyone needs a supportive culture and social ecology and a large measure of good fortune. But with a properly constituted framework for life that structures one's intellectual, emotive, aspirational, and volitional outlook and behavior, one will be able to give a good rendition of what it is to be a human being in whatever factual situation it is one's lot to live; and that is moral success even if one's life plan is thwarted or even aborted by circumstances beyond one's control. Indeed, humanity is often manifested at its best in the lives of people with frustrated or aborted life plans.

4

THE PRIMACY OF

FAMILY AND

COMMUNITY

The family is the primary institution. It is the social womb for children and a humanistic haven and general support center for adults. It typically provides food and lodging, health care, education, and entertainment, but its primary and enduring purpose, which cannot be taken over by other institutions, is to meet the deep humanistic needs of its members. Everyone needs to be grounded in, to identify with, and to be supported by a family that provides one with intimacy and a sense of belonging and unconditional acceptance; location in a kinship network that connects one with contemporary relatives, ancestors, and future generations; and a family story or collection of family stories in which one's own life is a developing chapter. This is our primary human way of being anchored in the world. A community, a nation, or a religion may supplement one's family, but there is no real substitute for a good family. Those without a good family experience not only lack an essential emotional support system but have a hollow place in the core of their being; and they are more insecure and lonely because of it. And when the family as an institution is in trouble, the whole social order is threatened by the weakened identity and the weakness of character on the part of the members of the society. A society has no greater responsibility than to tend to the health of the family as an institution, unless it is to protect the basic rights of individuals.

SEXUALITY AND KINSHIP

The family is based on and held together by sexuality and kinship. We often confuse sexuality with sex and kinship with genetic relations. We share sex and genetic connections with other animals, but not sexuality and kinship. Sexuality and kinship are humanized sex and genetic relationships; they are bearers of meaning. Sexuality and kinship are forces within us that move us toward higher values and a higher level of being. They are primary wells of meaning in our lives. One of the major sins of our modern culture has been the destruction, prostitution, or trivialization of the sources of meaning in our lives. There is little wonder that we complain about the loss of meaning. Many philosophers even claim that talk about the meaning of life is meaningless.

Sexuality is a powerful force in the lives of people. Freud, in search of the fundamental human motivation in terms of which all human behavior could be explained, seized on sex in much the way in which mechanists tried to explain all forms of change in terms of locomotion. Certainly sexuality is pervasive in human life, even in dreams, fantasies, art, and religion. It is the basis of our most intimate and life-enhancing relationships; it plays a central role in our search for meaning; it is an inner dynamic that draws us out of ourselves toward identification with something larger and higher than ourselves; it is a major force in society; and it is given expression in our highest cultural achievements.

Sexuality is built into our identity. We are men or women, sons or daughters, and perhaps brothers or sisters, fathers or mothers. We have masculine or feminine voices, outlooks, ways of dressing, modes of behavior, and some say ways of experiencing, thinking, and expressing ourselves. Kinship, which is linked with sexuality, is a strong bond among people. The lives of most people revolve largely around their parents, siblings, spouses, children, and other relatives. Many people are fascinated with their family genealogy. And, when we are at our best, we universalize our feelings of brotherhood and sisterhood. Some religions think of the ultimate generating power of the universe as father or mother.

Sexuality and kinship are fertile areas of our hearts that can be informed and spiritualized by higher values in ways that elevate and empower our lives, enrich our culture, and humanize our institutions. Some religions teach that these powers within us that move us toward higher values are sparks of the divine. Indeed, the divine just is that which manifests or works toward the realization of the highest values. Sexuality and kinship feelings, properly informed culturally, are such powers.

At the basic level, sex is the power within us by which we participate in the creation of new members of our species. But we are not merely biological beings. We are the only animals with the capacity and responsibility to inform this power with understanding and higher values. Precisely because of its great power and spiritual significance, sexuality, if not properly acculturated and integrated into our understanding of ourselves and our place in the creativity of the world, can be debasing and destructive. Animal sex in animals is natural; in humans it is beastly. Sex is not something to be left to the impulses or untutored choices of the immature and the inexperienced. Nor should its acculturation be left to a youth culture that is divorced from the experience and judgment of the adult community. Indeed, we all need the accumulated wisdom of a historical community and time-tested institutional structures and practices to guide us in the development and management of our sexuality. What we need is not just science-based sex education, but sex education that is an integral part of humanistic education for a meaningful and worthy life. All of us, especially the young, need to understand and to respect this creative but dangerous force within us. Only people who have put their sexuality in the service of their higher ideals and integrated it into their normative self-concept, life plan, and world view can manage their basic sexual feelings and desires in a responsible and constructive way.

But education in sexuality is not enough in our present cultural and social situation. Our humanistic culture and institutional structures are, as we indicated in chapter 1, in disarray under the forces of modern materialism and subjectivism. Sex is largely an unregulated energy in our society. Teenagers, some even in their pre-teen years, are sexually active. Children are having children. Casual sex is commonplace with people of all ages and classes. Promiscuity and marital infidelity are common. Sex has become a plaything for entertainment or escape from boredom. It is cheapened and debased in fiction, movies, television, and popular music in search of thrills and excitement for a jaded public. It is exploited for commercial purposes in advertising, even for promoting careers and business deals. There is no way of assessing the personal, cultural, and social cost of the despiritualization of sex — cutting it loose from our higher values and a humanistic understanding of ourselves as human beings in the world, and thus allowing it to sink into meaningless hedonism, trivial pursuits, or the demonic.

THE EROSION OF THE FAMILY

Marriage should not be simply a contract between two individuals that is registered with and regulated by the state. Contracts are based on the self-interest of the contracting parties. Traditionally marriage and parenthood more than anything else formed the adult identity of most people and endowed their lives with a larger meaning and purpose. Consequently marriage bore the mark of the sacred. It was regarded as a covenant of two people with each other and with their families and society in the presence of God, the ground of their being and their values, to establish a family grounded in love and to accept responsibility for each other and for any children they might have.

There is a good reason for the permanent monogamous marriage. The most perfect union requires faith in the wholehearted commitment of each to the other and to the relationship for life. Anything less is conditioned. No one can genuinely bond unconditionally with more than one person in this manner. Certainly there have been other family arrangements and many people violate their monogamous commitments, but experience and reflection support the claim that the permanent monogamous relationship grounded in and supported by mutual love and trust has the highest potential for the enhancement of life. The quality of such a relationship is diminished or adulterated if conditioned, if one shares one's heart romantically with another, or if one engages in behavior that violates the other's trust. A conditioned relationship, one with a divided heart, or one grounded in anxiety or doubt about the faithfulness of the other is relatively shallow and fragile. No number of such relationships can deepen and complete one's being and give meaning to one's life in the way in which an enduring, unconditional, and trusted union with one other person can.

Of course this is an ideal. There never were any perfect marriages and all too many have been unmitigated disasters. The traditional family was based as much on the inequality and economic dependency of women as on the ideal. But the ideal itself and the values it presupposes have been culturally undermined and are under open attack. Nevertheless, the ideal of the permanent monogamous relationship grounded in mutual love, faith, and support still structures the popular image of a meaningful adult life. It is what mature romantic love seems to demand, or at least to hope for; it is what the well-being of children requires of their parents; it is still the standard by which we judge success and failure in marriage and family life. When a marriage breaks up, the husband and wife don't just separate, they tear apart. It is usually painful and filled with regret and grief, and often with guilt. It leaves scars for life and frequently damaged children. Furthermore, the instability of the family is a threat to the whole social fabric.

Powerful cultural, social, and economic forces have had a destructive impact on the traditional family. In most cultures, and certainly in Western civilization until recently, the family involved male domination and often exploitation and oppression of women. The husband/father was the authority figure both with regard to the wife and the children, and the wife/mother cared for the needs of other members of the family, often with little time or energy for herself. Children were, for the most part, dependent on and at the mercy of their parents, with little societal protection from parental abuse or neglect. The home was the man's castle and often he ruled like a feudal lord. The state was hesitant to interject itself into the internal affairs of the family.

But the family could not remain a feudal island in the sea of modern liberalism. The doctrine of moral equality and human rights finally undermined the traditional family values that sustained the feudal family structure. Although some conservative religious groups still insist on it, the subjection of wives to the authority of their husbands was no longer tenable once the idea of the moral equality of human beings was introduced. In fact, the dissolution of the traditional family-authority system has gone so far that the authority of parents over their children is challenged and greatly weakened.

In our earlier predominantly agricultural and small-shop economy, the economic life of the society was located largely in or near the home. Mothers and fathers worked together and their children grew up working with them. With industrialization and the rise of urban life, the husband/father left the home for outside work to support the family financially and the mother was left to do the housework, to care for and to supervise the children, to organize the family's social life and entertainment, and perhaps to do volunteer work for a better community. The father became a more distant figure and less involved in the intimate life of the children. With the steady advances in household appliances and the market economy, more and more of the housewife's work was done by machines or transferred to the marketplace, including much of the child care, health care, and entertainment. Although she did much for the material welfare of the family and was largely responsible for providing for the humanistic needs of other family members, the wife/mother came to feel devalued because she was not a money-earner in the increasingly materialistic culture. At the fiftieth anniversary reunion of my high school class, one of my classmates expressed a widespread cultural attitude when it was her turn to make a brief statement about her life after high school. She said, rather apologetically, "I have never done anything important; I have been only a housewife and mother"; and she added, almost as an after thought, "We have five children."

Under the prevailing cultural values, power and status in the family, as in the society in general, go to those who earn or have money. So the full-time wife/mother who earns or has no money of her own feels powerless and increasingly worthless. The role of wife and mother no longer seems like a worthy, self-fulfilling position for a human being. Indeed, the position of wife/mother has come to be regarded by many as self-denying, stifling, even enslaving and destructive. This is, in part, because she is seen as serving others without monetary compensation. Housework and child care done for others for pay, especially when organized as a business, is respectable.

Consciousness raising about the impact of the traditional wife/mother role on women gave rise to the women's liberation movement. Only with full access to the money-earning and power positions in the society and the right to choose their own careers and to pursue their own interests are women considered free and able to live their own lives. The moral judgment that is made on the traditional position of the wife/mother is similar to that on slavery: it is a position that no human being can hold and fulfill its responsibilities without doing violence to or thwarting oneself as a person.

The women's liberation movement has transformed the traditional role of men as well as that of women. With wives less economically dependent on them, husbands have acquired a greater independence also, but usually without accepting equal responsibility for housework, child care, and the humanistic needs of the family. With greater independence on the part of both husbands and wives and with sexual activity largely freed from the fear of unwanted pregnancies by science and technology, sex has been liberated from the traditional morality that safeguarded and reinforced the family. But with the new sexual freedom, sex has lost much of its meaningfulness and has become casual and recreational for many. Nevertheless, human emotions still run deep over sexual relationships. We seem to have a higher level of abuse and violence on the part of lovers. Indeed, our emotions seem to rise up and veto our free-sex culture.

Under our present economic and cultural conditions, marriage has become less important to many people and families less stable. Marriage is often no more than a contract between self-interested partners, with each free to withdraw when the relationship no longer seems rewarding to him or her.

There were many evils in the traditional family structure, especially for women. In the feudal family, underwritten by the Judeo-Christian religion, women were not regarded as autonomous moral agents. Even in traditional wedding ceremonies today the father (or a close male relative) of the bride gives her to the groom. Back of this practice is the idea that a woman is under the guardianship of her father until the father transfers her guardianship to her husband. Under the economic and cultural conditions of industrial society, the wife's role, defined largely in terms of household chores and responsibility for the humanistic needs of the family and community, did not give her much status or power in the predominantly materialistic culture. Only full participation in the economic life and power structure of the society would do that. This is what the women's liberation movement seeks.

Furthermore, it was thought that women in the power structure of the society would be beneficial for all. Women would have greater independence and more fulfilling lives; families would have larger incomes with two money-earners; society would benefit from the economic productivity of women; husbands and wives would benefit from being more equal partners in their families: women would have more self-respect and be respected more; men would be humanized and come to have a closer relationship with their children by sharing more equally in family responsibilities; women in the work force and power structure would bring humanizing values to business and government; both parents would have quality time with their children and be able to do more for them financially.

All of this may be true in some cases, but in general it does not seem to be working out that way. The family as an institution is unstable, and in its present unstable condition it is not, by and large, meeting the needs of women, children, or men. It is very difficult for a young husband and wife to launch two independent careers and a family at the same time. The demands are more than many can manage. This is especially true for professionals, who are at the most critical point in their career development at the time of the maximum demands of the family. There are more stresses on marriages than ever before. Separate careers often result in commuter marriages or divorce. In most cases, women still accept and are expected to shoulder a greater responsibility in housework and child care; indeed, there are many more women than ever before with the full responsibility for home, children, and income. There are more children in single-parent or broken homes than ever before. There are more children shuttled back and forth between the homes of separated parents. There are more women and children living in poverty. More men lack an anchor in an enduring family. Often separated fathers have only limited or no contact with their children. There are fewer men and women who have the stability and support of a long and lasting marriage; and there are fewer children who have the foundation of a stable family within which to grow up and to give them continuing support. And nuclear families are less supported by an extended family and a caring neighborhood. With broken families, and with the greater fragility and weakness of the family in general, men, women, and children suffer from the lack of an important part of the framework for a meaningful life; being less securely anchored in the world, they have a more problematic self-concept and thus a less sure compass in life.

What we are witnessing is the impact of our materialistic culture and economic system on our basic humanistic institution. More will be required for the reconstruction of the family in a way that will serve our humanistic needs than simply preaching the old family values and the politics of virtue. Even if we wanted to, we could not and should not restore the traditional family with the husband as the authority and provider and the wife as housekeeper, child-care provider, and in general humanistic minister of the family. The traditional family of the industrial era is not the family we need. The moral judgment of the women's liberation movement on the role of women in such families cannot be refuted. We must work toward a family structure that will meet the humanistic needs of all members of the family, including the wife/mother as well as the children and the father. Such a change in the family structure is not possible without a basic change in the culture and the society, especially in the governing values and the practices of the major institutions in which most of the work of the society is done.

TOWARD A MODERN HUMANISTIC FAMILY

It has become clear that we cannot sustain the family as a humanistic island in a materialistic society. Although we cannot see clearly the fate of the family in our evolving society, without a shift in our governing values and a more family-friendly society, it is likely to become even more fragile and unstable. Our focus here is on what the constitution of the family should be as our primary humanistic institution. And if the dominant values of the culture and the other institutions of the society must change to make it possible, so be it.

It is not difficult to specify the major needs the family should satisfy and the conditions that it should meet. As long as we have family homes, there will be work to be done in them to meet materialistic needs. Wealthier people may be able to employ housekeepers, cooks, caterers, nurses, building and grounds caretakers, and the like to provide for the material needs of the family, but, in the typical family, most of these matters will have to be taken care of by family members themselves. When husband and wife share the economic responsibilities of the family, these family tasks should be shared by them in a communal spirit, with children taking on some responsibilities as they become competent to handle them. Sharing in the work to provide a home and an atmosphere which all members of the family can enjoy does more than satisfy materialistic needs; it makes family members feel that they are needed and that they are doing their part; it strengthens their self-respect and wins them the respect of others; it develops appreciation for meaningful work; it builds a feeling of family solidarity; and it enhances their pride in their home. The modern family can organize and manage these tasks in ways that would, to some extent, recapture something of the good aspects of the family communal life of the agricultural and family-shop era.

Some residential schools have realized the humanistic significance of shared responsibilities and cooperative work in meeting the needs of the school community. In the 1960s, my daughter attended a high school of this type. It was located on a two-hundred-acre farm. There were eight faculty families living in separate houses, and forty students (twenty boys and twenty girls) who were divided among the faculty homes. In meetings of the whole school population, they made or modified the rules they would all live by, and they all accepted responsibility for the welfare of the school community. Students were assigned in pairs to a specific task or set of tasks for a week at the time and then rotated to something else with different partners for a week and so on throughout the year. For example, two students would have full responsibility one week for preparing all the meals for the family and students who lived in their house; the next week those students might be assigned with a different partner to child care for certain hours in the day or some form of farm work, and so on. The whole community (the eight families and the forty students) met every morning to review the days activities and to discuss whatever problems existed in the community. The school had a strong academic program, but the most important thing that the students got from their years in the school was their development as responsible, caring, and cooperative human beings with self-respect, respect for others, and concern for the school community and the larger society.

On a smaller scale, families can be organized and operated in a way that would have something of the same humanistic benefits for its members, especially for children. But this kind of home life is not just for raising children. A husband and wife can benefit humanistically from shared responsibilities, cooperative work, and full communication in this manner.

For the most part, families will continue to have to support themselves economically by money-earning work in enterprises outside the home, but they may not have to spend as much time away from the home. New technologies will reduce the amount of long-distance traveling that will have to be done in business and professional work; indeed, increasing numbers of people may be able to do more of their career work in the home. And with new clusters of residential/shopping/business/school/recreational communities, more people will be able to work in their own neighborhood and have more time at home and be more accessible in the local community. These developments will make it possible for some parents to be more closely involved with their homes and neighborhoods. Their children will be more aware of their presence, even when they are at work. These developments should make for a somewhat more family-friendly society and provide a better home and neighborhood atmosphere for those affected.

Yet such developments are not without a price. All institutions need to develop their own culture and the loyalty and solidarity of their members. The isolation of workers in their homes would work against the institution's culture and solidarity. Furthermore, the removal of work from its institutional context might diminish its meaningfulness and deny the worker the support of the culture of the institutional setting and the spirit of solidarity with co-workers. Also the fragmentation of larger companies by establishing branches in all-purpose neighborhood centers would have something of the same effect on corporate culture and solidarity, even though smaller branches of a large corporation might provide a better and more supportive context for those who work in them.

Perhaps the biggest difficulty with the reorganization of our metropolitan areas into all-purpose centers is that they would never offer sufficient opportunities for a diverse residential population. The limited employment available in such communities would screen the residential population so that these centers would be, like present-day suburbs, more or less homogenous neighborhoods rather than cross-section communities. This would not be healthy for the society. It would not help people to identity with the complex problems of the society as a whole; it would not generate or sustain a common culture that would unite the whole society. It would tend to generate classes and factions rather than social solidarity and common purpose.

But what about the internal structure and culture of the family? As we observed earlier, the positions or offices in any institution should be compatible with personhood; that is, each position should be such that a human being could occupy and fulfill all the responsibilities of the position without having to compromise or shirk one's responsibilities as a person. The positions in a family (basically husband, wife, father, mother, son, daughter, brother, and sister) are natural rather than conventional, or at least they have a natural basis. Of course they may have a conventional aspect as well, which may be warranted or not. Whatever form these family roles take should be such that they support, nurture, and enhance the selfhood and enrich the lives of those who occupy them. Indeed, each family position should be such that, in being embraced in the identity of the individual who holds it, it would enlarge and ennoble his or her selfhood; a family member, in fulfilling his or her family role, would be fulfilling and enriching oneself as the particular person one is. This is so because the family just is first and foremost a humanistic institution. Its defining purpose is the development, empowerment, and support of its members in ways that enhance the quality of their lives, including the generation and upbringing of offspring to secure the future of humankind and civilization.

Relationships in a family should not be a matter of authority, duties, rights, justice, self-interest, or bargained agreements. When such issues arise, the family is already in trouble. Rather the family at its best lives by a spirit of love — concern for and devotion to the well-being of all members of the family, with respect, open communication, understanding, honesty, trust, support, cooperation, sharing, self-giving, and forgiving. A fully functional family has a spiritual unity; its members think more in terms of "we" than "I." A self not caught up in a larger spiritual unity is underdeveloped and impoverished. The family is the natural spiritual home of the individual.

When members of a family put themselves first and become self-seeking, when they become demanding, when they try to use or to control other members of the family, when they become angry and abusive, when they are insensitive to the feelings and concerns of others, when they are dishonest or show distrust, when communication fails and misunderstandings develop, the spirit that makes the family a living reality dies and the family disintegrates into a set of quarreling or sullen individuals. There are those who say that anger and hurt feelings should be vented, not repressed. Such venting in families often takes the form of verbal or even physical abuse. Although such venting may avoid the psychological damage of repression, it takes its toll on the bonds that hold a family together. Anger and other negative feelings should be neither vented in a way that corrodes relationships nor repressed in a way that does psychological damage. They should be dissolved by caring understanding and communication that show respect for, and elicit the cooperation of the offending party in solving the problem.

Of course parents are in a position of natural authority with respect to their immature children. They have the primary responsibility for the well-being and proper development of their children in their immaturity. Inherent in this responsibility is the right to make decisions about their children's well-being and to guide their behavior while preparing them to be responsible self-directing moral agents on their own. They should do this in such a way that they can justify their behavior to others and to their children in their maturity. The authority of parents diminishes progressively as their children become competent to make their own decisions in area after area of behavior until they reach a level of full autonomy. At this point, the children have the full responsibilities and the freedom rights of personhood; the authority of the parents totally evaporates, even though they will continue to have a responsibility to provide constructive support for their children.

But even in the children's immature years, the authority of parents is not absolute. It is conditioned on their competence and actual performance. The larger society has the responsibility to assure the right of children to be cared for and brought up in a responsible manner. This may include proscribing certain types of parental behavior in child rearing and in prescribing certain levels of welfare, health care, and education for the children; when parents fail to provide minimum requirements for the healthy development of their children, it is incumbent on the society to see that it is provided in some way. And, of course, there are needs of children that cannot be left to even the best of parents alone but must be provided for by society collectively, for example, education, a safe environment, and certain levels of health care.

It is wise for a society to leave as much freedom to parents as is consistent with the welfare of their children and the future of the society. Parents have a natural responsibility for, and authority over, their children, and, by and large, they have an unmatched love and concern for them. Furthermore, children need their parents; there is no substitute for a good parental family relationship for a child. But the freedom that a society can leave to parents in child rearing depends on the strength and health of the family. With the family a crumbling institution as it is in our society today, the society has to do more to protect the rights of children and to provide for their basic needs while trying to rebuild a strong and healthy family structure. Unfortunately, this places the society in a dilemma. The more responsibility the society takes on for the welfare of children, the weaker and more fragile the family tends to become. This seems to be an intractable problem; certainly there is no easy fix for it. Any real solution must involve deep cultural and social changes.

As we observed above, the family is in trouble in our society because the traditional family culture and the social and economic pressures that once made it work are no longer in force. Throughout most of human history the family was held together by the shared family culture, social pressures, and economic necessity. The family culture, supported by the general culture and social pressures, prescribed that sexual activity be restricted to married partners, a couple's shared life be defined largely by the goals and plans of the husband, with the wife in a subordinate but supportive role. The moral equality and economic freedom of women and the social tolerance of individual behavior under subjectivistic individualism (i. e., the idea that the values by which one lives are a matter of one's own choice without accountability to some objective principle or reality) has left the family stripped of its traditional support system and at the mercy of the feelings, preferences, and satisfactions or dissatisfactions of the individuals involved.

Certainly we do not want to shore up the family by restoring the traditional family support system. The moral equality and economic freedom of women are positive achievements to be preserved. And they both entail individualism, which has taken a subjectivistic turn in our scientific/technological culture. It seems clear that we cannot restore and maintain the family as a strong institution on these cultural foundations.

Communitarians maintain that we must accept the necessity of family, community, and certain other historically evolved institutions, roles, and practices and define ourselves in terms of them, and, if this means abandoning individualism, so be it. Indeed, they blame individualism for most of our social ills. But this way of rebuilding the family and strong institutions in general sacrifices the moral ground for the equality and economic freedom of human beings, including women. There has to be a better way.

What we need to abandon is not individualism as such but *subjectivism*. Our approach, as already indicated, is based on moral realism within a general realistic humanism. Accordingly, it is not up to individuals to *choose* for themselves the values by which they live. Even though individuals ought to be the authors and executives of their own lives (this is the individualism I defend), the value judgments by which they live are either true or false, and, as rational agents, human beings ought to live by *responsibly held value judgments*. This means that individuals, in learning about values and in forming their value judgments, have to draw on the experience and thought of others as well as their own just as they do in any area of belief. Everyone should have a healthy respect for the accumulated wisdom of humankind and the reasoning and judgments of others, especially those with more experience and proven reliability. When one comes to a conclusion contrary to the wisdom of qualified judges or that embodied in the institutionalized ways of the society, one should have good reasons that one believes would be convincing to any fully informed qualified person who would think the matter through properly, or at least one should be convinced that there are no counter reasons that would convince a clearheaded person that one was wrong. In other words, although individuals should live by their own value judgments, their value judgments are neither arbitrary nor simply expressions of their feelings, preferences, or choices. People are accountable in their value judgments to reality through their experience and critical assessment in collaboration with the experience and critical appraisals of others.

The problem we face is whether, and if so, how, we can find an adequate support system for the family (and the community) within the cultural framework of realistic humanism that preserves individualism and the equality and freedom of all people. We shall discuss these matters more fully with regard to the community, but we can pave the way for the more general discussion by focusing on the individual and the family at this point.

We observed earlier that the family is grounded in sexuality and kinship. So if we are to rehabilitate the family as an institution, we need to rethink our culture as it bears on sexuality and kinship. With our emphasis on individualism and social mobility, we tend to play down the importance of one's parental family and ancestors. In some societies with a strong family institution, the marriage of a young man and woman would be arranged by their parents with the approval of other relatives, but with the bride and groom having very little to do with the choice of each other. Although such a practice reflects the importance and strength of the family, no culture committed to freedom, equality, and individualism could tolerate such a practice. But until about midway in the present century, our culture taught a strong code of sexual morality and families carefully supervised the relationships of young men and women. Schools and colleges insisted on the same sexual morality young people were taught at home and continued the supervision of at least the relationships of young women. But by the 1960s, the old code of sexual behavior was in shambles and families, schools, and colleges largely abandoned their supervisory roles.

Even preteenagers were left, for the most part, on their own to cope with their sexuality without the benefit of established cultural and institutional ways to humanize and to manage the sexual energy surging within them. What cultural guidance most young people have today comes from their own peer group and from commercial and literary efforts to exploit sex for ulterior purposes. It is not surprising that the new sexual culture within the framework of subjectivistic individualism provides little support for an enduring monogamous family structure. The motto of the prevailing youth culture seems to be "Do what you want to do when you want to do it." A civilization cannot be sustained on that basis.

One of the great problems of our age is how to humanize sexuality and to develop it as an enriching, creative, and spiritualizing force in our lives and in the culture; a closely related matter is how we can strengthen our sense of kinship and build a strong family structure for generating, nurturing, and sustaining strong human beings who will be committed to worthy lives of their own, the well-being of their families, and a good society for all. These are not problems that can be solved simply by better education; they require serious rethinking some very fundamental matters in our culture.

The dehumanization of sex was of a piece with the general dehumanization of our modern culture. We dehumanized the world in understanding it in a way that would make it subject to our exploitation, but this process, as we have already observed, led ineluctably to the dehumanization of ourselves. It rejected the foundations in both knowledge and reality of the humanistic culture, and, furthermore, it required the naturalization of ourselves in order to make our existence and behavior intelligible in terms of our naturalistic world view. The revamping of our sexual and kinship culture must be part of the restructuring of our culture in general in terms of realistic humanism. But perhaps the plight of the family and the widespread dissatisfaction with our reproductive culture will spur us to look more deeply into these problems.

SEXUALITY AND MARRIAGE

Sexuality may be a fruitful place to begin rethinking what we are and what we are about as human beings. Unlike purely bodily needs and desires, our sexuality tends to draw us into humanizing relationships. In romantic love and in mothering or fathering a child, we feel ourselves involved in the mystery of creation in a way that profoundly affects our self-image and our sense of what we are about in life. There are grounds within all of us for the realization that sexuality is an awful thing to waste, to misuse, to debase, for sex in human beings has ennobling tendencies — it is transformed into love by reaching for higher values. Love elevates and enlarges our being and enhances the meaning of our lives.

By our very nature, we are not complete in ourselves. As individuals, we are a fragment and we feel it. Something within us cries out for kinship, for relationships with our kin, for offspring, for being part of something larger and higher than ourselves. A human being needs intersubjective relationships of varying degrees of intimacy, including in adulthood a romantic relationship in which one joins one's life with, and opens one's innermost self to, another with mutual love and devotion. This ideal union is approached most nearly in an unconditional commitment of a man and a woman to share their lives monogamously and to support each other in good and bad times. This is not simply a private matter, for it is the formation of a nuclear family that joins two kinship families and should, under normal conditions, become a link to future generations. That makes it a societal matter.

There is no experience that is more inherently resistant to intellectual naturalization than romantic love, parenthood, and child-parent relationships. It is not just that in these areas we take a humanistic stance and think in humanistic categories; we do that in all lived experience and in all thinking. While in some areas of the culture we seem to be able to distance the naturalistic reduction of the subject matter, but here we find an exceptionally strong resistance within ourselves to the naturalistic reduction and the unrepressible feeling that the theory is manifestly absurd on its face. The reality of our lived experience in romantic and familial relationships seems to refute the naturalistic theory of it.

We must understand the subject matter in these intimate relationships in terms of their indigenous humanistic categories, for otherwise we destroy the subject matter itself, not just our beliefs about it. This means that, in locating ourselves and these experiences and relationships in the world in a way that makes sense of them, we must acknowledge a humanistic context in which they have their place. This means, as we indicated earlier, that our humanistic culture must define our world view.

However much romantic feelings may be involved in a marriage, and they are important and should be continually cultivated and nurtured, the marriage should not be at the mercy of their waxing and waning, as they inevitably will. It should be grounded in a commitment, which is a volitional matter, not just an affective state. The vow "to love and to honor" one another is not a promise of romantic feelings; we cannot promise feelings, for they are not subject to our will. The vow "to love and to honor" one's partner in marriage is a commitment to make one's spouse's interests one's own and to treat one's spouse at all times in the manner appropriate to his or her station as a person and as one's spouse. A marriage commitment is not just an ordinary commitment; it is a commitment that enters into and reshapes one's identity; it transforms one's individual "I" into an enduring "we" in a way that alters one's decision-making from then on. No longer can one think and plan in terms of "my goals and what will be best for me." One commits oneself in marriage to think and to plan with one's partner for a shared life with shared goals, with each thinking of the other's interests and well-being as having the same standing as one's own. This is what it means for two people to become one.

For a family to be healthy and strong, the commitment of the husband and wife to the preservation and well-being of the family must be part of the framework in terms of which they make their decisions; in other words, the solidarity and well-being of the family must be presupposed by the decisions the husband and wife make together and by the decisions they make individually on matters that affect the other. In ordinary situations, any action that would likely kill or seriously damage oneself is ruled out as an option. In like manner, if a marriage is to be healthy and strong, any joint or individual action that would likely destroy or seriously damage the marriage or be detrimental to one's spouse should not be entertained as an option.

Whenever a marriage commitment becomes conditioned on a sacrifice-free or frictionless relationship, the marriage is in jeopardy. Most parents regard their relationship with their children as not subject to divorce. Whatever problems arise, they accept that the problems must be dealt with or lived with within the relationship; the problems never put the relationship in question. And even if parents should choose to walk away from their parental responsibilities and sever their relationship with their dependent children, the society would not look the other way. Social and even juridical pressures would be brought to bear. Of course the situation is not the same with spouses as with children. Spouses are mature moral agents. Nevertheless, the common marriage commitment in our culture still takes the form "for better or for worse, until death do us part," but apparently these words are widely regarded as merely ceremonial, with no binding force.

There are marriages that clearly do not work and cannot be made to work; they may be destructive for all parties involved, including children in many cases. There is no point in condemning individuals to live out their lives in broken and unredeemable marriages. After all, institutions exist for people, not people for institutions. But our society values marriage and the integrity of the family too lightly. There are few, if any, special relationships or behaviors still reserved for marriage, except certain legal matters pertaining to property rights. Men and women live together and many even have children without marriage; indeed, many unmarried women living alone have children, some even plan to do so. What is most significant about all of this is that it has become a socially acceptable life style in many circles. For those who choose marriage and the more traditional family life style, the breakup of a marriage, although often traumatic for the parties involved, is socially and legally acceptable on a no-fault basis. This is, no doubt, humane for the individuals who are in a broken and unrepairable marriage, but it may lead to hasty divorces and tend to weaken the married family as an institution.

The way to strengthen the married family, however, is not by coercive sanctions against or roadblocks to divorce. A couple should stay in a marriage only for positive reasons or to avoid the inevitable damage of separation, not because of socially imposed penalties. Nevertheless, it makes sense for the society to insist on procedures that would require couples contemplating divorce to go slowly, to rethink their relationship, to explore together (preferably with a humanistic counselor) ways in which they might yet make the marriage work, and to try again to salvage it if possible. It is more important, however, for society to examine and to rethink our culture, education, and social arrangements pertaining to sexuality, intimacy, reproduction, and the basic humanistic needs of both children and adults. It is also important for society to examine the impact of social and economic forces and governmental policies on marriage and the family. The family is such a basic humanistic institution that it should be second only to the individual person in importance. Other institutions and social practices should be judged by how well they support or damage the family as well as how they affect individual lives.

Given realistic humanism, three questions arise about our sexual culture and social structure: What form should marriage and the family take under modern conditions? What kind of sexual life is appropriate for the unmarried? And what about the sexual life of those with same-gender sexual affectivity?

In modern society, extended education pushes full adulthood (i.e., the state in which one is a self-supporting, productive member of society) for many into their late twenties or even thirties. And young people who do not take the long educational route often find themselves unqualified for or unable to get even a self-supporting job to say nothing of a job that would support a family. In contrast with earlier generations, young people are, for the most part, not in a position to take on the responsibilities of marriage and a family until relatively late, if ever. This is the source of many problems. It is not only that men and women mature sexually long before they are in a position to take on the responsibilities of a family, but this long period between childhood and adulthood is usually a time of personal ambiguity, a weak or fluctuating self-concept, and self-doubt. In modern society, one may be in one's forties, if ever, before one gets the kind of self-confirmation that firms up one's identity and makes one secure in one's person as an adult. While wandering in this wilderness of uncertainty and self-doubt, one's sexual energy is at its peak, and the need for recognition, the need for intimacy, the need for the support of a meaningful sexual relationship, and the need for unconditional acceptance in a humanistic haven are never greater. It is not surprising that we have such a high level of aggressiveness and irresponsibility among our youth, especially the dispossessed without hope. If people cannot find recognition, respect, and acceptance in constructive relationships and behavior, they are likely to seek recognition through destructive behavior and acceptance and respect in a fellowship of discontents or criminals.

All of this is part of the human fallout of our materialistic culture. We have no greater problem than how to grow human beings into responsible adults and how to develop a society in which they can thrive through all stages of life. Our focus here is on how to humanize sex and how to develop the social structures needed for our youth to mature as responsible adults with meaningful lives.

First of all, we need, as previously indicated, to develop and to teach a humanistic philosophy of sexuality. Children need to be taught to think of sexual reproduction as one of the great breakthroughs in the creative processes of the universe. They should be taught to think of sexual urges and pleasures as nature's invitations and inducements for higher organisms to participate in the propagation of their kind, and that there are collateral sentiments and impulses that lead them to prepare an appropriate context for and to nurture and to protect their offspring. In the animal kingdom, all these reproductive, nurturing, and protective forces are coordinated and regulated by nature, but in human beings the natural controls are eliminated and these forces are either regulated institutionally or placed under our individual rational management. Our institutional controls have broken down for the most part. If we think about nature humanistically, and I urge that we do, we must feel a tremendous responsibility in having the management of these creative powers in our hands without social guidelines. These powers pertain to the creation of our humanistic identity and life as well as the biological and cultural generation of new human beings. This responsibility is an essential part of one's vocation. In theological language, it means that we are partners with God in creation, not just instruments of the creator. Everyone needs to learn the proper stewardship of these wonderful powers.

If by "the divine" we mean a causal power working for higher values as I am wont to do, fully humanized sex is a divine, creative power, whereas unelevated, selfish sexuality is a demonic power, for it is dehumanizing and socially destructive. One of the persistent problems in human history has been how to humanize sexuality — how to inform and structure this powerful force with higher values and how to integrate it into the lives of people in meaningful ways that are life-elevating, life-enhancing, and socially constructive. Society should sanction and encourage the integration of the gift of sexuality into the lives of people in ways that are individually and socially constructive; it should disapprove of and discourage all forms of sexual behavior that are dehumanizing, exploitative, or socially destructive.

It is a verdict of reflected experience that sexual acts as expressions of mutually committed and responsible love between a man and a woman are meaningful, for they enrich the relationship and the life of each. Furthermore, such relationships grounded in sexuality are the foundation of the primary family on which the present and the future well-being of the society depends so heavily.

It is also a verdict of reflected experience that whatever devalues or adulterates the meaningfulness of sex or of a committed love relationship is unworthy of a human being. It is widely recognized that casual or promiscuous sex is adulterated or meaningless, and that sex acts that are expressions of power or conquest are exploitative and morally wrong.

Among the collateral human sexual sentiments and longings are feelings of incompleteness, romantic affections, and the relentless need all mature people feel for bonding with another with complete intimacy in a meaningful, shared life that involves having and raising children — children who will give them a larger purpose and a continuing stake in the future. Given the whole human sexual complex, it is irresponsible for any human being to manage his or her sexuality with regard for only sexual desire and pleasure. Indeed, it is worse than irresponsible; it is to treat oneself as less than a human being; it reduces one's sexuality to its animal level and ignores or even denies its distinctively human dimension. If the sale of sexual privileges is prostitution, management of one's sexual behavior simply for the gratification of sexual desire is prostitution also; it cheapens one's sexuality by treating it as though it did not have the humanistic status that it has. If one uses another person simply for one's sexual gratification, even if by consent, one shows lack of respect for the humanity of the other person and lack of respect for one's own sexuality and for one's responsibilities as a human being. One's sexuality should be shaped and guided by a full understanding of, and respect for, its complex and ramified role in human life.

Nature's basic inducements for procreative behavior emerge in teenagers or even in younger children, especially in males, before the development of the whole syndrome of human sexuality. This is one reason why teenagers are incompetent to manage their sexual behavior without strict cultural guidelines and supervision. They need to learn from the culture the full humanistic significance of sexuality, but they cannot fully understand this significance until they reach the level of maturity at which the collateral sexual sentiments and longings are in full play in their lives. Our society is woefully inadequate in humanistic sexual education and in adult supervision of the behavior of the immature. We have never had adequate sex education, but the chaperon system in force in this country until about World War II was a fairly effective method of supervision, and it taught the virtue of sexual restraint, especially for teenagers. If people fall victim to biological inducements to sexual behavior without proper regard for their deep humanistic sexual needs, they are likely to pay a terrible price. The culture should stand firmly against casual sex and promiscuity; indeed, it should oppose all meaningless sexual encounters. Sexual relationships that are not vested with meaning are always dehumanizing. It is vitally important for children to be brought up with a humanistic philosophy of sexuality and in a culture of sexual discipline and social practices that turn their sexual energy to constructive purposes and prepares young people for an adult life in which they integrate their sexuality into their lives in a way that satisfies their deep humanistic sexual needs in socially constructive ways.

With the protracted preparation of youth for a fully adult role in a modern society, so many young people develop their full complex of humanistic sexual needs long before they are financially ready for marriage and a family. This has been an increasing problem for young people throughout the century, but especially since World War II. It is important for human beings as they mature, certainly in their twenties, to develop meaningful sexual relationships, even if they are unprepared for the usual economic responsibilities of marriage. It is now a widely accepted practice for young couples to live together for a time without marriage. Perhaps such relationships should be institutionalized — not legalized, but based on a covenant relationship with each other and with their families, with social approval. The couple would commit themselves to be faithful to each other, with the intention to marry when they became economically independent, and, furthermore, they would agree to marry in case the young woman should become pregnant to provide a secure family environment for the child. The parental families should provide moral support and such financial assistance as they were able while the couple continued their education. In the absence of sufficient parental assistance, the society should provide assistance for such arrangements for worthy students to the extent that it was able. It would be part of a policy of putting people and their humanistic needs first.

If a couple in such a socially approved covenant relationship should find that, in their continuing growth, they had become incompatible with each other in their outlook and life plans, they could terminate their relationship without the legal entanglements that would be involved in the dissolution of a marriage and perhaps be in a better position for a new relationship. In sum, socially supported "trial marriages" in this age group might reduce casual sex, give rise to better and more stable marriages in the long run, and reduce the number of divorces, while meeting deep humanistic sexual needs of young people at this age in a society that requires a protracted education for a large portion of the population.

Societies for the most part have not developed or sanctioned ways in which people, who find themselves constituted with same-gender sexual affectivity, can incorporate their sexuality into their lives in a life-elevating and socially constructive way. Rather most societies have condemned their sexuality, made them feel unworthy because of their given sexual nature, and have allowed them no morally acceptable option but sexual repression or denial. This cultural and social situation has fostered guilt-ridden thwarted lives, hidden relationships, homosexual promiscuity, ruined careers, and the trampling of basic human rights.

It is past time for an enlightened society to find morally justified ways and a supportive social infrastructure for people with same-gender sexual affectivity to embrace their sexuality, inform it with and orient it toward higher values, and integrate it into their lives in meaningful and socially constructive ways.

In our effort to reverse the trend toward increasing adulteration, trivialization, and exploitation of sexuality in general, we should develop a culture that recognizes that sexuality in the service of higher values is a divine creative power within us and that it deserves our highest respect. We need to restore the meaning of the term "holy matrimony" as a union in which the power that brought the couple together, sustains them, and enriches the life of each in the marriage is divine.

Monogamous marriage grounded in mutual love, commitment, equality, faithfulness and supported by the culture and the community is the best social structure we know for integrating sexuality into the lives of heterosexuals for the enrichment of their lives and for the good of society. The society should open this institution, with all of its cultural and social supports, including religious sanction, to people with same-gender affectivity. This would humanize homosexuality, help strip away the evil involved in its denial and repression, and unleash its potential for human good.

If homosexuality can engender and sustain committed loving/caring monogamous relationships that enrich the lives of the couples involved, who can say that it is not a divine power moving them to higher values? Who will say that it is not a holy union? Indeed, it is in just such powers within the human heart moving us toward higher values that we find God at work, if we find God anywhere.

In sum, the first step toward a society that is fit for human beings is the proper constitution and health of the primary humanistic institutions, those concerned with the generation, growth, nurture, and empowerment of human beings. We must rid them of their historic defects and free them from the grip of the materialistic culture that has invaded them; we must infuse in them genuine humanistic values and ways of thought.

The family is our primary humanistic institution. It is, as previously remarked, the social womb for children and a humanistic haven and general support center for adults. We cannot have well-integrated, strong, morally healthy citizens without healthy families. The family in our society is suffering from structural injustices based on our historic sexism and anti-homosexuality; its moral foundation has been undermined by our cultural subjectivistic individualism and the egoistic contractual rationality of the market economy; and it is under impact from centrifugal social and economic forces that threaten to tear it apart. We must rid the family of its historic structural injustices, restore confidence in a supportive objective family morality, and protect the family from threatening social and economic forces.

If we are to have a society fit for human beings, we must have a full-fledged humanistic family structure. Negatively, a humanistic family must be free from oppression of women, children, or men and it must be open to people of both sexes with same-gender affectivity grounded in their natural constitution. Positively, a healthy humanistic family would be one that was responsive to all its members' deep and enduring humanistic needs, and it would grow, nurture, and empower children with moral character, commitment to higher values, and a humanistic vision of humankind, society, and the world.

COMMUNITY

A good family is not enough. Everyone needs a community, indeed, multiple communities, but they should fit together coherently in a nesting manner according to their comprehensiveness. A community consists of people who are related to and identify with each other on the basis of a shared form of life. A form of life has its identity and unity in terms of the culture that it embodies, especially the assumptions and beliefs that it embraces about some enterprise and the priorities and the ways of behavior for those engaged in it. A community may be based on a limited or a more comprehensive form of life. A limited form of life gives rise to a specialized community of people such as the scientific, academic, business, or art communities. A more total or comprehensive form of life would define one's human identity, basic values, and orientation in the world. The people in a community, whether specialized or more comprehensive, may live in a common geographical area or they may live in scattered places throughout the world. They usually feel an identity not only with their contemporaries, but also with past generations who generated and participated in their form of life and future generations who will inherit it.

Although the family in which one is brought up gives one an identity and an orientation in life with a set of basic values, the community or communities in which one participates also give one an identity, a perspective, and a set of values. It is best for one, especially in early life, for all of these to be mutually corroborative or at least consistent. If one is torn by contradictory forms of life or cultural teachings before one has a solid core and critical powers, one may fail to develop a strong identity with a focused life and inner strength. The family and community should cooperate in growing strong, purposeful human beings with a clear moral perspective.

A supportive community is not only essential for children and young people. Adults also need to live in communities and especially in a comprehensive community or state with which they identify and in which they feel at home. People are alienated by an institution or a society that embodies a culture different from or at odds with the culture that they have internalized in their own identity and way of life. This is why humanistic institutions and a humanistic society are so important. Only a humanistic society composed of humanistic institutions would be fit for human beings. In later chapters, we shall discuss something of what such a society would be like.

My form of realistic humanism holds that personhood, as far as we know, is the highest achievement of the universe. Society, with all of its institutions, including the family, exists to develop and to support persons and to provide social forms through which individual human beings may be more fully realized and perfected. The overall judgment on any institution or society is how well it fulfills this function. Although people can develop and find their fulfillment only in and through society, people do not exist for their society or have their worth solely through their part in the society. Society is not a higher reality for which people can be sacrificed. Collectivists often make this mistake. The common good may override the private good of individuals in many situations, but the common good must embrace and safeguard the basic worth and rights of each; otherwise the alleged common good would be only a factional good without moral force. The proper order of things, as indicated in chapters 1 and 2, is not to measure people by the greatness of the society that they generate and sustain, but rather to measure a society by the greatness of the people it generates and the success of the people in defining and living worthy lives of their own in and through the cultural and social forms of the society.

This kind of individualism is challenged by communitarians. Some metaphysical communitarians, Hegelians in particular, think of ultimate Being (the Absolute, God) as being expressed and coming into self-consciousness in human history. The highest form of the expression and self-consciousness of Being, they say, is not in individual self-consciousness but in the culture and institutions of a politically organized historical community, a nation state. And since historical communities or civilizations vary in the degree to which they express the Absolute and bring the World Spirit to fulfillment, some have thought that neither particular individuals nor the less developed civilizations have rights that limit the most advanced cultural community whose time has struck, for there can be no normative limits on the Absolute.

For metaphysical communitarians, the moral substance resides in the community, not the individual, for it takes a historical community to generate a culture and individuals have their identity in terms of the institutions and practices of the community. Moral judgments that do not express the form of life of their historical community are said to be purely abstract, without force. And they acknowledge no judgment on a historical community other than the extent to which it expresses the Absolute (or, what amounts to the same thing for Hegelians, the extent to which it embodies rationality) in comparison with other historical communities.[1] When a society has ceased to embody the World Spirit, according to Hegel, a great leader may emerge with a vision that expresses the World Spirit for a new age, a vision that grips the minds and hearts of the people as what they have been groping toward, and thereby move forward the culture and the society.[2] But the effective ethics of the people lies in the historically evolved institutions and practices of their society, which are the counterpart of instincts.

Most present-day communitarians do not have the metaphysical foundation for the normative primacy of the form of life of a particular historical community.[3] For them, the form of life of any community is simply what the lathe of history has wrought in a non-teleological process, much like the "functional" structure of a biological species is said to be what the naturalistic evolutionary process has brought about. And as the "functional" structure of a species is the norm by which we judge well-formedness and deformity, and health and sickness in the members of the species, the form of life of a historical community is said to be the norm by which we judge moral behavior of individuals. There is no basis, according to this view, for comparing the forms of life of different historical communities or ethnic groups; indeed, there is no basis for judging any particular community's way of life. It is simply what it is, but nevertheless it is the norm by which the members of the community judge themselves. The people have to fit the society. There is no moral basis for social and cultural reform other than perhaps internal coherence or repair of the damage that has been done to historically evolved institutions in the name of individualism by social reformers.

In justifying individualism within the framework of realistic humanism, we need to guard against possible misinterpretations of what the priority of personhood means. The priority of the individual does not mean that the individual's life should be self-centered or self-seeking above all else. The rights of others and the common good impose requirements on everyone. Furthermore, the person who does not incorporate into his or her identity various memberships and relationships has a very impoverished self, and the person who does not embrace some higher values in his or her comprehensive purpose cannot achieve greatness. Some higher values obligate everyone, and people who do not give themselves to something larger than themselves have little to live for.

This kind of individualism rejects both the organic view of society and social atomism. It rejects the organic theory because a society is unlike an organism in a most important way. We think of an organ primarily in terms of what it exists and is structured to do in the life of the organism as a whole. If an organ becomes a liability so that the organism would be better off without it, we have no qualms about excising it, for its normative constitution is defined by its part in the organism and the value it has is derived from the needs of the whole of which it is a part. The situation is quite different with a person who is a liability on his or her family or society. Personhood is not defined in terms of the society; it is a natural office grounded in the individual's nature as a knower-agent. Rather the normative structure of society, as we previously argued, is grounded in and derives from the rights and needs of human beings. We judge a society by how well human beings develop and thrive in it, and we judge human beings by their interpretation and rendition of what it is to be a human being in the circumstances of their existence. This includes the roles they play in society, but those roles are judged not only in terms of their contributions to the society, but also in terms of their appropriateness to one's humanity and individuality and how well one realizes and completes oneself through them.

Nevertheless, a society is not an organization of independently constituted individuals. One's most basic memberships, relationships, roles, and offices are taken up into one's self-concept and thus into one's identity. Furthermore, in the ideal situation, the culture that organizes and shapes one's inner realm, one's subjectivity, is embodied also in the social structures and institutions of the society. When this is the case, one identifies with the society and relates to it as one's larger self. One feels its deficiencies and injuries, enjoys its health, and takes pride in its heroes and institutions and their accomplishments. Yet individuals have within themselves grounds and powers for criticizing, judging, and reforming the culture and the society. The whole cultural/social edifice is accountable, through the knowledge-yielding and critical powers of the people, to the inherent normative constitution of a society, which is grounded in the normative constitution and needs of its members. A society is judged by how well it grows, empowers, fulfills, and serves human beings, including the well-being of their environment and the future of their civilization.

All of this applies to the individual in relation to the family as well as to the individual and the larger society. This means that the family or any other institution must be judged by how well it generates, nurtures, and sustains human beings and enriches their lives. We have no warrant for sacrificing human beings for institutions. When an institution becomes a hindrance to human development and well-being, or when it is less than the best we know for human betterment, it should be changed.

But an institution is not simply a social artifact. We cannot, or at least should not, develop a new design for a major institution or a society and try to impose it on the people. Some revolutionaries have tried to do this. Deep changes in a major institution or in society itself require change in the culture and thus changes in people and their ways of thought and behavior. Changes in the culture and behavior of people may work changes in an institution or in society without the institution or the society ever coming under critical review. Sometimes, however, the restructuring of an institution or a society may be deliberate. If so, it should be done through rational discussion, debate, and an agreed-upon-decision-procedure in such a way that all the people involved could identify with it. The subjectivity of the people must mesh with the social and institutional structures of the society, or else there will be trouble.

MULTICULTURALISM

Two further issues present themselves: multiculturalism and the right of a family to have their children educated in public schools but in a way that would not undermine or conflict with the ethnic, moral, and religious culture of the home.

A community, as we said above, consists of people who are bound together by a common form of life. Without a shared culture there is no community. While a limited-purpose community such as the people engaged in some common pursuit or enterprise may share only a limited culture that is related to their common endeavor, a state as a politically organized society requires a comprehensive culture. A well-functioning more or less self-sufficient and self-governing society must embody a basic culture in its social structure that is shared by the people. Otherwise the society would not be a coordinated, well-functioning whole, and the people would be alienated from it. It could function only by sanctions and rewards that made it the self-interest of each member to conform with the institutional ways and laws of the society. It would not be a society in which people would flourish, for it would not encourage and support people in defining and living lives worthy of them as moral agents in pursuit of higher values. It would rather encourage them to live as atomic individual self-interest maximizers. It would make what Christians used to call original sin the organizing principle of the society.

So a radically multicultural society is not a possibility. This does not mean that there cannot be many subcultures and different ethnic and religious groups in a society. A country of immigrants like the United States with many ethnic and religious subcultures is possible because the basic culture embodied in our political institutions can be embraced and supported by so many different subcultures, and the provision by which even its most fundamental principles are held open to ongoing questioning and debate. But a subculture that absolutizes itself as a rival to the basic culture and seeks to replace it with a culture that is not held rationally accountable is a real problem. It tests the limits of rational tolerance.

This is why the rise of the radical religious right as a political movement in the United States in recent decades is seen as a threat by many. It is not that religion is involved in politics. The United States has tried to keep government out of religion, but religion has always been involved in politics throughout our history. Religion led the way in the abolition of slavery, the prohibition of alcohol early in this century, the civil rights movement of the 1950s and 1960s, and many other social reform movements. In these endeavors, religion was a religious force for social reforms that had moral justification that all citizens could acknowledge regardless of their religious views and commitments. In these instances, religion was not "tribal" in nature; it in no way tried to absolutize itself as a rival to the basic civic culture. By contrast, the religious right today is seen by many as promoting a political culture and program for the society based on "tribal" beliefs and principles that are not open to debate and are not available to others on rational grounds. They are seen as a threat to a free society in much the same way as the Communist Party was. Any culture for the basic structure of a society is a threat to freedom if it absolutizes itself beyond the limits of rational justification or reconstruction.

What is most troubling about the present debate over multiculturalism is the cultural subjectivism and relativism that often frames the discussion. It is assumed by many that the culture embodied in our basic institutions is not universal and objective, that it is not subject to rational justification or reconstruction, that it is not such that it can and should be acknowledged by and embraced in various subcultures. Rather it is held that neither the dominant culture nor the subcultures are subject to rational validation, that the struggle among subcultures or the struggle of a subculture with the dominant culture is only a power struggle between different cultural groups. When such conflicts are seen as power struggles rather than as rational debates, a free society is in danger.

Democracy cannot work without faith in some form of realistic humanism, for democracy is premised on the possibility of a reasoned moral consensus about fundamental issues of the society. Without faith in the possibility of such a moral consensus, politics collapses into bargained agreements among interest or ethnic groups, and power, not reason, is the arbiter. This is not a free society; it is not a just society; it is not a democracy.

We come now to the second problem mentioned above, namely, the right of parents to have their children educated in public schools in a way that does not undermine the culture they are taught at home. With reference to a controversy in a local community about how different life-styles were being dealt with in the school curriculum, the chairman of a local citizens group said: "We are trying, as parents, to make sure that our values are not tread upon for the sake of someone else's values." The statement, taken at face value, implies an ethnic subjectivism and relativism that would, if it were widely accepted, be a serious threat to meaningful education, a free culture, and democracy.

It is a fundamental right of every human being, according to classical liberalism, to be brought up and educated, not necessarily in the culture of his or her parents, but in a free culture; that is, a culture that has developed out of ongoing experience and cultural conflicts and challenges under reflection and critical examination. A culture that is not the product of such a process and is not open to it on a continuing basis is not a free culture; it is the instrument of some power structure or ethnic group. Such a culture does not generate free people, for it manipulates the minds and hearts of people according to some group's preference; it does not equip and inspire children to develop by their own powers according to their own inherent normative constitution and the best available knowledge and wisdom. Furthermore, one has the right to be taught how one can examine, test, and correct errors in the culture in which one has been brought up and educated. One is not fully a free human being until one can make the culture that one internalizes truly one's own through one's own understanding and critical examination of it.

Of course early education, which is concerned primarily with developing the character and the inherent powers of children and equipping them with the basic cultural capital they will need for a successful human life, has to proceed in terms of a more or less stable culture that is not put in question too much in the process. But we need to be sure that this basic culture of elementary education is not the property of, and is not controlled by, any "tribal" or partisan group. By the time students reach senior high school, however, they should have a level of self-formation and a sufficient cultural base to be taught about difficulties in, and challenges to, the culture they have internalized, and how to take a reflective, critical approach in examining and reconstructing it. For at least half of the student population this will be the last formal opportunity for them to learn how to be free, responsible citizens in a modern democracy.

Christian fundamentalists, as well as other fundamentalist religious groups, are right in claiming that public education in America tends to undermine the culture of their homes and religious institutions. Their children cannot be educated in the dominant culture of modern Western civilization, whether in public or private schools, without undergoing a great deal of emotional and intellectual struggle. If the education really "takes," the children will acquire a new cultural perspective and a new world view. If they manage to keep an identification with the religion of their upbringing, it will be with a different understanding of it.

There is a deep chasm between Christian, Jewish, and Islamic fundamentalism and mainstream modern Western civilization. Indeed, there are profound logical tensions between historical religion in any form and our modern democratic, scientific culture. There may be interpretations of any traditional religion and modern culture that partially relieve the logical tensions between them, but it is very difficult, if not impossible, to preserve any orthodox interpretation and the fundamentals of modern Western civilization. The fundamentalists, recognizing this fact, are engaged in a political assault on the fundamentals of modern Western culture.

Modern Western civilization is committed to freedom — not only freedom of the individual from morally unwarranted external coercion, but also freedom from internal control by cultural manipulation. Commitment to freedom in this sense involves commitment to the development and use of the knowledge-yielding, critical, expressive, and creative powers of each individual. Furthermore, under the governing imperative of modern Western civilization to achieve mastery of the material conditions of our existence for the acquisition of wealth and power, we have developed modern science, which provides us with the kind of knowledge and understanding that is useful for making, manipulating, and controlling things. As we noted earlier, this development has resulted in widely shared assumptions about knowledge and the world that are antithetical to orthodox religion and all prescientific cultures.

In teaching how to think scientifically about a problem, we teach the scientific view of truth and knowledge. And in teaching the scientific account of some phenomenon, we teach the scientific world view, for to describe and to explain something scientifically is to place it in the world as the world is conceptualized in scientific thought. With the dominance of this view of knowledge and the world, as we pointed out earlier, the whole area of humanity and values (including morals, social and political thought, and religion) become highly problematic. Everything solid seems to melt into air.

So education in our culture generates logical tensions and intellectual problems for all of us, for we have trouble trying to place ourselves as human beings and the norms by which we live in the world as defined by the scientific conceptual system. Some turn to cultural pluralism, claiming that any life-style is as good as any other and that the individual's only guide in choosing one is his or her preference. This, I think, is a great mistake. It gives up the possibility of a basic moral consensus; and without such a consensus, a free society cannot exist. Religious fundamentalists turn to "tribalism," trying to absolutize their ethnic ways and values through their ethnic religion. They would give up our ideal of a free culture and freedom of the individual from internal manipulation in order to protect their cherished views from the challenges of modern thought. This, too, would be a great mistake. It would give up what a free society is all about. But none of us can afford to ignore the problems deep within our culture that the religious fundamentalists and the subjectivistic relativists are pointing out. We must acknowledge and confront these problems without compromising our commitment to a free society.

Some people seem to expect the young to absorb uncritically the value, philosophical, and religious dimensions of the culture, while teaching them to think critically about only mathematical and factual matters. We cannot sustain a free society this way, especially one with deep cultural conflicts and contradictions like ours. Students should be taught how to cope in a responsible way with the logical tensions in the culture that they internalize. We should try to develop all of their knowledge-yielding and critical powers and teach them how to think constructively about values and difficult moral issues, conflicting conceptions of humanity and the world, and rival views of the culture and its foundations. Also students should be taught how people with conflicting moral, philosophical, and religious commitments can participate in a responsible way in determining the constitution and ways of the society. This is a tall order for education. It makes high demands on the educational qualifications of teachers, and it requires extraordinary wisdom on the part of parents and citizens. Nevertheless, this is the price we must pay, if we want to sustain a free culture.

There is much to be said for a multicultural curriculum in education in our multicultural society. Each ethnic culture is a distillation of lived experience under the demands of life in certain historical circumstances. We all need to be open to the cultural products and verdicts of lived experience. Cultures grow from challenges and borrowings from other cultures. They always have. And we can acknowledge a great deal of cultural relativity without accepting cultural relativism or tribalism. But we cannot have a society, especially we cannot have a democratic society, without having a basic shared culture, for the culture of a society not only informs and structures the lives of individuals, but also the institutions of the society as well. Furthermore, we cannot have a free society without a free culture, and we cannot have a free culture unless it is a rationally formed culture that is open to on-going rational criticism and reconstruction.

5

EDUCATION FOR

HUMAN GROWTH

Education, broadly conceived, is the most important function of a society. It is the process by which human beings are culturally generated and prepared for defining and living a life of their own and for participating in the society in constructive ways. Education embraces all that the family, the immediate community, and the larger society do to help their members, and what individuals do for themselves, toward the development and expansion of their powers that lend themselves to self-management, the development of the character or constitution by which they employ and manage their powers, and mastery of or access to the accumulated cultural capital of humankind. These are not independent processes. The powers and character of human beings can be developed and expanded only by internalizing a culture and learning to operate within it. Even criticism or rejection of parts or aspects of the culture has to be an inside job. In short, education is the process by which the society culturally generates and grows human beings and by which individuals develop and expand their powers, form their character, master the culture, and learn how to define and to live their lives and to participate in the society in fruitful ways.

THREE HUMAN ENTERPRISES

We may distinguish three great human enterprises in which all of us are, or should be, engaged: *Moral, cultural, religious* (*moral,* for short) — constituting and empowering ourselves and defining and living lives that are worthy of us as human beings and as the individuals we are; *Civic* — fulfilling our responsibilities as members of society, including working with others to develop and sustain a society that is fit for human beings; *Economic* — the organization of work and creativity in providing the goods and services that we need or want, either directly or by providing goods or services for others for some medium of exchange.

These are, of course, overlapping and interdependent enterprises. The moral enterprise is the most inclusive and should be primary. It envelopes the other two and provides the framework in terms of which they should operate and be judged. The civic enterprise is an integral part of the moral enterprise; its goal is part of the moral goal. A morally good life for anyone must include being a good member of society; being a good member of society depends on being a basically good person. There is, however, a different relationship between the moral and the economic enterprises. Of course individuals, in so far as they are able, have a moral responsibility to provide for their own and their dependents' economic needs, to help others whose needs require their assistance, and to do their part in support of the proper functions of society; and so, bearing in mind the qualification "in so far as they are able," success in the moral enterprise entails at least sufficient economic success to meet these requirements. It is a moral fault for one who, for lack of will or self-discipline, ends up a debit on society or fails to meet his or her economic responsibilities to others. But an individual can have economic success and yet be a moral failure; one who fails economically by errors in judgment or for reasons beyond his or her control may have moral success; a society can have economic prosperity while suffering enormous moral aberrations and deficits, or it can be morally sound and economically impoverished.

The inversion of modern Western civilization in making materialistic values, the modern scientific way of thought, and the economic enterprise dominant has resulted in phenomenal economic growth, but at the price of the derangement of the culture, a severe moral disorder in the society, and a large number of spiritually impoverished and morally dysfunctional people. Our commitment to wealth and power, as we indicated in chapter 1, has generated a way of thinking and a world view that have given us a limited view of rationality, eroded the foundations of moral and religious modes of thought, and degraded and distorted the humanities; it has resulted in the disruption and weakening of our reproductive and nurturing institutions.

Consider again what has happened to the family as most of its functions have been transferred to the marketplace and the morality that supported it has gone soft or suspect. Under the pressures of economic "necessity" and status based on money-earning work, children are often housed in underfunded day-care centers with inferior, fluctuating staffs for eight to ten hours a day, and the homes of many children are little more than single-parent "night shelters," with limited time and energy for love and attention.

Although many people are still involved in and support a religion of one kind or another and there is a strong reactionary religious movement, religions have lost much of their significance in our society. They are not a part of our mainstream cultural life. In fact, our dominant culture undermines and discredits religion; it is not considered intellectually respectable. Our public schools steer clear of the subject under the doctrine of the separation of church and state. We turn to pediatricians and child psychologists for guidance in raising our children, and to psychiatrists and other science-based psychotherapists to help us with our anxieties, depressions, griefs, and other emotional problems. Increasingly, especially among those who consider themselves among the culturally more advanced, we marry, celebrate births, and bury our dead without a religious ritual. It is not surprising that children who grow up in our society often conclude that religion is irrelevant or even that it is a backward superstition that should be jettisoned.

Schools, many of which are divorced from the local community and lack a nurturing and empowering culture, are charged with the task of producing workers for a rapidly evolving high-tech economy and military establishment. The public supports education largely because it is essential for economic growth and the military strength of the country. Politicians put forward education programs under such titles as "Education for Economic Growth," "The National Defense Education Act," and so forth. Educational programs are judged by their success in producing the kind of workers needed in the economy and the personnel needed for the military system. It is not surprising that schools often find themselves unable to cope with sullen, alienated, aggressive students, much less educate them.

Some seem to think that private schools-for-profit held accountable for quantitative test results would do a better job than public schools. This would bring into our educational system the kind of rationality that has corrupted many other institutions. We know what the emphasis would be in such schools and what would be sacrificed for the sake of efficiency, economy, and profit. Think of the plight of human beings with only Promethean knowledge and power. Surely the Protagorean myth is correct in holding that, without a sense of justice and reverence, human beings would not be able to sustain a social order that would make cooperative endeavors possible, and that under these conditions technical knowledge and skill would be for nought.

Television is our most powerful cultural agency, but consider what has happened to its programing under the control of market forces. In a discussion in the early 1990s with the vice president for programming of one of our major television networks, I asked him to what extent he was concerned about the values his programs taught. He said that they were in the entertainment business and that his job was to get as large a share of the viewing audience as possible, not to teach values. Much the same is true with most of the publishing industry, especially videos, music tapes, and motion pictures. Also look at what happens to politics and government when citizens are expected to vote their pocketbooks and politicians to say and to do what will win elections. Government in general is preoccupied with, and is judged by, the state of the economy and the military strength of the country.

Someone said that no society is ever more than twenty years away from barbarism. Given the present condition of our reproductive and cultural institutions, can barbarism be far away? Indeed, it already prevails in some places and most communities are marred by it. What price economic prosperity! Without success of the moral and civic enterprises, even economic prosperity will be lost in the end.

If we come to realize that success in the economic enterprise requires an emphasis on the moral and civic enterprises, perhaps we will give them greater attention, even if for the wrong reasons. Once emphasized, however, the moral and civic enterprises might correct our priorities so that we would support them for the right reasons.

LIBERAL EDUCATION RECONSIDERED

Although education is a complex process in which the whole society participates, I shall focus on formal education in the schools. It is where we can come to grips with the issues in the most clearcut way. If the society could be persuaded to support the schools in preparing students for the moral and civic enterprises, even if it were done for the sake of economic benefits, the schools, in concert with the family, religion, and other humanistic institutions, might be able in time to change the governing values of the society and thereby change the culture and the society.

Until the last quarter of the nineteenth century, formal education in the Western democracies, although quite limited by today's standards, emphasized *liberal education;* that is, formal education focused on preparing people, as Thomas Jefferson urged, for the moral and civic enterprises, especially the civic. Its primary purpose was to prepare the people for responsible citizenship in a democratic society and a select few for the learned professions.

The approach was predominantly humanistic. Education for the economic enterprise was left, for the most part, to apprenticeship and informal learning. Prior to the Civil War, no college or university in the United States offered a laboratory science course. In 1863, the United States Congress passed the Morrill Act that provided for landgrant colleges that would apply science to the development of the agricultural and mechanical arts. This reflected the rising dominance of the economic order over the social order in the wake of the Industrial Revolution earlier in the century, just as the bourgeois emphasis on materialistic values had given rise to the reformation in science two centuries earlier. Ever since the Civil War, formal education has become increasingly oriented toward preparation of students for jobs in our scientific/technological/industrial/service economy. Science and technology have progressively displaced the humanistic disciplines, with the behavioral and social sciences taking over even the study of human behavior and society.

It is not simply that we have lost sight of the moral and civic enterprises. If that were the problem, perhaps a humanistic revival could be brought about more easily. There are many people with moral and civic concerns; indeed, there are calls from many quarters for a new emphasis on moral and civic education. Our major problem, however, is that, in our materialistic cultural perspective, we have redefined the moral and civic enterprises in terms of the language and logic of an autonomous economic enterprise that is widely regarded as a moral-free zone. We no longer believe that there is a human vocation and way of life, one that we can ignore only at our peril; we no longer think of citizenship as an office with inherent responsibilities that require us to think and act politically in terms of the good of the society rather than in terms of our own safety and economic advantage; and we no longer think that there is a natural normative constitution for a society that defines how it ought to be organized and how it ought to function. Rather it is widely held that rational living is a matter of maximizing utilities defined in terms of our own preferences, whatever they may happen to be; and that social and political arrangements are self-interested bargained agreements. Some hold that the players in the political drama are individuals, while others think that they should be ethnic or special-interest groups with shared preferences. Some may think of moral and civic reasoning as based on some minimal set of universal interests or instinctual preferences, but with each person moved only by regard for one's own feelings and interests. All of these ways of thought are, I contend, serious perversions of humanistic thinking; they reveal the derangement of the moral and civic enterprises in our materialistic culture.

With no conception of a human vocation as such, we do not know how to educate people for a human life. What used to be known as liberal education loses its focus and rationale. Without agreement on a normative conception of a human being, we cannot reach an agreement on what it takes to be an educated person. All such judgments are widely regarded as purely subjective. So we cannot agree on what would be a sound curriculum for a liberal education. The possibility of a reasoned consensus on such a matter is rejected out of hand. Under these conditions, the liberal curriculum disintegrates into a smorgasbord of elective courses driven by the preferences of students.

We remain fairly confident, however, about what it is to be a lawyer, a physician, an accountant, or the like, and so we can devise effective educational programs to prepare people for these careers. By mid-century liberal education had been largely replaced by what was called *general education.* The best we could do in the prevailing culture was to look for the common educational qualifications needed for the special career programs. This at least gave us a concept that we could understand and some guidance in constructing a curriculum. However, what it defined was largely a set of basic requirements geared to specialties that prepared people for pursuing particular ends, not the basic requirements for living a life worthy of us as human beings and as citizens. This approach fostered the attitude expressed recently in a letter to the editor of a major newspaper by a professional person who was opposed to a required course on Shakespeare in a high school curriculum. Confessing that he knows nothing about Shakespeare, he said: "I still survive in life; I have a nice home and own land, and I did it without classic literature."

But by the 1970s general education in the colleges and universities was in trouble. Specialization had progressed and disciplines had multiplied to the point that no agreement could be reached on what subject matter should be included in the general education curriculum required of all college students. The general education program was replaced in many places with the so-called *core* curriculum; it focused on the basic skills rather than the subject matter that all would need to master in order to succeed in any career in our scientific/technological economy.

Core education, as was general education, is conceived as the prerequisites of career education; and career education is, for the most part, driven by materialistic interests — the quest for wealth and power. Of course there are some people who pursue their careers for the sake of benefits to others, betterment of the society, advancement of the culture, or their own self-fulfillment in a humanistic sense. But even if one's career is driven by non-materialistic ends, one is greatly impoverished if one's identity and life are restricted to and defined by one's career. One is first and foremost a human being, a family member, and a citizen. One should have a career that is integrated into one's identity and life, not an identity and life that are one with, or integrated into, one's career. One's career is never enough and should not be the defining and all absorbing factor.

Neither general nor core education is an acceptable substitute for liberal education; neither prepares one for living an authentic human life. Realistic humanism opens the way for genuine liberal education — education that emphasizes development of our essential human powers and the framework of thought and commitment in terms of which we employ our powers in defining and living our lives and in participating in society. It must include, as we indicated in an earlier chapter, an appropriate normative self-concept and life plan, a normative concept of society, and a world view that makes sense of human existence.

DEVELOPMENT OF BASIC HUMAN POWERS

Liberal education is preparation for freedom, for a self-directed life in a self-governing society. It focuses on the development of all of one's powers that lend themselves to being brought under one's management, with the emphasis on reliable ways of employing one's powers in accessing and using the culture; in encountering, knowing, relating to, and coping with reality; and in defining oneself, living one's life, and participating in society. We are not free, in the most obvious sense, if we are subject to forces that deny us self-management of our own powers and our own lives. The person in prison, for example. Neither are we free to the extent that we are driven by forces within us that are not under our control. Consider an act that issues from an impulse or desire without reflected endorsement, or one that is the direct result of a fit of anger in which one loses control. Such acts do not emanate from the center of the self; they are acts that one does not endorse or put oneself behind. Furthermore, we are not free in an act that is endorsed but the endorsement is corrupted by the prompting desire or some strong emotion; nor are we free when we are moved to action by irrational or unwarranted beliefs. Our freedom is diminished even to the extent that our thoughts and decisions are shaped by unexamined assumptions and presuppositions. A liberal education aims at liberating people from the grip of the forces that impact on them or pulsate in them so that they can take responsibility for their own identity, for their own beliefs, for their own actions, and for their own lives. It helps people become intelligent, critical, and creative centers in the cultural and social dynamic rather than helpless vessels caught in the whirl of natural, social, and cultural events or conditions.

Infants are taught and encouraged even in the development of their basic perceptual and motor powers. They have to learn how to use their hands, their feet, their eyes, their ears; how to eat and how to control their body functions; how to feel and how to relate to people and their environment. In short, children have to learn how to do all the things that they bring under their own management. And wherever learning occurs, education has a role; it shapes and furthers the learning process. It brings the accumulated knowledge and wisdom of others to bear on the individual's learning process so that the individual can learn in a few short years much of what it has taken the human race thousands of years to learn. Culture and education are the universe's biggest breakthroughs since the development of the genetic code and procreation. Culture is our most important product; it is our most valuable treasure. And education, the access to culture and the world, is the greatest opportunity open to anyone; it is the best bargain one will ever get.

Certain body skills are acquired with maturation and from trial and error, but children have examples to imitate and are coached and encouraged in their physical activities by adults from the beginning. The more sophisticated uses of the body require more instruction and coaching. The development and maintenance of their general physical powers are important for everyone, but highly specialized skills like those of professional athletes, musicians, or skilled workers are neither possible nor desirable for all. But the body as a medium of expression is important for everyone, and in this respect mastery of the body is of great importance for all. There are people who seem to be more body than spirit; their body seems to be a dumb thing — not an expression of the inner self. And there are those radiant, graceful beings with eloquent bodies — people whose spirit so pervades and dominates their body that their bodies are indeed works of art, revelatory of their souls.

We wear selected clothes not just for physical comfort but to express our inner selfhood. We want to show that we are not merely natural beings but cultural beings with our individualized identity. But we do not depend on clothes alone; we want our bodies to cooperate in expressing our selfhood. Above all, one does not want one's body to show that it is out of control or an obstruction to the inner self. This is why we speak of a person's *breaking down and crying,* for crying indicates that the person has been *overcome* by a strong emotion.

Of course we need to distinguish between those who do not have mastery of their body through a lack of development or weakness of their subjective center and those who lack mastery through conditions in their body that limit self-mastery. While a recalcitrant body, whether because of weakness of the inner self or body defect, limits one's freedom, only the former kind reflects adversely on the person as such. Some paraplegics have a radiant spirit and are great persons in spite of, and sometimes because of, their physical disabilities.

A word of caution. The foregoing discussion should not be taken to imply a radical dualism. All subjective states and acts have their bodily dimension. They are, as indicated in an earlier chapter, semantic states and acts that have their identity and unity in terms of an inherent structure of meaning and a logical form, but they have a physical dimension much like our speech acts. The self is, I contend, an integrated system of such states and acts that is capable of self-correction and generation of new semantic states and acts. The causal dynamics of such a system resides more in the subjective domain and its normative structure than in the body, but the body processes are essential even though they are largely in tow to the subjective (the semantical and logical) dimension of the system. This of course means that the body is not a closed physical system in interaction with its physical environment. Many of the processes in it can be understood properly only in terms of the semantic, logical, and normative structure of the inner self.

Liberal education focuses on the development and self-management of our inner powers, mastery of the cultural tools and ways of expression that expand and extend these powers, mastery of accumulated knowledge and wisdom, enlargement of our semantic environment, and a deeper understanding of self and world.

Our inner powers are extensive. They include all the ways in which we interact, communicate, and express ourselves; the ways in which we receive or appropriate data, whether factual, semantic, logical, normative, or whatever; the ways in which we interpret, reconstruct, and organize data into a coherent view of self and the world; the ways in which we entertain possibilities, make inferences and predictions, and construct explanations; the ways in which we reflect, evaluate, appraise, criticize, and decide; the ways in which we construct images, concepts, theories, myths, fictions, and plans; indeed, all the ways in which we organize and empower ourselves, interact with and relate to our world, and live our lives.

Because our inner powers are semantic in nature or have a semantic dimension, they can develop only so far by maturation and natural learning; they need cultural development and education. At the heart of this process is learning cultural ways of expression and communication, especially language and cultural symbols. These are not just for communication; they are semantic tools that enhance and extend our innate semantic powers. In learning a langauge, a child learns not only how to talk, to write, and to read the spoken and written word, but also how to discriminate and structure things in experience, memory, imagination, and thought. Indeed, without language, we would be severely limited in all of our inner powers; we would not have an inner realm with sufficient power and integration to be self-transcending, self-directing, and self-correcting agents; we would not be functioning persons.

Language and symbol systems are historical, community products. Individuals left to themselves with their rudimentary semantic powers, no matter how great their powers were, would not develop a langauge. And no set of individuals left unto themselves with only their rudimentary powers would get very far in their lifetime toward developing a language. And, of course, in the evolution of human beings, the physiological base had to develop along with the cultural process.

The development of signs and symbols into a language expanded not only the subjectivity of individuals, but also the intersubjectivity of the group, and thus made possible the sharing of experiences, memories, thoughts, and aspirations. In short, language made possible accumulated knowledge and wisdom — the development of a culture, and the culture made possible a historical community. Without language, culture, and a historical community, we would not be human beings — that is, human beings as rational, intellectual, moral, political, religious, artistic beings. Culture, historical community, and persons have to emerge together;

they come as a package and cannot be broken apart. We are all developed by and within a culture, a tradition, which is the accumulative achievement of a historical community.

It is by learning and appropriating the culture that one becomes a member of a historical community and thereby establishes one's cultural identity. Learning one's primary culture is a process of self-formation, but in the early phases of this process at least it is more the culture's generation of the self than it is activity of the self in its own formation. Of course there is a measure of self-activity from the beginning, but it takes liberal education to bring the self into real self-mastery.

A spoken language, through the thought it makes possible, literally transforms our experiences, memories, and imagination, and imposes a discipline and refinement on them that would otherwise be impossible. And a written language, especially an alphabetical language, refines and imposes a discipline on the spoken language and increases its power. But what is of even greater importance is that a written language gives us powers of memory, reflection, and thought and extends the range of our intersubjectivity in ways that the spoken language alone could never make possible. A people with only a spoken language have limits on the extent to which their culture can develop; and individuals with only an oral language are severely limited in their semantic powers, even in their powers to think. In my work, and I am sure that it is true in many fields, I can go only so far in formulating and solving problems in silent thought or by thinking out loud. I have to turn to writing in order to get very far. It makes possible a new level of thought, which in turn refines and enhances the powers of silent and oral thought. Without a written language and symbol system, for example, only a rudimentary science and mathematics would be possible, historical knowledge would be severely limited, communication and transactions would be so restricted that only small communities and limited cooperative endeavors would be possible.

Language and symbol systems can be learned only by using them in semantic activity. Children can come to understand the verbal behavior of those around them and to acquire verbal skills of their own only within a prelinguistic intersubjective/interacting relationship in which they share somewhat a common semantic environment with their companions and have some measure of understanding of their non-verbal behavior as expressions of feelings, attitudes, wants, beliefs, expectations, and intentions. They come to understand verbal behavior of others as an extension of their non-verbal behavior. Each new advance in semantic power and skill moves from a preexisting base by undertaking new levels of semantic activity. One masters semantic tools by using them successfully in semantically appropriating reality, communicating with others, and coping with the world through its semantic presence.

There are natural functional structures. The heart, for example, is a biological pump. It exists and is formed as it is for carrying out its function of circulating the blood throughout the body. We may judge the heart to be well-formed and well-functioning according to how well it performs the function for which it exists. Much the same can be said about the human mind. Whatever is true about it as a mode of being, the human mind has certain functions — the semantic appropriation and communication of reality and possibility, and the guidance of human beings by knowledge and critical judgment. The human mind has an inherent normative structure, a set of constitutional principles, which may be spoken of as logical grammar. Cultural languages such as English and French provide different semantic tools and grammatical forms for performing common semantic and logical tasks.

We may distinguish between logical grammar, the inherent normative structure of the mind, which is, I think, grounded in and geared to the basic structure of the world, and the conventional grammar of cultural languages. The former imposes restraints and requirements on the latter. We may judge a language in terms of its effectiveness in the performance of semantic acts and the furtherance of the human enterprise. Obviously some languages may be better than others, for some may serve the human enterprise better.

There are masters in the use of a language. They are the ones who have refined and perfected the langauge with regard to the functions for which the language and the semantic powers of human beings exist. These masters should be models for others. Their ways of using the langauge are the ways we should try to learn and to teach. Once we have mastered their ways, we can develop our own style and make improvements in the language if we can.

The teaching of correct and good ways of speaking and writing is not just the teaching of another skill in competition with a dozen others for time in the school curriculum. It is the teaching of the art of thought and the art of expression and more; it is the teaching of the arts of observation, memory, and imagination; it is the teaching of the arts of reasoning, criticism, and the organization of thought; it is the teaching of the art of feeling, the organization and criticism of emotions and attitudes, and the deliberation and judgment of actions. In short, it is the development and expansion of our basic human powers; it is at the heart of what education is about.

So far I have spoken of teaching and learning a native language. Of course being multilingual is important for many purposes; and it deepens one's understanding of one's native language and expands one's literacy; it may enhance one's basic semantic powers. But mastery of a language is essential for human development.

Although language is the most important cultural tool for the development and extension of our semantic powers, it is not the only one. Music without words, nonrepresentational paintings, and dance express the form of feelings and emotions or, what amounts to the same thing, generalized feelings and emotions without specific content; they integrate feelings and emotions and give them form. Representational art, whether songs, poetry, paintings, drama, architecture, landscaping, or whatever, expresses and elicits feelings and emotions about some particular subject matter. Art is essential in the development and refinement of feelings and emotions about the human condition and the important events and circumstances of life and history.

We need to perfect, in so far as we can, a style of being, of relating, of doing, of living that is appropriate to us as human beings and as the individuals we are. The outward forms of our being and behavior reflect our inner self and our lived experience. And of course the refinement of the outer forms refines the inner life as well. Just as speaking and writing well are essential for thinking well, well-formed dress and behavior are integral to a well-formed inner life. And, in order to perfect ourselves and our behavior, we need to understand and to appreciate the works and lives of at least some masters of style. This is part of our effort toward self-development and self-mastery, and, as such, it is part of the moral enterprise. The ultimate personal achievement is a beautiful life that engages the responsibilities and challenges of one's existence with intelligence, wisdom, moral integrity, and style — a life that is a masterpiece of the fine art of living a human life.

CHARACTER EDUCATION

Certainly the development and refinement of our basic semantic powers is one of the most important tasks of education; it involves gaining mastery of much of the culture, especially the language and the more important symbol systems. Furthermore, it involves understanding the major art forms and the development of some artistic skills of one's own. But the single most important task of education, and this is not something distinct from but inclusive of the development of our basic human powers, is the development of character — the formation of the constitution by which we employ our powers in search of knowledge and understanding and in living our lives and in participating in society.

We usually distinguish, as observed in chapter 3, between intellectual and moral character because we distinguish between the search for knowledge and understanding on one hand and living our lives and playing our roles in society on the other. In formal education, we give much more attention to the development of intellectual character than we do to the development of moral character. We try to teach students how to pursue truth and understanding in a reliable manner, and we think, for the most part, that the proper way to do this is to teach by instruction and practice grammar and composition, logic and mathematics, and scientific, hermeneutical, historiographical, and critical methods of thought. All of these have to do with the development of intellectual virtues. Students are trained through instructed practice until they develop the habits of mind that have been found to be reliable ways of discovering, organizing, and communicating knowledge about what is the case and why it is so.

The development of a sound intellectual character, however, is not just a matter of habit formation. Good inquirers in any field know what they are about; they know how to criticize their efforts and to correct their mistakes; they operate with a framework of thought that provides them with principles of criticism and basic categories that define for them both knowledge and reality. Someone said that education is what we have left after we have forgotten everything we learned in school. What we have left after all the information and explanations have been forgotten are, of course, a basic framework of thought and the intellectual virtues that enable us to operate in it successfully. What stays with us is the intellectual character that we have acquired.

In the development of intellectual character, teachers have to use training methods; they have to instill in students by practice ways of observing and thinking and speaking and writing before they can tell them much about why they should proceed in the prescribed ways. But no one considers such training as the imposition of the ways of thought of the society on the students in a way that compromises their freedom, for we believe that the ways of inquiry and thought that are taught can be rationally justified and that the students, with greater maturity, will be able to justify these ways to themselves or use critical methods to make corrections and improvements in them. Students accept this framework of thought and the intellectual virtues required for its successful operation, not as something imposed on them by the community or some authority, but as the cultural development of the natural powers of the human mind. The training is accepted as genuinely educational, for it is regarded as drawing out and developing the students' own knowledge-yielding and critical powers in enhancing ways.

In the prevailing culture, we view moral education quite differently. Moral character, as previously indicated, is the normative constitution that governs us in organizing and living our lives and in participating in society. Many seem to think that moral education is a matter of establishing certain moral virtues as habits of the heart. Intellectual character, as we just observed, requires not only certain intellectual virtues as habits of the mind, but also a framework of thought that provides principles of criticism and categories of thought that define knowledge and reality. In like manner, good moral character, I submit, is not achieved by simply instilling a set of moral virtues as habits of the heart. It involves, as I contended in chapter 3, a humanistic framework of thought that defines the self, society, and the world in a way that gives us a comprehensive and comprehending orientation and purpose and provides us with principles of life criticism. Moral education is preparation for the moral and civic enterprises.

The difficulty in our modern naturalistic culture, however, is that it is widely believed that a humanistic framework of thought for morality can be taught only by indoctrination, for any such framework is regarded as faith-based, with no rational validation. Consequently, it's place in education is called into question and often banned along with religion from public education.

Classical liberalism embraces, as we pointed out in the discussion of multiculturalism in the preceding chapter, the principle of cultural freedom — the principle that everyone should be brought up in a culture that has been freely developed under rational criticism and that is open to justification or reconstruction by one's own critical powers in one's more mature years. To be brought up in a culture that has not withstood, or is protected from, such testing is to have imposed on one the arbitrary or interest-serving choices of the power structure of society or some ethnic community; it is to be culturally enslaved without having been taught a way of liberation, leaving one in a provincial culture with no apparent escape route other than abandonment of the moral culture one was brought up in, with nothing left on which to base one's life but factual beliefs and one's own interests and preferences, without a conceptual system in terms of which one's interests and preferences could be validated or reconstructed.

It is often said that only parents, or some private institution selected by them, have the right to teach or to indoctrinate students with a supportive framework of thought for moral virtues. Public education, it is argued, should teach or try to instill only moral virtues for which there is a consensus in the community, and should not try to teach a framework of thought that would provide principles of criticism and reconstruction or make sense of the moral enterprise. But indoctrination with a subjective, ethnic-based moral culture, whether by parents or their selected agents, would culturally enslave children. It would violate their human right to be brought up in a free culture and to be free self-directing agents in their mature years.

Of course the moral subjectivism that forces us to restrict "moral education" to instilling consensus virtues would deny us the ground for making any truth-claims about rights or even for talk about a free culture. Indeed, moral subjectivism cannot be consistently thought through without undermining the ethics of thought in general, for it leads inevitably not only to the question of whose moral values are to be taught, but also which rationality as well.

I accept the principle that children should not be indoctrinated in a culture that cannot be rationally defended and taught by sound educational methods. This applies not only to public schools, but also to private schools and even to homes and religious institutions. Indoctrination in a culture that is not subject to criticism and correction by human powers is always a violation of the personhood of those subjected to it. A free culture that is open to ongoing criticism and correction is the foundation of a free society and a free people. It is the birthright of everyone.

Cultural freedom, however, presupposes some version of realistic humanism. And, if realistic humanism is philosophically defensible, the humanistic framework of thought can be taught educationally; if the humanistic framework of thought can be taught educationally, genuine moral education is possible by acceptable educational methods. But without general commitment to some form of realistic humanism, the public will not accept genuine moral education in the public schools; they will accept only efforts to instill a list of consensus virtues, for they will continue to regard the teaching of the humanistic framework of thought as indoctrination. Yet moral virtues that are simply instilled in one's youth without being anchored in and supported by a philosophical view of self, society, and the world will not have the force and lasting power to govern one's life.

People, for the most part, get their philosophical views indirectly as the underlying framework of other areas of the culture, especially religion and science, without ever giving much thought to them. Many people look to religion for the supporting context for moral virtues. And there is good reason for this. The major religions present in powerful historically evolved literary and artistic ways a humanistic view of self, society, and the world that engages people emotionally and volitionally; this humanistic world view makes sense of morality and supports the human enterprise. But the singularity of a religion that is grounded in the unique historical experiences and cultural ways of a particular people makes it alien and unavailable to people with different cultural roots. Furthermore, religions tend to locate their substance in their historically evolved forms and to turn dogmatic and authoritarian in trying to protect these forms from ongoing criticism and reconstruction.

Another obstacle to invoking religion in moral education is the fact that the humanistic framework of religion is seriously challenged by the philosophical perspective of modern science, and, given the status of science in our culture, the humanistic view of self, society, and the world presented in religion is undermined and discredited in the minds of the people, especially among those more in tune with the direction of the culture. This cultural condition not only denies moral education the resources of religion, but it also undermines morality and character education as well. Without challenging the dominant intellectual perspective of our culture, perhaps we can do no better than to try to instill and to maintain certain more or less universally preferred character traits by whatever means that promise to be effective. Under these conditions, however, morality becomes a weak force, far too weak to restrain and to govern the unleashed passions and materialistic desires, especially when major institutions live by an amoral rationality.

Even if we could do something toward instilling and reinforcing certain more or less universally preferred character traits in individuals, there is the matter of the character of institutions and of the society as a whole. Individuals holding offices in an institution may find the character of the institution (the culture in terms of which it operates) in conflict with their personal character; they may be so dependent on, and locked into, the institution and so helpless to change its ways that they feel that they have no choice but to accept and to act by the governing values and ways of the institution. Furthermore, the character of institutions and of the society as a whole (the culture by which they are organized and by which they act) is likely to influence or even determine the character of individuals. Without a commitment to some form of realistic humanism, we would have no grounds on which to criticize and to change a historically evolved institution other than what would be fruitful for the defining purpose of the institution or by government legislation based on bargained agreements among interest groups. And the government would be shaped by the materialistic values of the culture and the distribution of power in the society. Few legislators today think of their role as that of moralists engaged in formulating into law the moral voice of the society on pressing issues.

In short, it seems that as our culture becomes more materialistic and naturalistic, it precludes meaningful moral education and undermines the moral and civic enterprises.

This work, however, challenges our governing cultural values and the intellectual vision of humankind and the world that our materialistic perspective has generated. It is committed to the priority of humanistic values and the correctness of realistic humanism. Not even many philosophers, however, will accept realistic humanism so long as materialistic values and scientific modes of thought are dominant in the culture, for philosophers, being products of the culture, mostly try to validate or make good the governing intellectual vision of the age. Nevertheless our concern is with a society fit for human beings, and we contend that only a society that embodies a humanistic culture and educates its people for the three great human enterprises (moral, civic, and economic) from within the humanistic perspective meets this requirement.

EARLY EDUCATION

Pre-school and elementary education is concerned largely with laying foundations. Much of it has to be training in basic skills. It should be for the cultural development of the children's innate powers in accordance with the inherent normative constitution of the human self and in ways that can be justified to them later. Early training should be guided and controlled by the objective of preparing children for responsible self-direction and learning in their more mature years.

Children should not be allowed irresponsible freedom in their immaturity. They must be taken care of, trained, directed, and guided until they form a self-governing constitution and acquire the requisite knowledge and wisdom to take control of their own lives. Of course the transition from a guardian-directed and tutored life to a self-directed life is not a sudden transaction. Children should be given progressively the freedom for which they have the competence to manage as they develop their powers and their character. One would never acquire the competence for self-direction without the experience of managing areas of freedom as one's selfhood takes shape and one's powers develop. Inevitably there will be a struggle between children and their parents and teachers during this process because children are prone to overestimate their competence for freedom and parents especially are likely to underestimate it. The struggle will become unbearable unless children learn from the beginning to respect those in authority and to trust their judgment, and unless those in authority prove to be worthy of the children's respect and trust and willingly accept their diminishing authority as the children mature. There is no greater abuse or miscarriage of authority than for children to be brought up with a culture imposed on them for some end other than their own development in according with their own inherent constitution and toward a responsible self-directed life of their own.

Moral education is the core of education for responsible freedom. It has to begin very early in life. Children should acquire a sense of what it is to be a person in a way that would give them a profound respect for themselves and for all human beings; they should acquire also an appreciation of and respect for the world that generates and supports them. Children should be taught progressively the responsibilities inherent in being a person, especially how to organize and to cope with their desires, feelings, and emotions; what is worthy of love, devotion, and commitment; how to relate to others and to the world around them; and how to renew their inner strength and to control their behavior and to take responsibility for their actions. They need to be immersed from early life in a culture that generates a sense of their own worth and of their proper place in the world, a sense of what their identity and status require of them in their circumstances, self-confidence as they develop and exercise their powers, faith that (for the most part) the world works or can be made to work for those who approach it in the right way and do their part, and aspirations and commitments that are worthy of them as human beings and the individuals they are.

Children should be brought up and schooled in a joyous atmosphere that celebrates life; human powers and their potential; growth of body, mind, and spirit; the gifts of nature and society that support and sustain us; and the contexts, relationships, work, and play that make our lives meaningful and worthwhile. The emphasis should always be on the good and the right, guiding children toward a positive regulatory self-concept and the love and pursuit of higher values. This does not mean that the darker side of life should be denied. Children must be prepared to face and to cope with reality as they grow up without being defeated or perverted by it, however threatening and destructive it may be. This is why children should learn about and participate in the celebration of the lives of people, both children and adults, who have faced great adversity and evil with inner strength and courage and grown in the process.

Such a life-affirming and person-generating-and-sustaining culture should animate all the people and institutions involved in child-rearing. Children should absorb this culture from the feelings, attitudes, and behaviors of their parents, care-providers, and teachers. Adults who do not share this culture should have no place in child-rearing, child care, or the education of children, for children learn the basics of life from those who care for and teach them.

A wise man said, "Let me write the ballads the people sing/And whoever will may be king." In our day, we may broaden this saying to include the selection of the songs, the poetry, the stories, the art, the videos, the television programs, the films, and the toys and games for children. The culture that children learn and in which they participate should introduce them to life and its possibilities in ways that children can comprehend; it should help them to understand and to deal with their fears and anxieties and to organize their deep feelings and longings; it should show them what are responsible and what are irresponsible responses and behaviors for human beings in various situations; it should interpret for them what it is to be human. Children should be presented with heroes and role models who engage and challenge them to do the right and to pursue higher values, and they should be presented with characters whose traits get them into trouble and spoil their lives. Children's literature should not preach but present characters in such a way that the lived experience of the characters renders a judgment on themselves and their lives.

The noted McGuffey readers in the nineteenth century did, in the cultural context of the time, a good job of giving children an elevating and challenging philosophy of life in the process of teaching them reading skills and appreciation of good writing. They not only instilled certain character traits, but also developed a positive self-image and provided a social and religious framework that made sense of and reinforced moral virtues and a life devoted to higher values. But it did this in terms of the culture of Protestant Christianity, which would be unacceptable in our secular, multicultural society.

No doubt there is truth that can be taught educationally in any historically tested religion, but the language, symbols, and forms of a historical religion are grounded in the historical experience and cultural forms of a particular people in a way that may obscure the universal truth the religion embodies, especially for people with a different cultural history. However, for those for whom a well-developed and historically tested religion is available, the language, symbols, and rituals of the religion may be very effective in teaching the truths of the religion in a way that engages their deep emotions, aspirations, and commitments. But even for the devotees of a historical religion, there may be much that should be discredited or reinterpreted to prevent the teaching of illusions and beliefs that have been shown to be false.

Nevertheless, we can learn from the McGuffey readers and most historical religions, for they have a record of some success in helping generate strong, self-directed, responsible people. With a culture that provided a humanistic philosophical anthropology, sociology, and world view, we could develop sound moral character by acceptable educational methods without relying on sectarian religion or any cultural forms that cannot be rationally justified to the students when their powers are more fully developed. We need to learn how to present indirectly through stories, poetry, songs, art, ceremonies, rituals, and practices an underlying humanistic philosophy of selfhood, society, and the world, and the norms and values by which to live meaningful lives. Of course this general whole-culture mode of presentation should be supplemented by direct instruction in these matters when appropriate, especially for older students. This should be done, when possible, in the context of other disciplines, especially in history, literature, and social studies.

SECONDARY AND HIGHER EDUCATION

Some seem to think that liberal studies in high school are primarily for those preparing for college, and that high school for those not college bound should be devoted more to technical training for some career. But quite the contrary.

The purpose of liberal studies, as already indicated, is to help all of us develop our sensibilities and feelings and to provide us with ways of conceptualizing experience and reality that will enable us to understand ourselves and the world, live meaningful and worthwhile lives, and fulfill our responsibilities as persons and citizens. A liberal education should enhance our capacity for cooperative living and for achieving and sustaining a free and just society and a peaceful world. High school for most of those who are not college bound is their last chance for a formal liberal education — for an education for the moral and civic enterprises. The society should insist on a liberal education for them as broad and as deep as their abilities will allow. And liberal education is always relatively superficial and incomplete without philosophy.

Conflicting views of events, public issues, and forms of life are often revelatory of underlying contradictory philosophical assumptions. Given our cultural situation, serious education should prepare young people to cope with the incoherence and conflicting tensions in the foundations of the culture. We can no longer afford to leave the basic framework for thought and life to indirection while we concentrate on mathematics, science, history, social studies, and literature. The naturalistic framework of thought that we teach in the major disciplines undermines the humanistic framework for a successful life; it threatens our identity as persons, the humanistic world view that makes sense of and supports human life, and the norms and values by which we should live and run our institutions. Under these conditions, moral education in the higher grades, especially in high school, must not only be embraced in the usual program of liberal arts, but should include philosophy. Children should not be brought up in an incoherent culture without being taught responsible ways of resolving the logical tensions and achieving coherence in the foundations of their thought and their lives.

Rather than spend precious years and resources on career programs in high school at the expense of liberal education, most technical career training should be provided in community colleges, technical institutes, and in apprenticeship and training programs in industry and government. And four-year colleges should require advanced liberal education for all of their students, with concentrations in the humanities, social studies, and the natural sciences. Studies that concentrate on the philosophical problems in the foundation of the culture should be a part of everyone's program, especially for those who are preparing to teach in high school and at the college level. Professional and graduate schools should presuppose and require such an educational foundation for all applicants.

There is, of course, a problem about prolonged years of schooling. In earlier societies, young people typically moved from their childhood home and culture into a responsible adult role in the work force from the age of fourteen to sixteen. They proved themselves as adults very early in life. They had no serious identity crisis between childhood and adulthood. With the addition of the four-year high school to grammar school, we created adolescence as a new phase in human development. The term was introduced only early in this century. The phenomenon it designates did not exist before the era of the universal high school. It indicates a phase of ambiguous or unsettled identity in life, with insecurity, shifting norms, and volatile emotions. And college years and graduate and professional education add yet another phase between childhood and full adulthood. In a modern society, it takes a long time for one to form a mature identity and become secure in who one is. And without a clear and stable self-concept, one has no sure inner compass.

With the long years between childhood and full adulthood, an adolescent and youth culture develops more or less independently of the adult culture. Our teenagers and youth live largely within their own age group and they establish their own ways and expectations of one another. And market forces support their culture by seeking to exploit it for economic gain. This cultural condition makes a major emphasis on liberal education more imperative at both the high school and the college level, for liberal studies broaden and deepen the students' cultural perspective and encourage them to think critically about their own identity and cultural matters in general. But this is not enough. We need to develop ways in which young people will be engaged in responsible work in the adult world while they are pursuing their formal education. We have various internship programs and many students have part-time jobs, but we need to find more fruitful ways of engaging young people in adult life as a regular part of the educational program for all.

CONTINUING LIBERAL EDUCATION

Regardless of how extensive and successful formal education may be in the early decades of life, it will not be sufficient for a lifetime under modern conditions. There is a growing need for continuing education in all professions and technical occupations that are based on rapidly developing knowledge and technology. It is important for everyone for this need to be met. There are also a growing need and compelling reasons for continuing liberal education, for it is just as essential, if not more so, for the quality of life of all of us and for the health of our culture and society as continuing professional and technical education. No civilization based on freedom and progress can be sustained for long without supporting moral, civic, and intellectual virtues and a high level of life morale grounded in a defensible and widely shared vision of humanity and the world. The public needs to recognize that the humanistic framework of thought is not identifiable with or dependent on any particular religion or ethnic culture, but justifiable or correctable on grounds that are accessible to critical judgment by methods that can be taught educationally.

Although the foundations of a good life have to be laid in early years, many of the most profound problems of humanity are peculiarly adult problems. Only later in life are we likely to worry and have sufficient background to think seriously and at length about the deeper structures of selfhood — our unconscious desires and motivations; our obligations to people in the wider world; problems of power and authority; freedom and justice; how to cope with failure; what makes life meaningful; art and its interpretations and revelations; how to grow old; death and dying; life despair and religious faith in our scientific/technological age; and the like. Of course we think about these things in our youth, but only as adults are we really ready to learn how to put it all together in a holistic way that will make for a meaningful life. It is only as adults that we have the experience to fully appreciate works of literature, art, religion, and philosophy and how they illuminate the human condition.

Regardless of the success of early education, the liberal arts remain of central importance to adults, for we live in a complex world that is changing radically and with increasing rapidity. Traditional ways of thinking break down, the contradictions deep in the culture show themselves, all that is solid seems to melt into air, and new interpretations of experience and the world proliferate with bewildering fecundity. Unless we are well prepared by our education and continue to work at it, we will likely be overwhelmed by "information overload" and the attendant problems of sorting out the important from the trivial and recognizing what is responsible and what is irresponsible thinking. Even those with the best educational backgrounds need time to reflect on and to test their perceptions, interpretations, and critical judgments in dialogue and debate with others.

Continuing liberal education is important not only as a benefit to the participating individuals, but also for the development of the society and the culture. Our modern culture does not support the fundamental framework needed for character building and successful lives. We need a humanistic cultural revolution. A broad-based discussion of, and debate on, our governing values and their bearing on our ways of understanding ourselves and the world, and how our dominant ways of cognition are affecting our identity, our lives, and our society, might pave the way for such a cultural change. Philosophers and other humanistic scholars and critics should lead and participate in organized studies and discussions on these cultural issues in communities all across the country. It is imperative for the society and for our universities to rethink their responsibilities for continuing liberal education and determine how they could best fulfill their responsibilities in this area.

But liberal education within the present state of our culture is not enough. The present state of philosophy and the liberal arts in general leaves much to be desired. The humanities have been weakened, confused, and misled under the prevailing patterns of intellectual respectability in our scientific/technological age. Only when the humanities have reestablished their true identity and legitimacy will they be able to play fully their proper critical, reconstructive, and integrative role in the culture. Only then will they be effective in helping the society to develop the intellectual vision, ideals, standards of excellence, and wisdom that are needed for character development and for guiding and sustaining an advanced civilization under modern conditions.

6

HUMANIZING THE

ECONOMIC

ENTERPRISE

In our discussion of the humanization of persons and society, the family and community, and education, we were concerned with inherently humanistic subject matter that has been undermined, distorted, or perverted in our materialistic culture with its scientific/technological ways of thought. Our effort was to restore them to their natural humanistic constitution and to suggest ways in which they might be developed to a higher level of perfection under modern conditions. Humanization of the capitalist economic system is another matter entirely, for the capitalist system is the embodiment of modern materialism. Humanization of it would radically transform its constitution — its governing values, modes of thought, and ways of operating. In fact, humanization of capitalism would reject the autonomy of the economic system and integrate it into a humanistically constituted social order. This, I think, would be the more natural condition for the economy. Unlike the welfare state that tries to put something of a humanistic face on the materialistic economy by external legal means, humanization of the economy would build humanistic values and ways of thought into the very constitution and practices of the economy itself. This would be such a radical transformation of our present system that the very thought of it is daunting. It would be the end of capitalism as we know it.

THE GREAT TRANSFORMATION

In all societies prior to the nineteenth century, the economy was only an aspect of the social order and was governed largely by the culture embedded in the social structure. But by late in the eighteenth century, the materialistic turn in modern Western culture had developed to the point that the economic dimension of the society took on a life of its own. Adam Smith, in *The Wealth of Nations* (1776), was one of the first to envision, and to understand the laws of, the more or less autonomous capitalist economic system that was then emerging in England.

This development was part of the general cultural revolution known as the Enlightenment. Where the Renaissance, in the wake of the collapse of Christian feudalism, sought to revive classical Greek and Roman culture and the Protestant Reformation tried to recover primitive Christianity, the Enlightenment sought to develop a new culture based on reflected experience and inquiry, preserving from the past only what could pass critical review in each generation. Broadly speaking, there were two emphases in Enlightenment thought — the humanistic and the naturalistic. The humanistic thinkers focused on humankind, society, and the culture in terms of which people organize and direct their lives and their institutions. Some of the leading moral and political thinkers, notably John Locke and Thomas Jefferson, subscribed to a version of the classical natural law theory of ethics, even though it was being undermined by intellectual developments already underway. It was on the basis of a natural law theory of morality that they argued for moral equality, universal human rights, cultural freedom, and democracy, although they were not prepared to put into practice the full social and political implications of their democratic liberalism for all sectors of the society. Some contend that these humanistic thinkers were at least reinforced, if not motivated by, the desire to free the rising middle class from the older aristocratic culture so that they could better pursue their materialistic interests bourgeois style.

The naturalistic thinkers took their lead directly from efforts to know and to master the natural world in ways that would further materialistic interests. For the most part, the naturalists, with their empiricist theory of knowledge and utilitarian theory of practical reason or some form of moral subjectivism, won out and continue to prevail, even though there has been, and continues to be, some opposition, most notably the Romantic revolt, the idealist movement of the nineteenth century, and recent communitarianism. In other words, as I contended in chapter 1, the dominant intellectual development growing out of the Enlightenment was the new scientific perspective and its intellectual vision that undercut the humanistic foundations of civilization.

The capitalist economic system that Smith described was not realized anywhere until the nineteenth century development of the factory system based on new energy technologies. The economy, however, did not become simply an independent sector of the society; it became the engine of the society and, in time, the values and logic of the new economic system became the controlling values and modes of rationality of the whole social order. Karl Polanyi calls this inversion "the great transformation."[1]

Capitalism is more than a way of organizing the production and distribution of goods and services in a society. It is a civilization — it is a way of life embodied in the social order, a way of life dominated by materialistic values, scientific/technological ways of thought, and individualistic utilitarian rationality of the profit-driven, free enterprise, market-regulated economy. Capitalism turns both Christianity and Buddhism on their heads. The New Testament says that no one can serve both God and money (Matt. 6:24) and that the love of money is the root of all evil (I Tim. 6:10). Buddha says that craving and grasping are the sources of all suffering (The first sermon attributed to Gautama Buddha). Lewis Mumford observed that capitalism has converted all of the seven

governmental regulation, control of the money supply, social investment to assure full employment and to address other unmet needs, and a welfare safety net generate their own problems for society. Furthermore, capitalist values tend to dominate the political culture and to pervert the government's efforts for justice and the common good.

Science and technology are essential to capitalism, for they are the basis of most consumer goods and services, they fuel the process of creative destruction, they are the geese that lay the golden eggs. So there is little wonder that the ways of thought of science and technology have come to define the intellectual enterprise and to dominate education in modern Western civilization.

As the culture of capitalism becomes implanted in the organizing and governing constitution of individuals and the social order, the morality of the common good undergoes atrophy and the morality of justice and honesty tends to be replaced with legality. Even the political system apes the economic order. No longer are political campaigns, legislation, and policymaking regarded as processes in moral reasoning about the requirements of justice and the common good that should be enforced collectively through governmental action. Citizens are expected to vote their pocketbooks and politicians are expected to seek their political advantage. Laws and policies are established by bargained agreements among legislators and governmental executives competing for political support from special interest groups. Being schooled in the mentality of the business world is considered proper training for positions in government. It is assumed that the democratic political system, in a manner similar to the capitalist economic system, will coordinate all of this self-interested behavior in such a way that justice and the common good will be served without anyone really taking thought of it.

CAPITALISM AND THE WELLS OF MEANING

It is difficult to comprehend the extent of the transformation that has been wrought in our lives, in the social order, and in the culture as capitalism has become all but supreme. In preindustrial societies, the great stabilizing factors and wells of meaning in people's lives were the land, family, community, work, and religion with patriotism playing a prominent role after the emergence of the nation-state in the early modern period. The people were committed to and embraced these sources of meaning in self-defining ways. These relationships entered into the identity of people, enlarged and enriched their selfhood, anchored them in society and in the universe, and focused their lives. These sources of meaning took on the character of the sacred, for, in and through them, the people participated in a higher reality in a way that defined and elevated themselves.

In advanced capitalist civilization, all of these wells of meaning have largely dried up or have been polluted. As people left the farms for urban centers, the land that was once sacred and eloquent in people's lives has been reduced, for the most part, to real estate. With labor converted into an economic commodity, work has lost its self-fulfilling meaning, and market forces have scattered people and virtually eliminated the extended family as a social reality; indeed, materialistic values and market forces have stressed and torn the nuclear family as the humanistic values that supported it have been undermined and weakened by our intellectual culture based on science and technology. The same forces and intellectual outlook that have eroded the family have undercut and weakened community life and religion. And as the economy goes global and the binding values of national life are undermined and weakened by both intellectual and economic developments, even nationhood loses its uplifting, binding, and defining power, or, in irrational reaction, patriotism or ethnicity may reassert itself in a demonic form. The drying up or polluting of these wells of meaning under capitalism, joined with the impoverished, one-dimensional intellectual vision of humankind and the world under our modern materialistic culture-generating stance, essays the plight of humankind in the modern world.

This work contends for a humanistic renaissance, based on a humanistic conception of ourselves as human beings, a humanistic view of society, and a humanistic intellectual vision of the world. No one can tell just how such a cultural transformation would actually play itself out in society. In earlier chapters, I have tried to indicate something of how it could be worked out in regard to persons and society, the family and community, and education. The task here is to consider how it could be worked out in the economy, with the emphasis on how land and work could be restored as wells of meaning in a modern society.

ELOQUENT PLACES

Until the Industrial Revolution, most people lived on the land and made their living from it. Often they lived on land that had been in the family for several generations. It was common even for European peasants to live on land where their ancestors had lived. Most immigrants to America settled on plots of land that were handed down in the family through several generations. There were always those who moved on to new land until the country was largely filled from coast to coast. But just growing up on a farm, helping work it with one's family, gives one an anchor that growing up in an apartment or a house on a small lot in a city does not. There is not only greater participation in the life and work of the family but a real sense of an organic relationship with the land and the whole natural environment. It involves a profound sense of working with and dependency on the land and the whole ecological and meterological system on which the productivity of the land depends. The land becomes woven into one's identity.

When a family lives on and identifies with a farm, they do not regard the land as an economic commodity. Although it may be put on the market at some point, it is not something produced for the market. It is a part of nature that generates and supports life. The land is a partner with whom one may cooperate, but it demands that its ways be respected. If abused, it does not cooperate. Those who live on and identify with the land have a peculiar love relationship with it. It speaks to and nourishes their soul.

I grew up on a farm that had been in my family for six generations. My grandfather, my father, and I were all born in the same house. Although I left the farm when I was seventeen years old and my parents sold it seven years later, it has remained in the core of my being. I have taken my children and my grandchildren back there, and often, when I want to relax and reconnect with first and last things, I visit it in my meditation as it was in my boyhood. I walk the woods, work in the fields, play in the creek, sit in a quiet place, enjoying the view and the sounds of nature around me. It remains the most eloquent place on earth to me; it still speaks to me in many voices.

Growing up on a family farm in the pre-electric, pre-mechanized, horse-and-mule days was hard, but it anchored one in reality in a very special way. On many family farms, as it was in my case, one felt oneself working not only with one's family, but often with the local community in shared operations such as barn raisings, corn shuckings, wheat thrashings, cutting matches, road work, caring for the sick, burying the dead, and the like. There were family stories about earlier generations who were buried in the family cemetery on the farm, which had to be cared for from time to time. One felt oneself working in cooperation with one's grandparents and great-grandparents who had cleared some of the fields, laid out the roads, and built some of the buildings. Furthermore, one felt oneself working with the land, the weather, the sun, the moon, and the stars. One could not but feel oneself situated in and a partner of the universe, although a very junior one to be sure. Yet one could, in cooperation with one's family and nature, make a great difference in a small place in a relatively short time. And by early teens, one could come to match adults at work in a self-proving and self-confirming way.

Throughout most of our history this was a common experience; but industrialization and urbanization that came with science and technology under capitalism changed all that. And land, for most people, has lost its humanistic status as an important source of meaning; all too often it has become simply a productive resource for an agri-business or merely real estate — an economic commodity in either case.

I don't want to over romanticize agrarian life of earlier times. It was a hard life with many privations. Everyone must agree that modern economic developments have made life easier and better in so many ways. The material standard of living of the average person was about the same in most parts of the world in the mid-eighteenth century, but it has increased since then eight times more under capitalism than in non-capitalists societies.[6] But it is not only the material standard of living that has improved. There is more moral equality and greater political freedom in democratic capitalist societies; there is less back-breaking physical labor and more time for educational and cultural pursuits and social life; people live longer and have to suffer fewer untimely deaths of loved ones; they are healthier and largely freed from the fear of many crippling or life-threatening diseases that were prevalent in earlier generations; there is a higher level of education, better communication, and greater access to cultural resources; there is more, faster, and easier travel; and so many other ways in which life has been improved in humanistic ways by the rising tide of material well-being. Nevertheless, there has been a price to pay. People are less spiritually anchored in the world, more concerned with profits and possessions than with being and doing, more dependent on an impersonal, economy-driven society, and, paradoxically, they are, in many ways, less in control of their own lives and of that on which they are dependent. On the farm in my boyhood, we went into a self-sufficient mode during the depression of the 1930s, and, with the folk-wisdom and ingenuity of my parents and neighbors, the family and local community could have lived for years with hardly any outside input. Very few people could be that independent today. Most importantly, people have lost an anchor and an inner resource. Few people today have an inner connection with land that has been made sacred by their self-forming experience with it.

Nobody wants to go back to "the good old days," for those days had their share of hardships and limitations. But we need to find ways in today's world in which people, especially while growing up, can find self-defining and self-confirming ways of anchoring themselves in the family and community and in the universe that would help develop and sustain inner strength, self-direction, and life morale. While children growing up on the land in earlier times were immersed in the family and community and had an organic relationship with the natural world, young people in modern societies are largely segregated according to age and have little sense of participating with either adults or nature in cooperative endeavors. Most of the adults with whom they are involved are in some instructional or supervisory role.

There ought to be cooperative endeavors in which young people and adults would work together. In chapter 4, I spoke of how families and schools could be organized for cooperative work on the part of all the members. Every community ought to provide workshops, work camps, or work projects of some kind in which teenagers could have constructive work experience along with adults. Most any community could organize teams to pick up litter on roads and in parks at certain times, to plant and care for flowers and shrubs to beautify public places, to do yard work or make repairs on homes of the poor and disabled, or whatever would be a worthwhile project in the community. The primary purpose would be to have teenagers working in a group with responsible adults on worthwhile projects. All involved, especially the young, would identify more with the community and develop a sense of civic responsibility. Equally important, the young would learn from and measure themselves by the performance of the adults, and they would gain self-confirmation and self-confidence.

The matter of developing and sustaining, under the conditions of modern life, a sense of an organic or ecological relationship with the natural world is a greater challenge. There are two aspects of the problem: the experiential sense of being in a dependent but a cooperative working relationship with nature, and the intellectual way we think about nature and our place in it.

No one can escape nature. While our civilization may distance us from the land, it cannot distance us from our bodies. Although one's self is, according to my view, primarily a self-monitoring, self-correcting, creative complex organization of intentional states and acts that functions as a whole in terms of its own inherent normative constitution with the focus of a center that expresses itself as I, everyone is aware that one's subjective center and inner states and powers are embodied in and involve one's body. And everyone is aware that many of one's bodily states and processes on which one is dependent are not subject to one's will. Furthermore, no one can escape being aware that one's body is emersed in and dependent on one's natural environment. But in living our lives in a modern society, our concentration is largely on the human-made world, especially the world of artifacts. Yet, we need and have an inner craving for the natural world. Most people want at least a few plants and flowers around them in their homes and offices and some shrubs, trees, and a patch of grass if possible. And we want public parks and wilderness areas to which we can escape from our world of asphalt, concrete, and machines. Children should grow up with some gardening experience, even if it is only growing flowers in a pot. Better if they can have a flower bed to plant and shrubs and a lawn to help care for. Some cities provide public land where families may have an assigned area in which they have a vegetable garden. The value of this is not just for the family's grocery budget, although in some cases it might help; it provides a wonderful opportunity for children, teenagers, and adults to work together and with nature in producing food for the table and to share with friends. Most any community could provide this kind of an opportunity for many of its citizens.

It would be good for everyone to have an identification with some special place where nature manifests itself boldly and beautifully. Families that can vacation repeatedly or visit frequently a place in the midst of natural beauty where their children would have significant experiences with nature might establish a self-defining connection that would be in memory and imagination a soul-restoring experience for a lifetime. Although it would be impossible to replace the role of the land in the spiritual life of earlier generations, we need to take seriously the importance of the nature-connection and to work at finding effective ways to enhance its role in our lives today, especially for children and teenagers.

A nation needs its sacred places — places where its values have been defined and its identity formed. The United States has its Jamestown, Plymouth Rock, Independence Hall, Yorktown, Mount Vernon, Monticello, Gettysburg, Appomattox, the White House, the Capitol, and many more. These are eloquent places that speak to us from our history about the values that define our identity as a nation and the ideals that unite us in a common life. In like manner, individuals need sacred places in their lives. Any place where one has been stirred by a vision of a higher reality or gripped by some ennobling experience or purpose may become sacred for one. Such a place may be a home, a frequently visited vacation place, a school or college, a church or temple. A school, for instance, should not be planned and run on strictly utilitarian grounds. Of course a school has the responsibility to help students develop skills and master important subject matter, but its primary responsibility is that of growing people. A school should be a beautiful, warm, friendly place with large, well-landscaped grounds. It should be small enough, personal enough, and students should attend it long enough for every student to establish a lasting, self-defining relationship with it. A school should be for the students a gateway to a higher reality and a larger world; it should provide students with opportunities for elevating, self-defining visions and experiences; and, if they have such experiences, the school will become a sacred place in their lives.

The ancient Hindus emphasized the importance of maintaining "the rituals of righteousness," for otherwise, they said, a society would be overcome with unrighteousness (*The Bhagavad Gita*, 1.40). A nation tries to maintain rituals that engender and keep alive feelings and commitments that unite the people and empower the governing institutions. In like manner, families, schools, civic organizations, and religious institutions need to develop and maintain appropriate "rituals of righteousness" for growing and empowering human beings and sustaining a humanistic society.

The "rituals of righteousness" should include celebrations that would cultivate proper attitudes and feelings toward our place in our natural environment. These might include spring festivals, flower celebrations, wilderness appreciation excursions, harvest-time thanksgiving ceremonies, and the like. They should relate us to the forces at work in nature, not in a materialistic, utilitarian way, but in a way that bears on our identity and place in the order of the world.

This brings us to the issue of how we should think about nature and our place in it. In our pursuit of power for the satisfaction of unlimited wants, we have become ecologically alarmed. The ecological crisis forces the question again about the role of value concepts in our descriptive/explanatory language and about whether there are normative structures in nature. Ecologists tend to be holistic rather than atomistic in their talk about ecosystems. This suggests that an ecosystem has a normative structure. A species is said to have a place defined by its function, a role for it to play, which it may in some way fail to do. Ecologists speak of "normal" environmental conditions. Does this mean environmental conditions that are the way they ought to be? "The balance of nature" has the ring of a *healthy* state; an "imbalance" within the ecosystem sounds like a *sickness*.

In other words, ecology seems to employ value language in a descriptive/explanatory role in such a way that, if we take ecology-talk seriously and at face value, which we are entitled to do on the basis of realistic humanism, human beings find themselves embedded in a normative structure of nature that imposes normative as well as factual limits on their will. Our modern culture-generating stance, in which we ask only "How can we get what we want and how can we impose our will upon the world and exploit it for our own purposes?," comes to be viewed from within such an ecological perspective as a failure on our part to understand ourselves and our place in nature, a failure which results in not only a perversion of ourselves but an imbalance or sickness in nature itself. Indeed, our modern culture-generating stance comes to be regarded as moral wickedness, giving rise to acts of violence against and rape of the environment.

Just as we should learn to live within our place in society, accepting the normative limits and requirements that impinge on us, we should learn to live within our place in nature, respecting the normative structure of our environment. And beyond our place in our social and ecological environments, we, with our human powers, have to consider our place in the order of being itself and how we relate to whatever is ultimate. The "rituals of righteousness" should prepare us emotionally and attitudinally for the proper nesting of ourselves in our multiple environments in ways that would be life-supporting and life-enhancing.

Work and the Normative Structure
of the Economy

Under capitalism, those who organize and run our economic enterprises think of them as existing for one purpose — to make profits for the investors. Everything is focused and governed by this objective. Many people argue that, for the most part, if an enterprise in a competitive market does not serve some social purpose, it will not be successful at making profits for long. We have to admit, however, that some enterprises that cater to human vices may succeed even though they are destructive for people and detrimental to the society. Consider trade in destructive substances, gambling, prostitution, and the like. But under capitalism social ends are left, for the most part, to Adam Smith's unseen guiding hand, without anyone taking thought of them in the policymaking and management of economic enterprises. It is argued that this is the best system because of human nature; we are, it is said, primarily self-serving individuals. The glory of the capitalist system, it is often said, is that it exploits this moral weakness in all of us and turns it to the common good. We may ask, however, whether human beings are atomic *materialistic* self-interest maximizers by nature or by culture. Only those who are well trained in a capitalist culture are good performers in a capitalist economy. Human beings have been culturally generated in other societies to live by quite different values. Of course we all have materialistic desires and we want the material means for satisfying whatever desires we have or may have in the future. But we have also other kinds of impulses, sentiments, and emotions that move us toward knowledge, understanding, beauty, friendship, intimacy, solidarity with others, justice, the common good, harmony with the universe, and the like. Even if self-interest is a powerful force in all of us, the form that it takes will depend on how the self and thus self-advancement are understood. Self-interest need not be in terms of material possessions or success in making money. It may be in terms of achieving excellence or rank in most any kind of endeavor, whether domestic, civic, educational, athletic, business, military, scientific, scholarly, philosophical, artistic, religious, philanthropic, or whatever. In the culture of some street gangs, self-interest may express itself in terms of being tough, mean, and brutal, even though this way of life may be understood as assuring an early death. In other words, self-interest may ally itself with and reinforce whatever wins self-respect and high social status in terms of the culture's conception of what one ought to be or ought to become. Self-interest focuses on wealth and material possessions under capitalism because human beings are conceived primarily as materialistic self-interest maximizers. Wealth is our heaven, poverty our hell. In a humanistic society, the governing values would be different, for the normative conception of selfhood and human perfection would be understood differently; self-interest would support the moral and civic enterprises and humanistic values would trump materialistic interests.

In a humanistic culture, under our realistic interpretation, a human being, in whatever office or position, would be recognized as primarily a person, never as a thing or an economic commodity. Everything required of one or done to one should be appropriate for a *person* in that position. One should never be required to function simply as a machine or treated as a mere economic commodity. One should never function simply as an individual self-interested utility maximizer. Negatively, every position or role in the economy, as in the society in general, should be such that a human being could occupy it and fulfill its responsibilities without having to compromise or do injury to oneself as a human being or as the individual one was; positively, every position should be such that the person holding it, in fulfilling the responsibilities of the position, would be fulfilling oneself in the work. In other words, work should not be just for an external benefit but meaningful and rewarding in and of itself. Anything less is a form of prostitution of one's humanity. From the perspective of a humanistic economy, we would judge jobs for which the paycheck was the worker's only motive and reward much as we now judge slavery in earlier societies. We should ask of the economy that it, along with the predominantly humanistic institutions, contribute to human growth and fulfillment as well as meet our materialistic needs. After all, the economy, however constituted, comprises so much of the human enterprise, especially in modern societies, that it leaves its imprint on our identity and all aspects of our lives as well as on the society as a whole. The economy should not be thought of primarily as society's way of organizing and managing the production and distribution of goods and services. That puts the emphasis on end-products — the goods and services. The economy should be thought of as our primary way of organizing and managing our creative and productive work in meeting human needs. When thought of in this way, meaningful, self-fulfilling work is taken to be one of the human needs that the economy must meet. It becomes an important objective of the system, along with goods and services for consumers, a market for those with goods and services to offer, wages and salaries for workers, tax revenue for public service and investment in the commons, and profits for investors. Hence, in an advanced technological society there may be a need for subsidized jobs that would provide meaningful, self-fulfilling training and work for those who for whatever reason may not be able to perform adequately in a more productive job. Appraisal of an economy has to be in terms of all of these objectives.

In capitalist societies, we distinguish between the way the society looks at and appraises the economy and the way in which owners and managers think about their enterprises. From the societal viewpoint, we consider as outputs of the system the jobs provided, the wages and salaries and other worker benefits, the tax revenue generated, and the consumer needs that are met as well as the profits for investors. But owners and managers think only in terms of profits. They count jobs, with their wages and salaries and benefits, and taxes as part of their cost, not part of their output. And they consider consumers only as a market for their goods and services, with little regard for the difference between goods and services that meet real needs and those for which a desire has to be created by marketing techniques, or the difference between goods and services that serve constructive purposes and those that are destructive. The governing issue is whether there is a market or one that can be created for goods and services that would make a profit for investors.

The logic of the capitalist system works to cut jobs; to cut wages, salaries, and benefits for the workers; to divide and to routinize work in a way that robs it of its meaning and diminishes the humanity of the workers; and to reduce or to evade taxes. Workers are forced to unite in an adversary relationship with the management; the government, which has a concern for good jobs and benefits for the workers and tax revenues for public services and investment in the commons, is forced into an adversary relationship with the owners and managers of private enterprises. Any organization of society would need safeguards against abuses, but it would seem that a society with less built in logical friction among its major players would function better for the good of all.

Socialism was an attempt to create a more humanistic economy by embracing it in the government and running it by command. The twentieth century has demonstrated serious difficulties with state socialism, even in democratic societies. And the difficulties are humanistic as well as economic. Even the welfare state is dehumanizing for those who become dependent on welfare without meaningful work. In fact, poverty in and of itself is dehumanizing quite apart from the material privations involved, especially in a capitalist value system. And poverty on welfare is even more devastating to one's self-esteem; it destroys one's inner self and guiding light while satisfying one's basic material needs only at a minimal level. Of course, everyone receives social assistance in many forms; no one is self-made or self-supporting. We are all generated and sustained by a complex cultural/social system. All production is social production. Given the accumulative nature of our social/cultural capital, perhaps all of us end up on the debit side. The only question is the magnitude of one's social/cultural credits in a life time. There will always be some who will need special social assistance part or all of the time. Social assistance in whatever form or amount should be humanized so that it would strengthen the recipient, not injure his or her selfhood.

What I am suggesting is not a capitalist, not a socialist, and not a welfare society as we know them; it is predominantly a humanistic free-market economy in a humanistic society in which private and public institutions cooperate in organizing the efforts of their members in trying to meet the humanistic and materialistic needs of all. The major ways in which such a system would be different from capitalism would be two. First, the rationality internal to private economic enterprises would be humanistic; the objectives sought would not be restricted to profits for the investors, but would include also meeting some set of real needs of the society without doing harm, providing secure jobs consisting of meaningful, self-fulfilling work with compensation proportionate to contribution but adequate for a reasonable standard of living for all those engaged in the enterprise, and reasonable taxes as social rent and cultural royalties for services and investment in the further development of the commons. The second major difference would be that all the members of an enterprise, managers and workers alike, would be able to function in their positions as full-fledged human beings in terms of the logic of humanistic rationality rather than as abstract economic men and women subject only to the utilitarian rationality of materialistic gain or as programmed machines carrying out routine, dehumanizing work assignments.

However, it would still be the case that the governing rationality in the policymaking and management of a humanistic economic enterprise would not be the same as that of the society in its evaluation of the success of the enterprise. Although all members of an enterprise should find added meaning and satisfaction in their work from the social good they do by providing a market for the goods and services they purchase from suppliers and from the taxes they pay, increasing these sums would not be an objective of the management. In fact, their attitude toward these costs of doing business would not be much different from that of managers in a capitalist enterprise, except that they would be less inclined to take advantage of the weakness of their suppliers or the technical loopholes in the tax code. The big difference in the management of a humanistic and a capitalist enterprise would be in the attitude toward employees, investors, and consumers.

In a capitalist enterprise, the workers, and increasingly lower and middle-management employees, are regarded, along with the machinery and equipment, as part of the cost of production; the objective is to keep all costs at the lowest possible level. The logic of the system forces the top management to treat employees as economic commodities to be bought for the lowest price on the market and to be managed in the most efficient way for maximizing their productivity. In the present labor market, for instance, many companies are turning to "temporary" or "contract" employees to avoid established retirement and health benefits for regular workers, even though the temporary or contract workers may be kept on for years. Furthermore, for the sake of increased productivity, the work is divided so that each worker may do more efficiently a limited number of different operations with a prescribed time set for each performance, even though such division of labor robs work of its meaningfulness and reduces the worker to the level of a machine. Adam Smith said that the practice, although profitable, had the effect of making the worker, who has no occasion to exercise his understanding, "as stupid and ignorant as it is possible for a human creature to become."[7] When workers are no longer needed or their productivity is not up to expectation, they are readily laid off or dismissed just as a machine would be shut down if not needed or replaced if not performing at top capacity.

In a humanistic economy, the situation would be quite different. Secure meaningful work for the employees would be just as important an objective of the policymakers and management as profits for the capital investors. The enterprise should be organized in such a way that on becoming a permanent employee, after a probationary period, one would be made a partner and would no longer be expendable for the sake of profits for capital investors. Partnership should be based on the commitment of oneself as well as on the basis of the investment of capital. All partners should have a voice in policymaking, including the allocation of work among the employees.

The salaries of the employees should be counted as profits, not costs of the enterprise. This would obviously require an adjustment in tax laws. Employee-partners should receive ownership shares over and above their salaries and benefits from the overall profits according to their contributions.

A primary consideration in the organization and division of the work to be done should be, in so far as possible, for all the employees to have what would be meaningful work for them. If there were work that had to be done but could not be made very meaningful for anyone, it should be shared by workers in such a way that the total work responsibility of each was meaningful and self-fulfilling. There is a lot of work that is sheer drudgery in any operation, but such work should be included in a total work responsibility that would redeem it.

Most any work can be meaningful for someone if it is properly organized and framed with meaning. And the meaningfulness of most any work can be destroyed if not properly organized and framed in a wider context. Consider the janitorial work in my building at the university. We had the same janitor for about twenty-five years. Our building was his building. He knew the professors, secretaries, and graduate students personally. He chatted with us on a daily basis, he came to our departmental parties, we recognized his birthdays and kept up with the news about his family, and so forth. He identified with us and with his work. He took great pride in keeping the building neat and clean and the furniture and floors shining. He loved his job and was happy in his work. The management of the janitorial services decided that having janitors assigned to particular buildings was not efficient. They organized janitorial teams that would go from building to building, working from 4 o'clock in the morning to noon. They made time studies and assigned people to specialized chores. No one any longer had identification with a particular building or with the people whom they were serving. There were supervisors telling them what to do and writing evaluations on their performance. Our janitor of twenty-five years no longer loved his job and no longer took pride in his work. He soon took an early retirement. Whatever efficiency in terms of work-hours and wages may have been achieved, but I doubt that it was much, the meaningfulness of the work was destroyed, the quality of the work deteriorated, and the family life of the janitors was disrupted by having to be at work by 4:00 A.M. There is no way that the rearrangement of the work was worthwhile from a humanistic perspective.

While the benefits of an enterprise to its suppliers are important in framing the work done in the enterprise, the goods and services the enterprise provides its consumers are of far greater importance. If the goods and services provided consumers serve only trivial interests or are actually harmful to the consumers or to society, awareness of this fact would rob the work of the employees of its meaningfulness. For workers to have job morale and a sense of self-fulfillment in their work, they must believe that their work is not only important in the internal operation of the enterprise, or that it makes profits for capital investors and for themselves, but they also must believe that the enterprise itself is worthy of them and of their best effort. Such worthiness of the enterprise comes from the significance of its goods and services to its consumers and to the society in general. So if providing meaningful work is a primary objective of an enterprise, as it should be, the policymakers and managers must consider the real value of their goods and services to their consumers. This is not an important consideration when the governing objective is to maximize profits for the capital investors.

Of course, in a genuinely humanistic economy, investors would want their investments and earnings to be meaningful. This would mean that they, too, would be concerned about the real worth of the goods and services on which they made their profits. Goods and services that did not meet important needs of consumers or were actually harmful to them or to society would not be regarded as worthy of their investment. A meaningful investment would have to provide meaningful work and worthy goods and services.

The amount of anticipated profits would no longer be the controlling consideration.

In summary, the ideal of a humanistic economy would be one in which all the participants would have positions in which they could function as full-fledged human beings and find a measure of self-fulfillment in the performance of their responsibilities. There would not be the same effort to keep the monetary cost of production down, nor the same effort to keep monetary profits as high. And profits would not be sought from trivial or harmful goods and services. But the situation might not be as bad for monetary profits as it might appear. With genuine identification with their jobs, satisfaction in their work, and high morale, workers would no doubt be highly productive. And of course there would be the humanistic "profits."

Some might question whether such an economy would generate enough investment capital. Of course the system presupposes that those who saved for investment would find satisfaction in the increased meaningfulness of their investment, but monetary returns should be substantial with the increased productivity of meaningful work. Much of the capital for investment should come from various forms of insurance and retirement funds and the savings of employees. If productivity were up and the society not so consumer-driven, there should be a higher level of savings. Many companies might be totally employee owned, with borrowed capital when needed. Of course, if consumerism of the kind we have now were weakened, there would be less market for many consumer goods and services and production would slacken accordingly, but many real needs not now registered in the market might take up some of the slack. In any case, it would be important for everyone to have his or her share of the work to be done so that no qualified person would be left out, even if this meant a shorter work week in general. Every able person has a right to meaningful work.

But a humanistic economy would not succeed even by humanistic criteria unless it were embedded in a humanistic society that was populated by people who internalized and were animated by a humanistic culture. If the people judged themselves, others, and the institutions of society in terms of humanistic values, then self-interest and social pressures would reinforce humanistic ways of thought and behavior. Economic enterprises that tried to function by capitalist values would be in ill repute and unsupported by the employees and by the public.

NOT-FOR-PROFIT INSTITUTIONS

Even a successful humanistic economy of the kind I have sketched would not meet all the needs of a society. A private for-profit humanistic enterprise, even though its inner rationality were humanistic, would be appropriate only where what was best for the enterprise from the viewpoint of its policymakers and managers was also best for the consumers and for the society in general. This would be the case more often in a humanistic economy than in a capitalist system, but wherever the inner logic of an enterprise, even though humanistic, worked against the best interest of its consumers or the society, the society would have to impose requirements that would bring the good of the enterprise in line with the good of the consumers and the public. Where this could not be done effectively, the goods and services in question should be provided by either public or private not-for-profit institutions whose rationality was harnessed directly to the good of the consumers and the public.

Although such institutions or agencies would be free from concern for profits for capital investors, they would still have a responsibility for the well-being and morale of their employees. If the goods or services a private not-for-profit institution or public agency provided consumers should cease to be needed, the management would have a responsibility to find, insofar as it was consistent with the public good, socially beneficial work to secure the employees jobs. Providing meaningful work should be one of the objectives of any enterprise, including not-for-profit institutions and public agencies, but it cannot be the only objective. If it were, the work would not be meaningful. The work of such institutions

and agencies should meet real needs that would otherwise go want-
ing, needs for which the society has a responsibility.

Among the needs that cannot or should not be left to for-profit enterprises subject to market forces are the need for laws and
their enforcement; the need for military defense of the rights of
the state and of its citizens; the need for essential goods and services
that people have a right to by virtue of their humanity or mem-
bership in the society but are inappropriate for, or cannot be assured
by, private for-profit enterprises; and the need for goods and services that would be corrupted by the profit system.

Obviously the making of laws and enforcing them are things
a society has to do for itself. In the very nature of the case, there can
be no private for-profit lawmaking firms competing for a contract
to provide a society with laws; nor can a society contract out its
judicial function to private firms on the basis of competitive bids.
Laws and judicial decisions made in this manner would lack all
authority, and, for this reason, they would not be laws and judicial
decisions. Neither should a society contract out to private businesses its police or punishment responsibilities, but this apparently is not unthinkable for some in our rush for privatization. In fact,
several states have already contracted out prison responsibilities to
private prisons-for-profit. This is the prostitution of punishment.
Some things are not a moral option for the sake of economy. The
society cannot invest the private operators with the moral authority to carry out their functions. The operators do not have the
moral purpose required for the responsibilities involved in administering punishment and correctional programs. Their primary rationality would be hitched to profits for the investors under capitalism and to profits for investors and meaningful work for
employees in a humanistic economy. Prisoners in resisting the
guards would be resisting only power, not authority. Furthermore,
the business of making profits from punishment is morally offensive. Think of Executioners for Profit, Inc. Society's punishment
should be motivated only by moral responsibility. Any other motivation perverts the act, defeats the objective, and morally corrupts the agent. If prisons are to serve their moral purpose, they
must be managed in such a way that the inmates can realize, even

though many may fail to do so, that they were at fault in their crime; that society was morally justified in physically depriving them of their freedom after they had morally deprived themselves of the right to freedom; that they were still human beings who could regain their right to freedom by fully accepting their responsibility to live a morally justified life; and that this was what society was encouraging them to do. Therefore, those who are in charge of the prisons and who supervise the prisoners should be agents of the state, with the moral authority and concern of the people behind them, and with responsibility only to the state and to the prisoners as human beings. It is unthinkable that a civilized society would adulterate the state's moral responsibility by delegating it to private for-profit enterprises.

The same arguments apply to the responsibility of a society to protect the rights of its citizens and to defend the sovereignty and territorial integrity of the state. By the nature of the case, these responsibilities and the authority to carry them out inhere in the state and cannot be contracted out or transferred to an army-for-profit or any non-state agency.

Private for-profit churches, temples, or mosques to minister to the religious needs of people would be equally absurd. The service to be rendered would be prostituted by the profit motive. The same would be true for love-for-profit or friendship-for-profit services.

Private for-profit schools, hospitals, and health-care clinics are also questionable. Here we are concerned with essential, universal needs of individuals that bear heavily on the good of the society as a whole and for which the society has a responsibility. Certainly we cannot rely on for-profit enterprises to satisfy all the needs for education and health care. However many for-profit schools and health-care enterprises we might have, the society would have to pay the cost for many individuals at these enterprises or supplement them with public and/or private not-for-profit institutions. Of course we have many more for-profit health-care enterprises than schools. That may be simply because there is more potential for profits in the health-care field. But the primary issue I want to raise is whether the profit motive is an appropriate way of rendering either of these services. With the possible exception of certain discretionary educational and health needs or wants, restrains on service in the interest of profits in growing human beings educationally and morally and in ministering to their health needs seem morally inappropriate. Teachers, doctors, and nurses, like ministers of religion, lawmakers, judges, police, and other servants of clients and the public should be able to perform their professional services with a singular regard for the welfare of the people they serve and the general public. Any limitation on needed service because of cost should be for the sake of providing service to others in as great or greater need with the resources available, never for the sake of profits for investors as such. Furthermore, students are dependent on their teachers and patients are dependent on their doctors for information about what their needs are. This makes it especially important for teachers and doctors to have a responsibility to only the welfare of their clients, the professional judgment of their peers, and the public good. It might be argued that profits would bring in investment capital that would make more resources available for greater service to more people. Nevertheless, the profit motive would compromise or pervert the motivations required for success in the service and for morale in delivering it.

In summary, a humanistic economy would consist of a private-enterprise economy supplemented with private-not-for-profit institutions and public agencies. No doubt many will say that a humanistic economy would not be successful, but we must not judge success in terms of the present capitalist criteria. The question is whether a humanistic economy could be successful by humanistic criteria in a humanistic society. We will never know unless we try it. What seems clear is that we cannot have a society fit for human beings with a capitalist economic system, for the values, ways of thought, and practices that constitute the capitalist system have a way of dominating the whole culture and society and drying up or polluting the wells of meaning. The humanistic vision of, and aspiration for, a society fit for human beings must include a humanistic economy embedded in a humanistic social order.

7

GOVERNMENT AND THE CIVIC ENTERPRISE

The civic enterprise is, as we indicated in chapter 5, part of the moral enterprise; it is defined by the responsibility of individuals and groups to develop and to maintain a well-formed, healthy society, and by the responsibility of the society collectively to provide the culture, the institutions, the social structures, and the environment in which the people can flourish in living worthy lives as human beings and as the individuals they are. Government consists of the institutions by which the society acts to fulfill its collective responsibilities and to advance its well-being.

Government, properly constituted, is the moral voice and arm of the society. This is what gives it its peculiar authority; it is the foundation of political obligation. When a government persists as the voice and arm of a power clique or a faction, it is a mere power structure and must rely upon cultural manipulation and coercion to govern. It is a de facto government only. It has no right to govern and the people have no moral obligation to obey its commands and requirements; self-interest is the only reason for anyone to comply with it; and if one's self-interest is best served by disobedience, one is free to do so without moral fault. In fact, one is morally obligated to try to reform a factional government or even to try to replace it if it is beyond reform.

A factional government, however, may acquire authority by seeking it — by pursuing justice and the common good while working to become the moral voice and arm of the inclusive society. This is the case with a revolutionary government with a moral purpose that comes to power by overthrowing a factional government. It may take time for a moral consensus of the society to be formed, but a government that works for justice and the common good under the best judgment possible while seeking to become the moral voice and arm of the society already has some measure of authority and may be worthy of support.

THE MORAL VOICE OF THE SOCIETY AND THE AUTHORITY OF GOVERNMENT

This brings us to the crucial question about what it is for the government to be the moral voice of a society. But first, a look at what a society is. People occupying a given geographical area do not make a society. As we indicated in chapter 2, a society is a more or less integrated, self-sustaining, and self-governing complex system of institutions and offices formed by a division of responsibilities in the cooperative endeavors of a people in living their lives and promoting the common good. A people is not just a collection of individuals; a people has an identity and unity by virtue of having a common culture and form of life. The individuals must recognize in the behavior of one another and in the institutions of the society a set of basic assumptions, values, and principles that they share, or else they will feel alien to one another and there will not be a functioning social order. The collection of people would be simply that, a collection — a multiplicity; there would not be an integrated system of offices and institutions, there would not be cooperative endeavors over time nor the benefits that derive from such efforts.

Only history can generate a people, for it takes time to develop a culture and the institutions and practices that embody it.

In order for a society to have a government with authority it must be able to speak with, and to act under the guidance of, a more or less univocal moral voice. In a culture that understands the morally right as the will of God as interpreted in the accepted religion of the culture, the government may be understood as deriving its authority directly from God; indeed, it may be understood as the voice and arm of God in history. Such is the case with fundamentalist Moslem states; this was the case with Christian states in the West when they had an established religion that defined the morality of the culture as God-given and based the authority of government on the divine rights of kings. Wherever there is a widely accepted authoritarian moral voice in a society, the authority of the government is taken to be grounded in it. A free democratic society became a possibility only with the Enlightenment recognition that the people did not have to depend on some authoritarian source, religious or otherwise, for their social ideals and moral judgments, but could in principle reach a rational agreement on such matters through reflected experience and informed rational debate. It was on this basis that the religious wars of the early modern period in the West finally came to an end.

Value subjectivists and moral nihilists, as well as moral authoritarians, are a threat to a free society, for they reject the fundamental basis of freedom. In response to widespread moral skepticism and nihilism, many today are turning to one or another authoritarian source for moral guidance. People who seek political power in support of authoritarian moral judgments that are regarded as not subject to rational justification or reconstruction are a threat to a free society. That is why so many people feel threatened by the role of the religious right in today's politics but did not feel threatened by the political role of other religious groups and their leaders in various civil rights and social reform movements of the past who pleaded their cause before the critical judgment of humankind.

Some people think that the fundamental freedom is economic freedom; others think that it is political freedom, but the fundamental freedom has to be cultural freedom — the freedom of inquiry, thought, and expression, for all other freedoms depend on it. And nothing is more damaging to cultural freedom than authoritarian morality. Some who think that they know what the moral truth is say that there is no freedom to do what is morally wrong, but there must be freedom in the search for moral truth as in all other areas of the culture. Without cultural freedom, especially in the area of morals and value judgments in general, the inner core of the people is manipulated. Their beliefs, feelings, attitudes, and wills are controlled by those who shape or maintain the culture. This is so even if the culture embodies moral truth. The people are denied self-mastery and self-direction, often without awareness of their cultural slavery.

A government with authority is possible under cultural freedom only if the people can reach a reasoned consensus on the basic moral issues confronting the society, or, if not a consensus, at least positions with which all can live until the issues can be reopened and debated under procedures with which all agree.

Consent of the people is important for the authority of government, but it is not enough. It is possible for all the people of a society to consent to a governmental action without their consensus being the moral voice of the people. An obvious example might be universal support of the people of a society for conquering and plundering another country for their own gain. The people might even universally support some domestic policy because each expected to gain by it; they might support some policy that they thought would be for their immediate advantage, even though it might be costly to them later or to the next generation; they might favor some policy without being fully informed about it and without having thought it through in terms of what it would mean to themselves, to some subgroup, or to the society as a whole. Universal consent under any of these conditions would not constitute the moral voice of the society.

Commitment to and promotion of justice and the common good are important for the authority of government, but they are not enough either. For a government to have authority it must protect the rights of the people and promote justice and the common good on the basis of societal judgments. In a society in which the people are in a state of tutelage (that is, a society in which the culture holds, and it is widely believed, that the people have to be told what is morally right and wrong and what is obligatory by some authoritarian institution), a government that accepts and governs in terms of the moral wisdom proclaimed by that institution may have a measure of authority to the extent that the authoritarian moral voice is defensible to the enlightened. Such a government is the arm of the only moral voice the society has. Although this kind of society may be the best that is possible under some cultural conditions, it is not, and never has been, fit for human beings, for in such a society most of the people are undeveloped human beings; they are not what they, by their nature, ought to be or ought to become; they are not autonomous moral agents. A good society is one that grows human beings to the highest level of perfection possible. That means that the members of a good society are autonomous moral agents who live responsible, worthy lives in cooperation with other members of the society in pursuit of justice and the common good.

A government with authority under the conditions of freedom has to act on the basis of the moral voice of the people about what justice and the common good require the society to do collectively. In other words, for a government to have authority it cannot be the voice and arm of a faction, not even the *moral* voice and arm of a faction. Neither can the government be the agent of the confluence of the self-interested voices of most or even all of the people, for governmental actions based on such grounds would not impose obligations on those who might opt out. Only when the government acts in response to the moral voice of the society about the requirements of justice and the common good does it obligate its people. Of course the moral voice of the people can be in error, even systematically so for an extended period of time; but so long as the government works in good faith at forming a genuine moral voice of the people and acts on it in a responsible manner, the government has authority, even when it makes mistakes.

The authority of any government is a matter of degree, depending on how inclusive it is. As long as any group of people's rights and interests are not given proper consideration in the laws and policies of the government or the members of the group are not allowed to participate in the formation of the society's moral voice, the government is the voice and arm of a faction and lacks full authority. Consider the United States throughout its history. Women and certain minorities were not given equal protection under the laws and they were not allowed to participate in the electoral process until relatively recent times. Unfortunately, the amount of consideration any group receives in governmental decisions is still largely based on their political power, not on the requirements of justice and the common good. A good government strives for ever greater authority, even though complete authority is unattainable in a large, complex society. In general, most will agree that the government of the United States has increased its authority with respect to inclusiveness in the twentieth century, even though it remains too responsive to groups with political power and too indifferent to the rights and needs of those who are politically weak.

For a society to have a moral voice it must have a culture in terms of which, and the institutions by which, the people, either directly or through representatives, can reach reasoned moral conclusions for governmental implementation, conclusions in which all the people can concur, or at least go along with provisionally while working to correct what they believe to be errors. It is vitally important for there to be institutional ways for dissidents to argue their case in the government and with the public.

Furthermore, it is important for there to be limits on what the government can require of people contrary to their own moral judgment. The government should not, for instance, coerce any well-intentioned citizen to perform an act that would violate his or her normative self-concept as a human being, except in some unusual case where it was necessary to protect the rights of someone else. This is the principle under which we exempt conscientious objectors to war from compulsory military service. We should broaden the application of this principle, especially to include conscientious objection to a particular war one judged to be morally wrong and to include particular weapons or methods of warfare one found morally unacceptable.

Some contend that the exemption should be extended to paying taxes that would support activities one found morally offensive such as war or abortions for the poor, but the case for this is not so clear. Exemption from a societal requirement on the basis of conscientious objection is for the protection of one's moral integrity. It is not obvious that one is personally at fault morally in paying taxes that are used in the performance of a societal act that one thinks is morally wrong. One does not oneself personally perform the morally offensive act in the way in which a soldier may perform an act of violence. As I shall argue later, properly assessed taxes are largely society's share of the people's economic productivity; they are best thought of as cultural royalties and social rent. How the society spends its share is not one's personal responsibility, except in one's role as a citizen in making that determination. But the people who pay their taxes and fulfill their responsibilities as citizens in the society's decision-making have done their moral duty. Of course, one may refuse to pay taxes to protest a societal decision one thinks is egregiously wrong, but such an act would not be for the protection of one's own moral integrity, but a way of meeting one's moral responsibility as a citizen.

It is one thing for the government to force a person to do something that one sincerely feels would do violence to one's personhood (that is, force one to violate one's inherent responsibilities as a person) and quite another thing for the government to require one to refrain from doing something that one wanted to do or even something one thought was the right thing under the circumstances. Consider the abortion issue. Many people in our society sincerely believe that abortion is morally wrong under most circumstances and should be prohibited by law. Many others who have moral objections to abortion sincerely believe that a woman has the right to decide for herself whether to make her body host to an unwanted fetus and that the government should not prohibit abortion. Still others sincerely believe that early abortions are not morally wrong. If the anti-abortion party should succeed in getting abortions outlawed, the government would not be coercing people who would otherwise have had an abortion to do something that they felt violated their normative self-concept. They might feel that the society had violated their right to choose, but they would take this to be a moral fault of society, not a moral fault of their own.

Laws in a free society have to be such that they can be justified to the informed and well-intentioned people who have to live under them, or at least they must be such that a plausible case can be made for them so that the unconvinced would be willing to defer to the societal judgment with the matter still open to further debate. But when dissidents reject, not just the case for a particular law but the very foundational framework of that case, they are less apt to be willing to comply with the law at a major personal sacrifice. They would regard the law not just as a mistake subject to correction, but as grounded in superstition or metaphysical nonsense, and thus beyond rational justification. This would be the attitude of many people in our society toward a law against abortion, for they would reject the metaphysics on which most moral arguments against abortion are based. Past history shows that many otherwise law-abiding women with an unwanted pregnancy would have an illegal abortion without self-reproach; furthermore, many other respectable citizens would not regard their behavior as criminal. Indeed, even those who claim that an abortion is murder, do not seem to favor the criminalization of abortion for the women who have them. Whenever good citizens recognize no reason to comply with a law other than the penalties imposed for violation, the law is not an expression of the moral voice of the society. Such laws undermine the authority of law; they make for bad government, not for good people or for a good society.

The genuine moral voice of a society is not infallible. Informed, public spirited individuals or groups may have sounder judgments about the responsibilities of the society than the collective voice of the society. But, like an individual, the society has to act on its own judgment, even though its judgment may be faulty and its action unwise. This is why the society's official position on issues must be open to public criticism with procedures for correction on a continuing basis.

CITIZENSHIP AND

THE POLITICAL ENTERPRISE

Citizens have a responsibility to work for and to support a good society in many ways, but our focus here is on the role of the citizen in politics and government. The political process is the way a society collectively organizes itself for, and carries on, the society's business. The business of a society is defined by the responsibilities of the society — the needs of the society and the requirements that impinge upon it in a way that morally obligates the society collectively.

As we observed in chapter 2, a society has a normative constitution with respect to which it is well-formed and well-functioning or not; it is, by its own nature, under an inner imperative to provide the social space (the freedom and opportunities) and the necessary protective and support systems for the members of the society to flourish as human beings and as the individuals they are. So a society, like an individual, has moral obligations — what it by its own inherent constitution ought to be and ought to do. When a society fails to organize itself and to function in accordance with its own inherent normative constitution, it is morally at fault. Whatever morally obligates the society morally obligates the members of the society to do their part in the collective effort to fulfill the society's responsibility. In other words, the business of society is the collective part of the moral enterprise; it is the matter of assuring justice, promoting the common good, and fulfilling the responsibilities of the society in general, including its responsibilities in the world community. The government of a society consists of the institutions through which the society acts collectively in conducting its business.

In a society in which the government operates on the basis of an authoritarian moral voice, the members of the society are subjects; in a free society, they are citizens and collectively they are sovereign. Of course there are historical anomalies. The people of

Great Britain, for instance, are still called *subjects* for historical reasons, although Great Britain led the way in the modern democratic movement and its people are really citizens. Citizenship is the basic political office in a free society. One of the primary responsibilities of citizenship is to participate in the formation of the moral voice of the society on which the society acts. The political process should not be a power struggle but a process of education, inquiry, and rational deliberation, first, about how the society should organize itself and act collectively in fulfilling its responsibilities, and, second, about what its specific responsibilities are and how it should fulfill them.

Although citizenship is the basic political office in a free society and its responsibilities and requirements are considerable, we should not overestimate the role of citizens in policymaking and lawmaking, especially at the level of the national government of a large state. Most of the needs and responsibilities of a modern society require a level of information, critical assessment, and rational debate among parties with different interests and perspectives that is beyond even the best informed and most rational citizens. Most of us are by necessity preoccupied with our private lives, careers, and other institutions in which we are involved. On most matters before the government citizens have to rely on representatives who are in a better position to study and to understand the issues and to debate them with people who represent various perspectives and concerns. Even representatives in legislatures and policymaking officials can be well-informed on only a few issues in today's complex world. They have to rely on their professional staffs, expert consultants, and hearings, but even then they have to depend on the work of other representatives and offices on most problems. A member of Congress told me that of the hundreds of votes he casts every year he feels informed on, and has a good understanding of, only the issues that his staff and the committees on which he serves have investigated; on all other matters he said that he has to accept the recommendations of colleagues who serve on committees that have studied the particular matter at issue. For legislators and policymakers to follow public opinion polls on specific issues simply sums public ignorance and prejudice. It is like putting proposals on specific issues on the ballot in general elections. These practices do not make wise decisions on complex matters. Rather they make for bad legislation and bad policy. What legislators and elected officials owe their constituents and the country are careful study and rational conclusions in light of all relevant considerations about what justice, the common good, and other responsibilities of the society require in the way of legislation or policy on specific matters. Of course they have the responsibility to give their constituents a clear and honest account of their actions and the justification for the laws or polices they support. At best, citizens are competent to judge only the most basic principles and policies by which a society should be organized and governed and to participate in the election of those who represent them in making laws and in policymaking offices.

Citizens, however, cannot perform the responsibilities of their office without the proper civic culture and education. They must be prepared to resist corruption and appeals to their self-interest and lower impulses. They must not ask: "Will I be better off economically or have an advantage over others with this party in office or with that policy enacted?" They must vote neither their pocketbooks nor their prejudices. They should ask: "Will the society be better, will justice and the common good be served better, with this party or that policy?" In other words, citizenship obligates citizens to think primarily in terms of justice, the common good, and the moral responsibilities of the society. This requires character training and education in civic humanism.

Universal public education was first advocated as necessary for responsible citizenship in a democracy. But, as previously observed, education has become increasingly geared to the economic enterprise, and as the capitalist economic system, with each one seeking his or her own advantage, is said to promote the common good without anyone's having to take thought of it, we have come to think that the democratic political system will take care of the common good with each one thinking only in terms of his or her own economic or political advantage. This simplistic faith in capitalism is, as I have contended, not only unwarranted but evil. The governing values of capitalism lead to cultural derangement, pathological social conditions, and amoral human beings. Reliance on the democratic political system, with citizens, politicians, and officials in a self-seeking mode and growth of the economy as the measure of governmental success, is one of the most dismal consequences of capitalism.

Consider the way in which it has become rather common to think about lawmaking and the practice of law. In addressing a group of state legislators, I referred to them as the state's official moralists. This was a novel idea to most of them. Some of them said that they were representatives of a clientele engaged in bargaining with the representatives of others for benefits for their clients. One official said that politics was a matter of "green stamps." When legislators wanted to pass a bill in the interest of their clients, he said, they obtained the votes of others by giving them "I-owe-you"s that could be cashed in when they themselves needed help on some legislation for the benefit of their clients. A representative of a state bar association, in administering a state bar examination, is reported to have told the three hundred or so candidates at the beginning of the examination that nothing stood between them and a license to steal but the examination before them. A practicing lawyer told me that lawyers, whether as prosecutors or defense attorneys, are not after truth and justice; that their purpose is to win. Perhaps he thought that the judicial system would take care of truth and justice without anyone's having to be concerned about it. Even the jury selection process has come to be based on a sociopsychological analysis of candidates in search of jurors with prejudices that would favor one's side in the dispute rather than intelligent, fair-minded jurors. If lawmaking and the practice of law are viewed in this manner, how long can the moral authority of law be sustained? How long can a free society endure?

In the search for intellectual respectability in our materialistic, scientific/technological culture, high school courses in civics have become part of general social studies and departments of government in universities have become departments of political science. In both cases, the normative approach has been replaced by historical and scientific methods of studying political organization and behavior. Although important, knowledge of the facts is not enough. Citizens need to think responsibly about the fundamental values that should govern society and its various institutions, especially government. These social and political issues cannot be divorced from a clear philosophical understanding of the human enterprise and an intellectual vision of the world that would make sense of the human phenomenon.

Responsible citizens must be prepared to give priority to, and to think politically in terms of, justice, the common good, and the responsibilities of the society. They must recognize that these are the proper concerns of government; they should insist that governmental institutions be structured to serve these ends effectively; and they should demand that officeholders, especially elected officials, be committed to and pursue these objectives. Citizens should have no tolerance for politicians who replace rational discussion of issues with the manipulative tactics of advertising agencies addicted to the marketing practices of capitalism; they should have no patience with politicians who corrupt the political process by trying to destroy their opponents with slander or misrepresentation; they should not support politicians who pervert their offices by favors to special interest groups for their support or by following public opinion polls for the sake of political popularity; they should demand that politicians and elected officials provide real leadership. Indeed, citizens should not support candidates who seek to gain office or reelection by any tactics other than honest proposals and rational debate about the problems of the society and what should be done about them. Of course politicians and officials should fully share in and be guided by civic humanism, but even if some politicians refuse to participate in the perversion of the political process for the sake of winning, there will be others who will take the low road so long as they can win that way. Only the citizens can keep the political process clean and rational. This is one of the most important responsibilities of citizenship.

Citizens cannot fulfill the responsibilities of their office without a culture geared to, and universal education for, the moral and civic enterprises. And without responsible citizens a good society is not possible.

THE PROPER BUSINESS OF GOVERNMENT

The business of society in general is defined by the society's inherent normative constitution, which, as we contended in chapter 2, is grounded in the inherent normative constitution of human beings. Thus, the business of a society is, first, to provide, insofar as it is able, the freedom and opportunities, along with the necessary support and protective systems, cultural resources, and social order for its members to define and to live lives of their own that would be worthy of them as human beings and as the individuals they are; second, to fulfill the responsibilities that it has as a society in the world community; and, third, to provide for its own development, health, and well-being so that it will be able to continue to fulfill its responsibilities to its members and in the world community.

The people of a society, in establishing a formal constitution for a government that defines its responsibilities, organization, powers, and ways of operating in doing its business, are attempting to formulate, and are responsible to, the society's inherent normative constitution as a society and as the particular society it is in its historical circumstances. The formal constitution of a society is to the society what an individual's normative self-concept is to him or her. And, just as an individual's normative self-concept may be in error, a society may go wrong in establishing its constitution. An error in a society's constitution may mislead the government and harm the society in much the same way as a misformulated normative self-concept may be self-destructive for an individual and dangerous for others.

Basically, the business of a society consists of whatever normative requirements impinge on it by virtue of its inherent constitution and its particular circumstances. But in light of the role of the moral voice of the people in forming a government and in its operations, we have to qualify this account. We have to say that the business of a society consists of what is defined as its business in the society's formal constitution or what the society decides by a constitutional process to make its business. But the decision-making at each of these levels is based on or consist of societal judgments about either or both the inherent normative constitution of the society and the normative requirements that impinge on the society in its concrete situation at a given time. An action of a government in response to a situation obligates its citizens only if the action is based on a constitutionally formed societal judgment that there is a need or normative requirement that obligates the society. The obligation imposed on citizens may involve doing or refraining from doing something in support of the governmental action, or it may be only a matter of their recognition and acceptance of the validity of the action. For example, when the people of the United States elect, in a constitutionally proper manner, a particular person as president, all citizens, regardless of whom they were for in the election, are obligated to recognize and accept the one elected as their president. Yet, in the establishment of the society's political constitution, the focus has to be on the society's inherent normative constitution, and, in making laws and public policy to deal with concrete situations, the appeal has to be to what, if anything, the situations in question require of the society collectively. The point is that regardless of what the inherent constitution of a society may be or what a situation may objectively require the society to do, neither a formal constitution, a statutory law, nor a governmental policy obligates the citizens to support it unless it is based on a properly formed societal judgment. So we may say at one level that the business of government is whatever the society ought to do collectively; we may say at another level that the business of society is restricted to what is properly judged to be the responsibilities of the society, for only the moral voice of the society has the authority to obligate people politically.

When a government undertakes to do something that does not politically obligate the citizens, it is acting without authority. Of course the assessment of whether the citizens are obligated in a particular case may be controversial. But whenever there is considerable agreement that citizens are not obligated to support the government in its actions, the government is not the moral voice and arm of the people and it has lost its authority.

Many of the responsibilities of a society may be, and perhaps should be, fulfilled by the actions of individuals, private enterprises, or non-governmental institutions. Individuals should always be alert and responsive to not only the needs and well-being of the people around them, but also to the needs and well-being of the organizations and institutions in which they are involved and the social order in general. Indeed, contrary to William H. Vanderbilt, the railroad magnate, who said "I work for my stockholders; the public be damned," the policymakers and managers of limited-purpose organizations and institutions, including for-profit corporations, should always be mindful of the needs of society and the impact of their actions on people and on the common good. The business of society is the business of everyone, but much of the business of society would not get done if it were left to everyone. Some of it requires collective action. Government, as we previously observed, is the institution or complex of institutions by which a society acts collectively in defining and conducting its business.

There is a continuing debate about what part of the business of society should be the business of government. This is a matter for the society to decide through a political process. In one sense, all the business of a society is the business of government in that the government decides, or at least the society decides politically, how and by whom the business of the society is to be conducted and the government has the continuing responsibility to monitor how well the society's business is being done regardless of who is doing it. It is quite possible for a society to assign all or most of its business to its government, but this would not be wise. A government may undermine itself by trying to do too much, especially in trying to do things that could be left safely to individuals, the family, or other institutions. But the government has the responsibility to see that the society's needs are met and its responsibilities are fulfilled somehow.

There is general agreement that it is the business of government to protect the rights of individuals and institutions, to assure justice, to keep the peace, to be trustee of the society's common wealth and guardian of the common good, and to protect the society's rights and to fulfill its responsibilities in the world community. Of course there will be controversy about what all of this amounts to in concrete situations, but there is no answer for a society other than its own properly formed political judgment on such matters.

On what grounds should the society decide these matters? One criterion seems clear: Whatever need or responsibility of a society that requires collective action with the peculiar authority that only government has is properly the business of government — a need or responsibility of a society that requires collective action in such a way that the society would be justified in enforcing compliance with or participation in the action on the part of its members. But are there proper tasks for government that do not require enforcement authority? It seems that there is little that government could do that would not involve the use of public funds or resources in some way; some argue that, since the people are required to pay taxes, they are thereby forced to participate in or support whatever the government does. Some have claimed, as we previously observed, that, if pacifists should be exempt from military service on the grounds of conscience, then they should be exempt also from paying taxes that support a war or even a military establishment; indeed, some have claimed that no one should be required to pay taxes to support a governmental action that one found morally repugnant, for paying taxes in support of the action would make one an accomplice in violation of one's conscience.

This argument is faulty on two counts. First, it assumes that the state has no resources other than what it appropriates from the earnings and wealth of individuals and private enterprises. This is an error. The government is the trustee of, or has responsibility for, the common wealth of the society — its territory, its cultural heritage, and the physical and social infrastructure that makes the society viable.

Only the society collectively has a right to decide how the land and other natural resources in its territory are to be alloted for development and use; it should decide on the basis of what would be fair for all and best for the whole society, including future generations. We recognize that there should not be private ownership of the beaches at the seashore or of natural resources under the sea.

Arguably there should not be private ownership of natural resources beneath the surface of the earth. There are extensive public lands in the United States and in many other countries. Private "ownership" of land is a right granted and protected by the society, but the society reserves the right to control the use of the land, or even to claim it for non-payment of taxes or for a public need. In fact, private "ownership" of land might be best thought of as a transferable lease for an indefinite time and taxes on it as public rent. The society cannot relinquish its collective responsibility for the preservation and use of its natural resources, including its land, rivers, and bodies of water. It has to decide how these societal responsibilities can be best fulfilled.

The cultural heritage of a society is perhaps even more important in its life and welfare than its territory and natural resources, for without the culture most natural resources would have no utility or economic value. Consider, for example, how advances in the culture within the last one hundred or so years gave petroleum its great economic value. But the culture not only gives or enhances the economic value of our natural resources, but it also makes us what we are as human beings, and it makes our institutions and social structures what they are. In addition to the wider culture, most any society has its unique cultural heritage. The culture of a society is the larger part of its common wealth. A society has a collective responsibility to preserve, to correct, and to advance its culture; it has a responsibility to make its culture accessible to the people and to train and to educate them so that they can access and employ the culture in their lives and in the institutions and the life of the society.

Another very important part of the common wealth of a society is its social and physical infrastructure. This includes all of the basic social and institutional structures of a society in terms of which the relationships and behaviors of people are organized and coordinated, and all of the foundational physical structures required for a well-functioning society such as roads, bridges, ports, communication networks, means of transportation, power plants, and so forth. The social infrastructure of a society is the product of a historical community. It may be well-formed and healthy, or it may be malformed and sick, choking or perverting the institutions and enterprises of the society and the lives of the people. The society has a collective responsibility for the well-being of its social and institutional structures. Although part of the physical infrastructure of a society may be privately owned and operated, the society collectively has a responsibility to see that an adequate physical infrastructure is in place and well functioning, for the welfare of the whole society depends on it.

The point is that the enormous common wealth of a developed society like ours, of which the society collectively, and thus the government as its agent, is trustee or guardian, contributes heavily to the economic productivity of everyone and of the society as a whole. It is difficult, of course, to assess just what is the common wealth's share of an individual's, a corporation's, or the society's total economic productivity. How could we assess, for example, the contribution of public schools and universities to our productivity? Or the contribution of the research and cultural development that is publicly financed? Or the contribution of roads, bridges, airports, seaports, peace and order, and on and on, to say nothing of our natural resources that should be owned in common? Two things are clear, however: Without the common wealth we would produce very little and most of us would perish; the more complex and successful the productive process becomes, the larger share the common wealth has in its productivity.

Taxation, then, is, for the most part, the government's collection of the common wealth's share in the productivity of individuals and for-profit enterprises. But if it should be necessary for the government to assess additional taxes to meet some of the society's extraordinary responsibilities for national defense, the needs of its people in some natural disaster, or to provide some service required by social justice or the common good such as welfare security, social security, or health security, this kind of taxation should be based on the society's reasoned judgment about the individual taxpayers' fair share of the society's burden in meeting the collective responsibility.

So in properly assessing and collecting taxes, the government is never taking the taxpayers' money but is only collecting what the taxpayers owe the society. And when the government spends its properly collected tax money, it is spending the society's money, not the individual taxpayers's. Of course the taxpayers are among the people who collectively make up the society and are thus trustees of the common wealth in their time and should be active participants in the society's decision-making.

In light of the above discussion, it seems clear that the government can justifiably undertake enterprises that do not require the enforcement authority of the state. Indeed, most governmental projects on behalf of education, the culture, the economy, health care, welfare, and the common good require only voluntary participation. Of course governments use their enforcement authority in collecting taxes, but that, as we have insisted, is a matter of collecting either the society's share in one's productivity or one's share of the burden for the society's responsibilities as determined by the official moral judgment of the society.

It is a fundamental thesis of this work that it is an inherent responsibility of a society to provide, in so far as it is able, the opportunity and the necessary protective and support systems for the people to define and to live lives that are worthy of them as human beings and as the individuals they are, and to promote the conditions that make for human flourishing. It is generally agreed that this is not just a collective responsibility, but the responsibility of everyone and of every enterprise. But it is uniquely the responsibility of government to assure that the society provides sufficient opportunities and the necessary protective and support systems for individuals to live worthy lives. It is the business of government to monitor the adequacy and the health of the institutions and social structures of the society and to find ways to overcome inadequacies and to keep the whole institutional and social order healthy and well-functioning. When the society as constituted fails to provide sufficient social, cultural, and job opportunities or the necessary protective and support systems, the government should take the lead in seeing that they are provided by either private or public enterprises, according to which way would be best under the circumstances.

THE CULTURE OF GOVERNMENT
AND PUBLIC SERVICE

The culture of government and public service, like the culture of citizenship, is different from the culture of private pursuits and enterprises. Remember the government is the moral voice and arm of the people; it is the institutionalization of the collective moral enterprise. So moral values and ethical ways of thinking not only provide the framework and the basic guidelines for decision making and behavior, but are, or should be, the principal culture for governmental action and for public service. Experience in a capitalistic enterprise does not prepare one for public service. Even experience in private humanistic economic enterprises of the kind proposed in chapter 6 would not suffice. In fact, experience in either would teach one ways of thought and behavior that would have to be set aside or overcome for success in a government position, especially in a legislative, policymaking, or administrative role. The rationale of government is shaped by its mission to promote the health and well-being of the society and to assure that the society fulfills its responsibilities to its own people and in the world community.

Where the mission to make money for the capital investors in a competitive market imposes a severe discipline on capitalistic enterprises, the needs and responsibilities of the society and the appeal of a better social order and world should discipline governmental enterprises in the use of their resources in much the same way as the needs and responsibilities of the family and the desire for a better future impose a strict discipline on most of us in the management of our family budgets and activities. Yet cynics say that the mission of public institutions does not in fact discipline their behavior. And they are right under our modern cultural conditions. Of course there are dedicated, public-spirited people in public institutions who use all the resources available to them to fulfill their mission, but the general culture of the society and even the operating culture in the government work against it. The political process makes it very difficult for public-spirited people who really want an elected office to work for the good of the society to get elected. The system favors the power-driven individuals who will do whatever it takes to win and to hold office. And governmental agencies are organized bureaucratically so that most civil service workers cannot see or feel the social benefit and the meaningfulness of their work or have the satisfaction of self-fulfillment in it. For many of them a government job is just a job with a paycheck and benefits; the public often sees them as self-serving and part of the cost of a bloated government, living off of and wasting the taxpayers hard-earned money. I heard a former editor of the *Wall Street Journal* say that everyone on the public payroll was a social parasite. With all the hostility toward and attacks on government in recent years, it is difficult to see how government workers could have any job morale. There is no wonder that they are prepared to join a union for protection of their jobs and to press for their advantage along with workers in capitalist enterprises.

No institution will work unless the culture embodied in the institution is shared by the people who work in it and by the people who support it. The source of the present plight of government is the same as the source of our human identity crisis and the plight of morality, family, religion, education, and the humanistic culture in general. It is the dominance of materialistic values in our way of life and the resulting reformation of our intellectual life and transformation of the social order. With the shift in our culture-generating values and the humanistic revolution that we propose, a big order to be sure, an efficient well-functioning government under the discipline of its mission to meet the needs and to fulfill the responsibilities of the society could become a reality. At least that is our faith and hope.

Some people, even in our materialistic culture, pursue careers with a primary concern for the work they do and the good they accomplish rather than for external benefits. They work from a sense of mission and from love of the work itself. The mission makes the work meaningful and worthwhile. When the workers identify with their work and find fulfillment in it, they love their work and gain self-respect and life morale in doing it well. This is often the case with the scholar, the scientist, the philosopher, the poet, the novelist, the artist, the physician, the nurse, the clergy, the counselor, the teacher, the welfare worker, and the like. And there are some people in most other lines of work who have a sense of mission, find self-fulfillment in their work, and love it. We find them even in what we consider the most menial jobs. But our materialistic culture and social organization emphasize the external rewards of work. A wealthy man reportedly said, in offering a toast to a group of graduating honor students in my university: "May each of you be able to say, when you come to retire, 'I got mine.'" That toast expresses the dominant values of our culture.

With a humanistic culture internalized in the minds and hearts of people and embodied in the institutions and social structures of the society, government would come into its own as the moral voice and arm of the people. It would have a culture appropriate to its mission and the people would support it in doing its work. The offices of government at all levels could be organized so that officeholders could understand their role in public service and have a sense of the importance of their job and find self-fulfillment in their work. These offices should be filled with people committed to public service and to assisting the government in fulfilling its noble mission.

Our human-development institutions, including the family, the church, the school, and other character-forming and cultural institutions, should encourage young people toward service vocations, including public service; our educational system should prepare people for mission-oriented public service jobs with all the seriousness it now prepares people for jobs in the private economy and the professions.

In a sense, of course, all jobs are service jobs, but we need to distinguish, as we indicated in chapter 6, between the service involved in making the external conditions of people better and that involved in making them better in mind, body, or spirit. And, by extension, we need to draw the same distinction among jobs that serve society and the culture. There are those that contribute to the material wealth of the society and those that better the culture or the social order directly. People, society, and the culture have both external and internal needs. These roughly but not entirely parallel what we have called "materialistic and humanistic needs." The need for food, for example, is an internal but materialistic need. We may speak of external and internal services according to whether they pertain to external or internal needs and the goods that satisfy them. Our present discussion concerns internal service jobs.

Those involved in most internal service jobs, certainly the basic ones concerned with health-care, education, religion, advancement of knowledge and understanding, and the health and well-being of the social order should have a commitment to and be strictly under the discipline of the needs served and the goods sought. An emphasis on material gain for oneself or profits for investors would tend to pervert the service. The rationality of the capitalistic economy, as indicated in the preceding chapter, is inappropriate for most internal goods and services. Such goods and services, for the most part, should be provided by either private or public not-for-profit institutions. An exception may be made for food, clothing, shelter, and medicine so long as the society guarantees the necessities. Those preparing for internal service jobs should be committed to and educated in the culture appropriate for the institutions in which they will work.

There are those who say that human beings are self-centered and self-seeking by nature and that we need to build our institutions in a way to exploit this natural bent of human beings. Of course self-interest plays a powerful role in human behavior, but, as we observed in chapter 6, the form that self-interest takes is determined by one's sense of identity, by one's governing self-concept. With the right self-concept, self-interest can be harnessed to higher values. Our most powerful emotions are tied to our sense of identity and social status. People will risk their material wealth or even their lives to protect their good name. The military knows how to shape behavior by appeal to duty and honor even in the face of great hardship and mortal danger, behavior that could not be sustained for the sake of material gain. With the proper culture and education, people can be strongly motivated by moral and other higher values anchored in their selfhood in a way that enlists the support of self-interest.

Public service and other forms of internal service are the most honorable and meaningful vocations. And with an enlightened humanistic culture and properly educated people committed to internal services, governments and public and private not-for-profit institutions will work. Contrary to Representative Richard Armey's maxim ("Government is dumb; the market is rational"), government and public and private not-for-profit institutions should not operate on or be judged by the rationality of the market. They have their own rationality; they are under the discipline of providing maximum internal goods and services by meaningful work with available resources. And when functioning properly by their own normative constitutions, government and other public and private not-for-profit institutions are rational.

8

THE MILITARY

The Peculiar Institution

As we have previously contended, every society, by virtue of its inherent normative constitution, is defective to the extent that it does not provide the necessary protective and support systems for all its members to define and to live lives worthy of them as human beings and as the particular individuals they are; and all the members of society have a responsibility, grounded in their personhood, to work for and to support such protective and support systems.

Historically the maintenance of a military force has been regarded as perhaps the primary responsibility of a politically organized society, for it has been regarded as an essential protective system, required by both the common good and the rights of individuals. It has been regarded as a moral responsibility of every citizen to support the society's military forces, including service in the military forces, if qualified and needed to assure the security of the society.

Yet a military office makes very unusual demands on those who occupy it. It requires not just discipline, hard work, and the acceptance of risk and sacrifice; it requires not only that its holders place collective ends and the commands of superiors ahead of their personal ends and their own judgments, but it also demands that soldiers do these things when there is no self-advantage in doing them, even when they may have to sacrifice their lives. Furthermore, the state may conscript people for the office or extend their term of service against their will and not allow them to opt out when the judgments and orders of their superiors seem wrong or the risks and sacrifices seem too great.

There are good reasons why the military profession has been regarded as a noble profession, perhaps the noblest of all. Duty and honor play a greater role in the military than in any other occupation. Self-interest cannot be given the same play in the life of a soldier as in the life of others. Nevertheless, there is no office in society that is more morally ambiguous or more morally hazardous to one than the military.

Remember two primary moral judgments are made on any conventional office of a society: Can the person who holds the office fulfill the responsibilities of the office without doing violence to oneself as a person by having to shirk, or fail in, one's primary responsibilities as a person? And does the office serve, or at least is it compatible with, the common good?

The women's movement in recent decades, to consider just one example, has made a moral assault on the traditional office of womanhood. This office, to place it in the best possible light, was defined by the responsibility to be a homemaker, wife, mother, and, in general, a caring, nurturing, humanizing member of her family and community. It was an office to provide services from love and caring, not for materialistic self-gain; it was an office that would only be prostituted and cheapened by having a price placed on its service. It, along with manhood and personhood, was considered a natural office, not a conventional office that one could choose or resign. But with increasing materialization of the culture and marketization of services, monetary income became the most significant measure of a person's contribution to society and of one's own worth. Regardless of what could be said for the traditional office of womanhood under traditional conditions, in modern society the office has been progressively reduced in responsibilities and devalued in the culture. The position seems to be one in which many women can no longer live meaningful and fulfilling lives. Indeed, the office, as we observed in chapter 4, is widely understood as perverting and thwarting, as one that does violence to the personhood of those whose identities and lives are framed by it.

Some might contend that it is still not clear whether abolition of the traditional office of womanhood was justified in terms of the common good, for it profoundly affects, perhaps adversely, the family, our ways of rearing children, and our ways of promoting the higher values and the common good. Nonetheless, we have to say, insofar as the traditional social position of womanhood is dehumanizing to women and does violence to their personhood in modern society, it morally has to be abolished. Furthermore, it is not only morally wrong to try to promote the common good by social arrangements that violate the human rights of any group, it is logically impossible to achieve the common good in such a manner, for the benefits to society must be calculated within the framework of justice for all. In other words, the common good is logically tied to justice for individuals so that the common good cannot be achieved by arrangements and practices that are unjust to any individual.

In spite of the clear moral responsibility of a polity to provide for its own security and the security of its citizens and the responsibility of citizens to support and to serve in the military, the office of the soldier has seemed to many to be morally suspect. Worrisome questions have been raised about the military office on several grounds: (1) the virtues of a soldier, the trained habits of the heart and mind that make one a good soldier, seem to be contrary to the moral virtues of personhood; (2) the soldier, some have charged, is required by the peculiar structure of military authority to surrender his or her moral autonomy and thus to abdicate the office of personhood; and (3) the work of the military is violence (or, at least the threat of violence) against persons and property; yet inherent in the defining responsibility of personhood is the requirement to respect the rights of persons.

THE CONFLICT OF VIRTUES

The charge that the virtues of a soldier are incompatible with the virtues of a person so that one cannot be both a good soldier and a good person is perhaps the oldest criticism. It was the basis of the early Christian pacifism. Love was at the heart of the Christian religion from its inception; it was the fundamental Christian virtue. The Christian life was defined in terms of love of God and love of one's fellow human beings, including one's enemies. Yet the mission of the soldier is to destroy the enemy; the attitudes, the emotions, and the way of thinking about the enemy that enable one to be an effective killer are the exact opposite of Christian love and service.

After Christianity became the official religion of Rome and of the Roman army, St. Augustine attempted to reconcile the Christian conception of the good person with the Roman conception of the good soldier. He still insisted on pacifism in one's private life; he even held that a person should not defend oneself against a violent attack with any act of violence of one's own, for one could not do so without having thoughts, passions, and motivations contrary to Christian virtue. Yet he maintained that a person in a military office could perform acts of violence in fulfilling the responsibilities of the office while respecting and loving the persons he injured or killed.

Contrary to St. Augustine, however, military establishments, especially when engaged in actual war, try to instill in their combat soldiers denigration and hatred of the enemy. This is considered important for two reasons: (1) it helps to generate the spirit and motivation considered necessary to be an effective fighter; and (2) consideration of the enemy as diabolical or less than human protects the soldier's civilized self-image as a person from psychological damage by his or her acts of violence.

If there is a moral defense for the martial virtues, it must be that the mission of the soldier becomes incorporated in the moral responsibilities of some persons under certain conditions so that those persons cannot be good persons without being good soldiers.

It follows, however, that a soldier is a soldier- person and that a good soldier has to be a good soldier-person. This means that the virtues of a soldier cannot be defined independently of the virtues of a person. If the office of a soldier and its virtues were defined in such a way that a person would have to become perverted in order to be a good soldier, then morally we would have to condemn the office and reject the responsibilities that define it; or else accept the fact that, in this regard, human beings are tragic beings in that under some conditions they have, as persons, incompatible responsibilities that require of them incompatible virtues — a conflict that tears them apart and destroys them from within.

If the office of the soldier is to be reconciled with the responsibilities and virtues of personhood, two conditions must be met: (a) the responsibilities of soldiers must be defined in such a way that soldiers are not required to do anything for which they do not have moral immunity as persons; and (b) the attitudes, motivations, and ways of thinking developed in training soldiers and the characteristic of good soldiers in combat must be compatible with the moral virtues of personhood.

With regard to (a), in the long history of moral thought about war, something of a consensus developed to the effect that soldiers have moral immunity for acts of violence against human beings only if those targeted, through some act of their own, have forfeited their basic human rights vis à vis the attackers. This has been understood to mean that in war the only legitimate human targets are the combatants of the enemy. The combatants are considered a legitimate target in that, as instruments of violence of their country (whether voluntarily or by submission), they have forfeited their human rights in their relationship with the soldiers of the enemy. Thus, it is held that combatants in fighting combatants do not incur moral guilt. But if combatants target noncombatants, including combatants who have laid down their arms or have been disabled so that they are no longer instruments of violence, they are attacking human beings with their rights intact; they have no moral immunity for their violence.

It has been generally acknowledged that under the conditions of war, military forces may in fact kill and injure noncombatants as an unintended side effect of morally legitimate acts of war. Such injuries and deaths are considered accidents of the war; the victims just happened to be, or took the risk of being, caught in the violent forces of the war just as one may be caught in the destructive force of a tornado. Nevertheless, it has been widely acknowledged that an army has a moral obligation to try to minimize such unfortunate results of their acts; that soldiers who participate in military actions with a reckless disregard of the rights of noncombatants are morally blameworthy. It has even been acknowledged that military actions should be foregone if it were known that they would result in extensive civilian casualties. It has been acknowledged through the centuries, for example, that a city should not be put under military seige without advance warning and without provision for an escape route for the civilians.

Even if the acts of soldiers were restricted so that they had moral immunity for them, it would be difficult for the habits of mind and heart of good soldiers to be compatible with those of a good person. Many think that it is necessary for military forces to train their soldiers to denigrate and to hate the enemy for them to be effective fighters. Yet it is difficult for one to have the attitudes, motivations, and ways of thinking of an effective soldier in combat and be ready to accept as a person, with the appropriate attitude and behavior, the enemy soldier who surrenders or who is wounded and falls into one's hands. Even though it may be possible for certain individuals to be effective soldiers in combat without having morally corrupting attitudes and emotions, it would be very difficult to train large armies to be effective fighters without morally corrupting them. And it is very difficult for a nation to get fully behind a war effort without its citizens being moved by morally corrupting ways of thinking and feeling about the enemy.

MILITARY AUTHORITY AND

MORAL AUTONOMY

The basic moral imperative, grounded in the nature of personhood, is for a human being, with normal, mature powers, to define
and to live a life of one's own, under one's own knowledge-yielding and critical powers, that would be worthy of one as a human
being and as the particular individual one is.

This is a person's primary responsibility; it defines the office of
personhood and grounds human rights. Yet the structure of command in the military requires one to be subject to the commands
of one's superiors. This is not just a provisional submission to commands in which one reserves the right to resign the office if the
commands should become unacceptable; it seems to be, in effect,
an unconditional submission, with no live option open to one but
to obey the commands, however abhorrent they may be. In other
words, it seems that a military office may not only be incompatible with the office of personhood but may require one to abdicate
one's personhood. If this were, in fact, the case, the military office
could not be morally justified, for one could not preserve one's
personhood in the office any more so than one could in the position of a slave. If people became convinced that this were the case,
they would have to condemn the military on the same grounds as
they condemn slavery.

The structure of command is required by the function of the
military. And the function of the military requires that soldiers
cannot be allowed the choice of either obeying orders or quitting
the service when they receive an order that is morally repugnant to
them. We try to preserve, to some extent, the rights of personhood
by allowing exemption from conscription for military service for total
conscientious objectors (those who morally object to military service as such) and the right of soldiers to refuse to obey clearly illegal orders. But this only partially alleviates the tension between
personhood and the military office. It works fairly well for soldiers

in a war that they think is both morally justified and conducted in a morally justifiable way. But there is a profound problem for soliders fighting in a war that they, after careful and informed reflection, think is morally unjustified or that they think is fought in a morally unjustified way. There is no relief for their moral dilemma in the claim that they are not responsible for the war or for the orders they receive from their superiors. This would be abdication of their personhood. They cannot be good soldier-persons in such a war. The responsibilities of the two offices are in open conflict. In being good soldiers, they do moral violence to themselves as persons; in being good persons, they must fail in their responsibilities as soldiers.

One solution to this problem would be to allow exemption for conscientious objectors to particular wars and for conscientious objectors to the use of particular weapons and methods of warfare. Of course there would be practical difficulties for any society in administering fairly such provisions for exemptions from military service or from participation in particular military operations. But a society that rejects such policies should realize that it is brutalizing some of its conscientious citizens and undermining its own moral authority.

There are special problems for career soldiers, and, indeed, for all soldiers in a peacetime military force, whether volunteers or conscripts. They are subject to being ordered into combat in new conflicts and wars about which they have had no opportunity to form a judgment. The only way in which they can preserve any measure of their moral autonomy is for them to have a justified faith that their government would not commit them in a morally unjustified cause; nevertheless, they would have little recourse if they should find that their faith had been betrayed. Furthermore, many of them may be in positions in which they would be coerced to participate in a kind of attack they had come to regard as morally unjustified, for example, population bombing or the launching of nuclear missiles. In order to maintain their moral integrity, they might have to refuse to obey orders at a crucial moment at a great price to themselves and in a way that might jeopardize others.

An important consideration for any soldier, especially in a peacetime army, is the philosophy of military force held by the political leaders of the society. There are basically four theories: the reasons-of-state theory, the holy war theory, the classical just war theory, and the modern restricted just war theory.

The reasons-of-state theory holds that a sovereign state has the right to use its military power to protect or to promote the interests of the state, with the only rational restraint being prudential; that is, it should undertake only actions judged, with all things considered, to be beneficial to the state. In other words, on this view, states, in interstate relations, are not moral agents and their actions in this sphere are not subject to moral requirements and appraisals.

The holy war theory, in its original form, held that a state was justified in any military action that was in obedience to the will of its god (or to its interpretation of the will of God). In modern times, the theory has been extended to include the moral justification of military action in terms of a nation's values or ideology. Wars to make the world safe for democracy or to promote world communism would fall in this category.

The classical just war theory held that a state, *A*, was morally justified in military action against another state, *B*, only in response to a wrong that *B* had done to *A* or to its citizens and had refused to make a satisfactory correction. The military actions undertaken should be such that rational, informed people of all nations would recognize and approve them as morally justified.

The modern restricted just war theory holds that the only wrong that justifies a military response would be a violation of a state's basic rights, its rights of sovereignty and territorial integrity. In short, the theory holds that only defensive military actions are morally justified. This means that military power is not a morally justified way of dealing with non-military problems between states. Yet when states build up their military forces and position them for defensive purposes, others may feel threatened, and, in some situations, a state may be convinced that another state is about to attack it and strike first as a purely defensive action. So it is possible for a war to begin without an aggressor, unless we count whoever strikes first, regardless of intent, an aggressor.

The problem with which we are concerned is the moral problem of soldiers in the army of a state whose political leaders subscribe to an unjustified theory of war, or at least a theory that the soldiers think is wrong. For example, soldiers who believed in only the restricted just war theory while their political leaders subscribed to the use of military force to promote national interests could not preserve their moral autonomy even in the limited way indicated above, for they could not have a justified faith that they would not be ordered to participate in an unjustified war.

Unquestioning obedience to the orders of superiors is considered an essential military virtue. But a person can submit oneself to such obedience and maintain one's personhood only within a framework of justified faith in the moral integrity of the government and of the command structure of the military forces and only if there is an effective way to avoid obedience if that faith should be shattered.

VIOLENCE AND HUMAN RIGHTS

As we observed earlier, something of a moral consensus was reached in a long historical process to the effect that soldiers in combat have moral immunity for their acts of violence against soldiers of the enemy, but not for acts of violence against non-combatants. Yet, under the conditions of modern technology and total war, these historically achieved moral restrictions on the conduct of war have been largely abandoned both in practice and in long-term planning, if not in the codes of war. In World War II, both the Germans and the British resorted to terrorist population bombing early in the war and the Americans joined in, first just to show the Japanese that their cities were vulnerable, and later to hasten the end of the war in both Europe and the Pacific. Since then the major nations have based their military strategies on weapon systems that cannot discriminate between combatants and noncombatants. This gave rise to the policy of mutually assured destruction. Although, with advances in our missile guidance systems, we have developed a counter-force strategy, the major population centers of the United States, Western Europe, and Russia were targeted with nuclear missiles until the end of the Cold War. And even counter-force strikes with nuclear weapons would take out large population centers and perhaps endanger the lives of people in other countries as well.

We still do not consider that footsoldiers with their rifles or sub-machine guns have moral immunity to target civilians; but we seem to hold that those who fly bombers and launch missiles have moral immunity for attacks on populations. Does the difference lie in the fact that footsoldiers with their weapons can discriminate between combatants and noncombatants whereas the bombers and the missile launchers cannot? But in World War II, certainly in the bombing of Dresden, Hamburg, Tokyo, Hiroshima, and Nagasaki, the civilian populations were targeted. What is the moral difference between the bombers in these cases and the footsoldiers in the My Lai massacre in the Vietnam War? Can anyone seriously believe that the bombers and the missile launchers have moral immunity for their acts but the soldiers at My Lai did not? If so, do they base the difference on the grounds of military necessity — that the actions of the bombers and missile launchers may be necessary for the prosecution of the war but that the killings at My Lai were useless? Even if the massacre at My Lai were useless, an army of footsoldiers could terrorize the civilian population in a way that might be useful in coercing the political will of the society. If so, would soldiers have moral immunity for such violence against noncombatants?

With our modern weapon systems, many have come to question the moral distinction between combatants and noncombatants. It is widely believed that, in a modern society at war, the whole population is implicated in the war and involved in the war effort in such a way that no one has moral immunity to attack. Perhaps it is not surprising that our moral thinking, instead of governing the means of war, becomes adjusted to the technological imperatives of warfare. But this merits critical review.

In what sense have all the citizens of a country at war forfeited their basic rights before the enemy? Is it because they support the war effort of their country? Certainly the children in a country at war are not involved in the war effort; nor are they implicated in the moral responsibility for the war. Can there be moral immunity for killing them in attacks on population centers? Or do we set aside their injuries and deaths as unavoidable accidents of war?

In what sense does a civilian, by virtue of supporting the war effort, forfeit his or her basic rights before the military forces of the enemy? It seems clear that soldiers cannot have both the responsibility to perform violent acts against enemy soldiers and also a right that morally shields them from attack, for, insofar as their responsibility as soldiers vis à vis the enemy takes precedence over their responsibility as persons in relation to the enemy as persons, they yield their responsibility as persons and the rights grounded in it. But I do not see any inconsistency between the responsibility of civilians of a country to support their armed forces in a war with another country and their human rights that give them a moral shield against violent attacks by the soldiers of the enemy. Supporting one's nation in an unjustified war may involve moral guilt, but it is not moral guilt that nullifies the rights of soldiers and makes them morally vulnerable to violent attacks by the enemy forces; nor does it seem plausible that the moral guilt of the citizens in supporting an unjust war dissolves their moral shield of rights as persons before enemy soldiers.

If soldiers have moral immunity for attacks on civilians of an enemy country, it would have to be based on the fact that the citizens accepted the responsibility to support their soldiers in *violent attacks on the civilian population of the enemy country*. Certainly the citizens of a country could not consistently claim that it was their responsibility to support military attacks on the population of their enemy and that attacks on them by the military forces of their enemy violated their human rights.

Even this, however, would not make the civilians and the soldiers of a country equally morally vulnerable to attack. One cannot be a soldier without accepting, either freely or under coercion, the officially defined responsibilities of the office. The situation is much more nebulous with regard to both what the responsibilities of citizenship are and whether one accepts them. Many citizens in a country at war may not accept, and may not be engaged in carrying out, the alleged responsibility to support the war effort. This is clearly true of children, incompetent adults, and foreigners who may be trapped in the country. And many citizens may refuse to participate; they may even be in prison for refusing to serve in the armed forces or for refusing to support the war effort as citizens. Many may support the war effort in countering the military forces of the enemy but reject any responsibility to support military attacks on the enemy population. Some may give up jobs that are geared to the war effort or sacrifice income on which they would have to pay taxes that would support the war effort. It seems unwarranted to say that such citizens were morally vulnerable to attack.

Furthermore, there is widespread agreement that there is a difference in moral vulnerability to attack on the part of the agents of violence and of those who support them. For instance, many feel that there is a difference in targeting the workers in a munitions factory, especially when they are not in the factory, and in targeting soldiers. The difference seems to be that they do not accept, and live under, the responsibility to perform acts of violence even though they accept the responsibility to help supply those who do.

We feel that the terrorist attack with a car bomb that kills passersby on a busy street as a way to coerce the will of the government is morally abhorrent precisely because it violates the rights of those killed or injured and the right of all citizens to security on their streets. We do not consider their involvement in, or support for, a repressive established order as having nullified their human rights. Nor do we think that the government or some group of citizens would be justified in countering terrorist attacks with terrorist attacks in a community of the repressed who supported the terrorists. We would think that violent counter attacks would be justified only against the terrorists themselves. There does not seem to be much moral difference between a powerless group's (or a powerless country's) resorting to terrorist tactics to achieve its purposes and a great nation's resorting to population attacks to coerce the political will of the enemy as we did in World War II.

In a major nuclear war, the victims of violence would not be limited to the population of the enemy country. Populations in other countries, perhaps all over the earth, would suffer. Surely there can be no moral immunity for those who participate in this kind of violence.

We need to rethink the legitimate use of military action in international affairs. Is it to limit the military power of, or to disarm, an enemy country to keep it from violating the rights of one's country or that of others (and perhaps, in some extreme cases, to overthrow the government in a country for "crimes against humanity" against its own people)? Can it ever be a legitimate use of military power to coerce the political will of an enemy country by terrorist attacks on its population?

THE LOGIC OF POWER OR THE ETHICS OF PEACE?

We are living in a troublesome age in which our historic ways of thinking about national security and military force must be reconsidered. Science and technology have ruined war as a way of dealing with international conflicts when other means fail; it has ruined war even as a means of national defense. As horrible as World War II was, many think that, given the policies of Germany and Japan, it was morally necessary for the other powers to try to defeat them militarily and that the world is a better place because they did. But no one could judge any conceivable outcome of a war among the major powers today as a justification of the war. There are no conditions or ends that could make such a war a rational choice. Yet, the major nations prepare for the possibility of war with one another as if it might be an option under some set of circumstances.

This situation casts a moral pall over the modern military establishment. The primary function of a country's military forces is to defend the basic rights of the country and of its citizens against its adversaries. Yet, this is a function our military cannot fulfill, for it does not have the means to do it. Furthermore, there is no amount that we could invest in the military that would provide the necessary means. The only security the military can provide is by deterrence. This of course is the best kind, but the deterrent power of the United States military against a major adversary lies in its readiness to do what it would be madness to do, namely, unleash nuclear weapons. Instead of an act of defense, this would be national suicide; it would bring destruction on much of the rest of the world. There is no framework in terms of which such an action could be justified.

This places military personnel in a most peculiar situation. They must be trained and prepared to perform acts for which there could be no justification. They must have the beliefs, the attitudes, the dispositions, and the will to participate, on command, in unthinkable and unredeemable acts of violence for which their office can provide no moral immunity. In short, to be a good military officer under these conditions is to be morally corrupt; it is to have a set of military virtues that are immoral. No more severe moral condemnation can be made on any office in a society. In our advanced scientific and technological age, the noble soldier has been reduced to a tragic figure.

No longer can the major nations depend on their military power for national security; search for security in this manner increases the insecurity of all. No longer can a few, not even a few million, provide security for the population of a nation by risking, or even sacrificing, themselves. The major powers pursuit of security by modern military means puts everything at risk, even the survival of civilization, perhaps even the life-support system of the planet.

Paradoxically, war has been regarded as morally elevating. It is true that when a nation is wholeheartedly at war, as the United States was in World War II, the people transcend their self-centered lives and are prepared to make sacrifices for the sake of the good of the nation; they are bound together by loyalty to the nation and commitment to the cause for which they fight in a way that lifts them out of their self-centeredness. Often nations are said to have their finest hour in war. This is why William James said that we need a moral substitute for war, something that would give the people the same elevation of spirit and moral quality as war but without its down side.

While war may be elevating, it is also limiting. Partial views and limited values tend to be absolutized, and, to the extent this occurs, both rationality and morality are compromised. People become corrupted in their virtues, in their habits of mind and heart. The nation becomes the object of the people's highest devotion and loyalty; they organize all their values in relation to it; it becomes their god and patriotism becomes their religion. The absolutizing of the relative in this manner is always demonic; it blocks commitment to higher values and gives rise to a systematic misevaluation of all values.

In general, military establishments tend to generate a culture that alleviates the moral dilemmas of the military office. They do this, if unchecked by a wider culture, by promoting a blind patriotism. Service to the state in the form of unquestioning obedience to its will as expressed in the command structure of the military is presented as the highest and noblest service open to a citizen. It is cast in the same terms in which many religions think of service to God and unquestioning obedience to God's will; indeed, it is not uncommon to present one's state as "God in history." Patriotism of this kind eliminates the conflicts between the moral virtues of personhood and the martial virtues of the solider by transforming those of personhood into those of the soldier; it eases the tension between one's moral autonomy as a person and obedience to the command structure of the military by holding that there is no office in society more honorable than a position in the military and that the highest responsibility of one as a person-in-the-military is to obey the commands of one's superiors, and since, on this view of patriotism, the highest moral obligation of soldiers is to obey orders of their superiors, they cannot be morally blameworthy for any acts of violence they perform in obedience to such orders, regardless of the rights of their victims. Those who subscribe to this view of patriotism tend to regard the rights of people as imposing no normative limits on the acts of soldiers in obedience to commands of superiors in the way in which orthodox Jews and Christians seem to think that the rights of Isaac imposed no normative limits on Abraham in his plan, according to the biblical story, to sacrifice his son as a burnt offering in obedience to a command of God.

The fact that militaristic patriotism "resolves" the moral dilemmas of the military profession in the way in which it does is the reason that many enlightened citizens regard it as demonic. This kind of patriotism is evil in that it perverts morality and personhood. It tries to ease the tension between the ethics of personhood and the virtues required by the military institution by adapting ethics to the military rather than by holding the military accountable to the requirements of ethics. This has given militarism and patriotism a bad name.

The moral dilemmas of persons in the military are symptoms of deeper troubles in our culture and social order. Many of our fundamental ideas, values, and institutions must be rethought, for they are evil in that they are morally corrupting and have the human race set on a self-destructive course. We must find new institutional and cultural ways of organizing and structuring human activities and providing for security. This does not mean that the military will be abolished, but it does mean that its mission must be redefined and that the military office must be reconstituted in a way that is compatible with personhood.

While our problems are vast and deep and the way to solve them is not clear, it seems imperative for nations, as a first step, to temper their nationalism and to abandon their search for empire. National security can no longer be achieved by military power; it must be sought in a just world order. The civilized nations of the world must be prepared to compromise their national "interests" for the sake of justice in international relations, to work for and to support institutions that work for justice in international affairs, and to restrict the use of their military forces to the defense of their national rights and the rights of other nations and in ways that will respect the rights of all involved.

Unlike the protection of national interests, the protection of national rights is not partisan; it does not require a morally perverting patriotism that makes it virtually impossible for any nation to face international problems objectively and fairly. A nation cannot rationally defend its own rights by violating the rights of others; when the rights of any are violated, the rights of all are made insecure. Defense of one's rights is a defense of the rights of all; and defense of the rights of others is a defense of one's own rights.

No nation can live unto itself; the human world has become one. A global economy is not enough; it cannot stand by itself. We must have political institutions coextensive with the problems we face, if we are to have a peaceful world. We must think in terms of, and work toward, a just global society in which the people of the world can live worthy lives. What is even more basic is a universal humanistic culture that is grounded in, and held accountable to, the inherent normative constitution of humankind and society. Multiple cultures, yes; but historically generated cultures should share, and be held accountable to, a transcending human and social normative framework.

9

RELIGION AND

THE ARTS

Religion and art are two of the oldest and most persistent forms of culture. They are quintessentially humanistic and at the heart of the human enterprise. Yet they have been intellectually undermined and subjectivized and marginalized in modern Western civilization. With realistic humanism, they could and should regain center stage and play a central role in integrating the culture on humanistic terms and in humanizing the society.

Religion and art not only give expression to but also enter into and integrate our complex lived engagements and the life-world implicated in them. Lived engagements involve all of our intentional modalities — sensory, emotive, volitional, behavioral, imaginal, intellectual, or whatever. An art work may highlight some aspect or complex of features of an object or situation that is emotively experienced, but it has a transcendent aspect. Like a religion, it integrates its subject matter into a wider context in a way that is revelatory of its meaning or lack of it. There is something of the religious in all art, either in a positive or a negative way.

THE ROLE OF RELIGION AND ART IN LIFE

John Dewey emphasizes the positive role of both religion and art in life. He speaks of the religious dimension of life as consisting of attitudes that have "the force of bringing about a better, deeper and enduring adjustment in life . . . the attitudes that lend deep and enduring support to the process of living."[1] Concerning art, he says:

> [T]he work of art operates to deepen and to raise to great clarity that sense of an enveloping undefined whole that accompanies every normal experience. This whole is then felt as an expansion of ourselves. . . . Where egotism is not made the measure of reality and value, we are citizens of this vast world beyond ourselves, and any intense realization of its presence with and in us brings a peculiar satisfying sense of unity in itself and with ourselves.[2]

But there are negative life attitudes, the feeling that there is no point to life, that the human struggle is absurd, that nothing really matters, that the larger world in which we dwell is alien or barren, that it lends no support to us in our quest for meaningful experiences, meaningful relationships, and a meaningful life. In fact, some of the best of modern art expresses life despair. T. S. Eliott's *The Waste Land,* regarded by some as the greatest poem of the twentieth century in the English language, presents a scene where there is nothing but stony rubbish, a dead tree, a dry rock, and fear in a handful of dust. The world enveloped in it is revealed as a desert, totally unsupportive of a meaningful life. And there is the absurd world in a Franz Kafka story where nothing makes sense; and the value-free world in an Albert Camus novel where nothing really matters.

These negative life attitudes are religious, if we define the religious, as I am wont to do, as our deep feelings and attitudes toward ourselves as human beings in the world. Negative life attitudes are the opposite of religious faith; they are the denial of the meaningfulness and worthwhileness of life. All religions seek to counter negative life attitudes and to promote a positive religious outlook. Art gives expression to lived experience, whether positive or negative. George Steiner speaks of great art, whether literature, music, or painting, as expressing "a more or less articulate consciousness of the presence or *absence* [emphasis added] of God in and from human affairs."[3] Art is interpretative, expressive, and revelatory, but, unlike religion, good art does not advocate, it does not preach.

Propaganda is not the business of art. This is not to say that the interpretations, revelations, and feelings expressed in an art work, or even the work of art in its own being, may not carry some recommendation or condemnation. But whatever recommendation or condemnation that is involved must be embodied in the work of art itself and not be an external purpose for which the work of art is only a means.

But is a work of art such as Eliott's *The Waste Land* or Samuel Beckett's *Waiting for Godot* totally negative in import? There is not only what is presented or expressed in the work, but also there is the work of art itself. It, in so far as it is good art, has aesthetic unity and integrity, including the appropriateness of form and medium to what it expresses. Is there a transcendent aspect to the work of art over and above what may be presented or expressed in it? Does it in its own being, purely as a work of art, reveal or express something about the world? And, if so, must it exemplify or somehow intimate the world in positive tones? Steiner speaks about the way a great work of art seizes us and "compels the question of creation." "We ask ourselves," he says, "whether there is in the genesis of great art and in its effects upon us some analogy to the coming into being of life itself." He further speaks of "'the real presence' in the symbolic object, of the 'mystery' in the form."[4] If all works of art have such a positive import, then there is an inconsistency in a work of art like *The Waste Land.* The poem in its own being opens to us a world in sharp contrast to that presented in the poem. It itself is a lilac in the desert that compromises the desert scene.

In other words, can there be art in a senseless world? Indeed, can there be a life or any humanistic phenomenon in a meaningless world? Perhaps this indicates that the negative religious attitude is grounded in some confusion, that it cannot be consistently thought through.

In the art of a culture, we find expressed the verdict of lived experience on life and the world view formed within the culture. It may reveal and judge something about the human condition in the large, or it may be a verdict on only the particular culture that shapes the life and world view of the people in question. For this reason, the art of a people is a rich resource for humanities scholars and cultural critics in their interpretation and evaluation of the lived experience, the social structure, and the culture of the society.[5] But our interest here is in the role of art in lived experience, with the focus on its role in the religious life of a people — its role in both forming and expressing the deep emotional, aspirational, and volitional dimension of individuals and communities.

Next to the family, an enlightened and responsible religion, whether Christian, Jewish, Islamic, or whatever, is the most complete humanistic institution. It addresses deep humanistic needs and engages profound humanistic emotions, aspirations, and commitments of individuals and communities. Neither the family nor religion, not even the government, can succeed in the modern world without comprehensive humanistic education in the schools and a humanistic culture in general. All four institutions (the family, religion, the government, and the school) are complementary and essential for a society fit for human beings, but they are weakened and threatened in our materialistic culture and economy-driven society.

The primary enemy of religion has always been our lower sentiments and desires and the resulting self-centeredness, narrowness of vision, and perversion of our understanding. The distinction between higher and lower or noble and base sentiments and desires has never been much in dispute. Even those on the low road often admire those who take the high road. Of course there have been controversies about some sentiments and desires, but there has been considerable agreement throughout history about the motivations and characteristics of people that are worthy of admiration, promotion, and celebration; there has been equal agreement in regard to the motivations and kinds of people that have been disfavored and condemned. There is no contest between objective and biased judgment; between constructive and destructive behavior; between a life motivated by love and compassion and one based on hatred and resentment; between goodwill and ill will; between the self-giving and the self-serving; between broad and narrow vision; or between spiritual and materialistic values.

Where scientific thought is geared toward the kind of understanding that would give us power and control over things in a way that would make us more able to satisfy our materialistic needs and desires, religion seeks the kind of understanding of self and world that would lead to salvation — that is, conversion from a materialistic to a spiritual life: the formation and empowerment of people for living meaningful and worthy lives in the pursuit of higher values.

Modern naturalists, with their intellectual vision shaped in its foundations by the priority of materialistic interests, have often charged religion with softheadedness and lack of nerve for projecting meaning and value structures into the universe for the sake of emotional comfort. They take pride in being tough-minded intellectuals who embrace the cold reality of the scientific world view without whining or flinching. They boast that they are prepared to dismiss meaningless questions and to live without the emotional warmth and satisfaction of myths, poetry, and illusions.

W. T. Stace, although he later modified his position, expressed a widely held naturalistic view when he wrote:

> There is no reason why we should have to give up the
> host of minor illusions which render life supportable.
> There is no reason why the lover should be scientific
> about the loved one. Even the illusions of fame and
> glory may persist. But without the Great Illusion, the
> illusion of a good, kindly, and purposeful universe, we
> shall have to learn to live. And to ask this is no more
> than to ask that we become genuinely civilized. . . .

> Man has not yet grown up. He is not adult. Like a child he cries for the moon and lives in a world of fantasies. . . . Can man put away childish things and adolescent dreams? Can he grasp the real world as it actually is, stark and bleak, without its romantic or religious halo, and still retain his ideals? . . . If he cannot, he will probably sink back into savagery and brutality from which he came, taking a humble place once more among the lower animals." [6]

But the hardheaded naturalists may not be as hardheaded as they like to think, for their position cannot be consistently thought through. On the tough ground of logic, or so I have argued, they run into inconsistencies between their one-dimensional world view and the humanistic presuppositions of all human activities, including the scientific enterprise itself. Indeed, modern naturalism suffers from narrowness of vision that resulted from the materialistic turn in the modern Western value system that placed the intellectual enterprise in the service of interests that could be satisfied by manipulatory power over things. Its puritanical epistemology is inadequate to accommodate the semantics and ethics of even scientific thought, to say nothing of the ideals that make civilization possible. On the other hand, realistic humanism, as I argued in the first chapter, meets the hardheaded test of logic and reality. It is justified in terms of the broad spectrum of the semantic and knowledge-yielding powers of the human mind; it provides a theory of knowledge and a unified world view in terms of which the whole culture can be interpreted and integrated without breaking down in logical inconsistencies and antinomies. Furthermore, a humanistic culture with proper regard for materialistic needs promises more success for individuals in defining and living worthy lives and for societies in organizing themselves and running their institutions in ways that support the human enterprise.

THE RELIGIOUS DIMENSION OF CONSCIOUSNESS

All human beings have religious needs and concerns. One cannot be a human being engaged in living a life with knowledge-yielding and critical powers without deep feelings and attitudes toward oneself and concerns for the life one is living — feelings, attitudes, and concerns grounded in questions and beliefs about whether oneself and the life one is living makes sense in the ultimate context of human existence. One may have religious feelings and attitudes focused on oneself as the individual one is and the life one is living, or feelings and attitudes that encompass all of humankind and human history. In the first case, one may feel disoriented and lost in a profound way, even that one is worthless and that one's life is meaningless, but that the fault lies within oneself. Religions often focus on "the salvation" of this kind of "lost" person. But their "salvation" does not address the most virulent form of life despair in modern culture.

Modern life despair is profound; it is the feeling that the whole human situation is absurd — that the life-world presupposed in the human struggle is an illusion. It is not just a matter of whether one's own life is meaningful and worthwhile, but whether human beings matter, whether the human phenomenon makes sense, whether the universe is a context in which the human enterprise is meaningful. Was Shakespeare's Macbeth right when he said of life: ". . . it is a tale / told by an idiot, full of sound and fury, / Signifying nothing"?[7] Or as Albert Camus would have it: Are we absurd actors playing our part without a stage?

The religious problem is a matter of alienation. One does not feel comfortable with clothes unless one "recognizes oneself in them," one does not feel at home in a house unless one finds oneself expressed in it in some way, and one feels alienated in a society unless one finds one's beliefs and values embodied in the behavior of the people and in the institutions of the society. In a similar manner, one feels alone and estranged in the vastness of the universe, unless one identifies in some fundamental way with ultimate reality and the forces at work in the world. Religions seek to relate the wisdom that gives form and direction to human life at its best to the wisdom embodied in the unfolding universe. Hindus, Buddhists, and Taoists identify the moral way of life for human beings with the way of the universe. When the early Christians thought they saw the Wisdom of the universe — the self-expression of God, what the Greek philosophers called the "Logos" — incarnated in the person and manifested in the life and teachings of Jesus whom they called "Christ," they concluded that they could and should become new creatures by identifying with and participating in the mind and spirit of Christ.

Organized religion is ill prepared to face the religious problem in its modern cultural form. Its traditional modes of advocacy speak to only those already culturally disposed to hear its message. Its effectiveness is largely limited to like-minded cultural enclaves, with little influence on our mainstream culture.

THE CULTURE OF RELIGION

Religion had its beginning in our early ancestors' emotional comprehension of themselves as beings in the world as their rudimentary powers of self-transcendence and world-awareness emerged. They must have given expression to their deep feelings and concerns in behaviors that in time took the form of rituals, dances, prayers, and songs — various forms of participation in or communication with the forces they felt to be in control of their destiny.

Religion trades in myths, dramatic stories, poetry, and other art forms. These are its natural medium, for religion engages the whole person and speaks in terms of the whole human situation as imaginatively and emotively grasped; it speaks to and gives form and voice to the deepest emotions and aspirations of the human soul. In contrast with the abstract conceptual language of the intellect, the language and symbols of religion are expressions of the emotionally charged imagination; they are the product of, and have their full-bodied meaning in terms of, the life and death experiences of a people. The language and symbols of a religion are fully viable for only those who can identify with and share in the life experiences that generated the religion. Some religions, of course, migrate and take root in the life of another historical community, but not without connecting the two cultures while transforming and being transformed by the new community. Consider the way in which Christianity, for example, has penetrated and been influenced by other cultures. But converts to Christianity in whatever culture have come to identify in some fashion with the historical experience of the Jewish people and the early Christians as well as with their own history. They have come to share in what was perceived as the divine power at work in the deliverance of the Hebrews from Egypt and in their nation-forming experience under Moses, and they have come to participate in the early Christians' encounter with what they took to be the divine in the person of Jesus — a spiritual power that transformed them and even human history.

All historical religions try to solve the religious problem of ontological alienation by humanizing the universe — by seeking intelligibility of reality in terms of the conceptual system grounded in selfhood and lived experience. They find backing, in one way or another, in the ultimate constitution and dynamics of the universe for the power and authority of the sentiment of rationality, the pull of the moral ought, the call of the universal and the transcendent, and, in general, the power of higher values to move the human heart. Religions, through myths, stories, rituals, symbols, teachings, and practices, cultivate and reinforce our nobler sentiments and impulses, stress the formation and nurture of character for living a worthy life, and build life morale through a vision of ourselves as human beings in the world — a vision that makes sense of and supports the human enterprise defined in terms of humanistic values. Indeed, they typically interpret the human struggle toward higher values, not only as in concert with and supported by the ultimate constitution of the universe, but also as the universe bringing itself to a higher level of perfection in our struggle for a higher mode of life for ourselves and our society.

MEANING AND TRUTH IN RELIGION AND ART

Although myths, stories, symbols, songs, poetry, rituals, and practices of a religion are its primary modes of comprehension and expression as well as the principal source of its power in human lives, a religion, in a culture with an abstract theoretical mode of thought, may take a theological turn, especially when facing logical challenges from other cultural developments. This happened with Judaism and Christianity when they encountered the challenges of the Hellenistic world. Theology is an effort to formulate in abstract conceptual language, and to defend intellectually, the truth embodied in the vital mythic, poetic, symbolic culture of the religion. This is called "sacred theology."

Sacred theology, as distinct from the humanistic intellectual discipline known as natural theology, is an intellectual discipline conducted by devotees of a particular religion; it focuses on the sacred culture of the religion — the culture made sacred to the adherents of the religion by opening to them the divine in a way that defines for them their identity and the meaning of their lives. Sacred theologians assume that the religion is true in its basic claims. Their first task is to determine just what the essential truth-claims of the religion are; their second undertaking is to find an interpretation of these essential truth-claims in abstract conceptual terms that would be not only consistent with one another, but also with all the other well-established truth-claims that they feel compelled to accept; their third function is to show how the truth-claims of the religion can structure the lives of believers so that their lived experience will vindicate the religion; and their fourth function is to show how the truths of the religion and all other well-substantiated truths can be organized and integrated into a coherent, defensible intellectual account of lived experience and the world.

The meaning and truth in the myths, stories, symbols, and rituals of a religion are more like the meaning and truth in poetry, novels, drama, and the other arts than like the meaning and truth in history, science, or philosophy. In intellectual discourse, the aim is to keep the meaning of words and sentences relatively thin, clear, and well defined so that the logical and evidential relationships may be clearly discerned and the validity of inferences and the truth-value of statements can be established in a way that can be agreed upon by competent investigators and critics. Furthermore, in intellectual discourse, the clarity and truth of a complex theory is dependent on the clarity and truth of its elements and the validity of the inferences involved. The whole theory may collapse by virtue of a faulty element or inference. Just the contrary is true in mythical, literary, and other symbolic modes of expression. In all of these, the meaning is thick, multilayered, imagistic, and holistic. The discourse expresses the whole person, often the experience and spirit of a whole community or a mega-historical experience. The meaning and truth of a myth, a religious historical story, a novel, or a poem may not at all depend on the truth of its elements or the validity of its inferences. The meaning and truth of Tolstoy's *War and Peace,* for instance, has little, if anything, to do with the historical reality of the individual characters and events presented in the novel. Its meaning and truth lie in what it shows us about human behavior, social institutions, civilization, and the inner constitution and the interior climatic conditions of human beings in ordinary situations and at the limits of challenge, violence, and disaster. This meaning and truth would not be diminished even if Napoleon had never invaded Russia. In fact, some have questioned whether there was an actual Trojan War. While most historians reject this thesis, no one would hold that the meaning and truth of Homer's *Iliad* would be undermined or its value diminished if this claim should be found to be true.

What bearing do these considerations have for the task of sacred theology in interpreting, for example, the meaning and truth in the Judeo-Christian religion? None of the early characters in the biblical story up to Abraham appears to be a historical figure, and even Abraham is a shadowy figure at the edge of history, more legendary than historical. Not much can be known historically about such a pivotal figure as Moses. Like Homer's story of Agamemnon and Achilles, who may have been contemporaries of Moses, the record we have did not take its historical form until several hundred years later. Much of the positive developments in the Hebrew religion and culture up until the Babylonian exile in the sixth century B.C. came to be attributed to Moses to give them the authority of this commanding legendary figure as their principal spokesman for God. Philo, the Jewish philosophical theologian, who was a contemporary of Jesus, spoke of Moses as the Platonic world spirit who moves lower beings toward the Logos, which he thought of both as the Word of God and as Platonic Ideas. In other words, Moses became not merely a bigger-than-life legendary figure, but, like Jesus in the Christian tradition, a mythical character.

The religious significance of Moses and Jesus and of the teachings attributed to them does not depend on truths that can be established or refuted by historical scholarship. Some Islamic scholars have contended for centuries that Jesus survived the ordeal on the cross and shortly thereafter migrated with his mother and some close associates to what is now Kashmir in northern India. They claim that he lived to a ripe old age and became a revered religious teacher in that area. In fact, there is an ancient tomb in Kashmir that some claim is where Jesus was buried.[8] The point I want to raise is this: If historians should establish this story as a well-authenticated historical truth, would it falsify the Christian religion? Or does the essential meaning and truth of the Christian religion transcend this kind of factual information?

What constituted the resurrection? A historical bodily event or a spiritual experience? Was the early disciples' reported experience of the resurrected Christ similar to Paul's experience on the Damascus road? Apparently Paul thought that they were comparable. What must be acknowledged as historical fact is that a small band of disappointed and frightened followers of Jesus came together after his death, united and possessed by a spiritual power that changed history. Was the appearance of this life- and history-transforming spiritual power in the little band of disciples the truth in the resurrection story? The early Christians identified the amazing spiritual power they felt at work in themselves with the spiritual power they had witnessed in Jesus during his lifetime. Was the earlier appearance of an overwhelming spiritual power in Jesus the truth expressed in the claim that "in him all the fullness of God was pleased to dwell" (Col. 1:19)?

If this is the truth about Jesus as the incarnate God and about his resurrection, must Christian believers accept the early disciples' metaphysical interpretation of the spiritual power they witnessed in Jesus and then found in themselves? Or should present-day Christians find a metaphysical interpretation acceptable in our time? And can they do this without compromising the religious truth in the Christian story? Christian theologians from the first century have taken the position that the theological interpretation of the truth in a religious story is not given with the story; it is something that they have to work out within the framework of a metaphysics acceptable to them. This has meant reinterpretation of the truths of the religion in each age according to the available world view of the time. First, there was the interpretation in terms of first century apocalyptic Judaism. This was followed by St. Paul's syncretistic interpretation in terms of apocalyptic and Hellenistic Judaism and the Gnostic world view, and the Platonic interpretations of the Fourth Gospel, Clement of Alexandria, and Origin. And there have been the Neoplatonic interpretation of St. Augustine, the Aristotelian interpretation of St. Thomas, and the Existentialist interpretation of Paul Tillich, just to mention a few.

We need to ask in our time: What is spirit? What is spiritual power? What is a spiritual person? The concept *spirit* has a long history. Whatever else may be involved, a basic truth about spirit is that it is value-seeking power, especially the power to bring about or to work toward the realization of higher values. The primary spirit that we know is in ourselves. It is here that the concept has its ground and is most at home. We think of ourselves as having a spiritual dimension. In us, spirit is the capacity to discern and to be moved by values, by what ought to be, especially by higher values or the more comprehensive normative requirements that impinge on us. Of course we talk about evil or mean-spirited people. These are people who, according to our view, systematically pursue what is bad or at least only a limited or partisan good. What we usually mean by a spiritual person is one who is focused on, moved by, and pursues higher values — intellectual, artistic, moral, and religious values, especially moral and religious values. The spiritual person stands in contrast with both the self-centered person and those preoccupied with materialistic values.

With a humanistic world view, we take the ultimate causal power of the universe to be not merely value oriented, not merely oriented toward the highest or most comprehensive values, but the actual constraint or pull of the normative constitution of the universe toward its own fulfillment; that is, we take the universe to have a normative constitution that is a teleological causal power in its own right, one that is causally efficacious in its own realization. This is what a theistic world view amounts to intellectually. This, I suggest, is the basic truth that is presented symbolically by the character God in the biblical story and the deity by whatever name in other theistic religions.

In other words, the theist takes what we regard as the highest and the best in ourselves as our best clue to the ultimate mystery of the universe. Religions are, in this sense, anthropomorphic in their world view in contrast with the mechanomorphic way of thought in modern science. The humanist, contrary to the scientist, does not seek to understand the whole in terms of its parts, complex things and situations in terms of their elements and antecedent conditions, the end state of a process in terms of the antecedent physicalistic causal factors; rather the humanist seeks intelligibility of a subject matter in terms of the whole of which it is a part, the lower in terms of the higher, the causal means in terms of the normative end of a process. The key to the difference lies in the role of value concepts, or the lack thereof, in the two frameworks of intelligibility. Even more basically the difference lies in what modes of experience are taken to be knowledge-yielding — the humanist looks to our total experiential engagement with the world; the scientist typically looks to only our sensory encounters. Back of this divide lies differences in the values that define the perspective of the knowledge-seeking enterprise.

It cannot be emphasized too much that religion focuses on the motive power of higher values and the pull of the universal and transcendent normative requirements on the human heart. It seeks out and nurtures all the impulses and sentiments we find in ourselves that thrust us upward and forward in life-enhancing and life-advancing ways and binds us together in solidarity and mutual support for the common good and the betterment of all. Religion strengthens these elevating impulses and sentiments and gives them authority by interpreting them as the divine at work in the human heart.

A humanistic culture is, in general, hospitable to and supportive of intelligent, responsible religion, for the religious problem is the supreme humanistic problem and religions have always focused on humanistic values and employed humanistic modes of thought and expression. The intellectual battleground in modern culture is not over the existence of God but over the nature of human beings. If we are compelled to accept a humanistic view of the human phenomenon, we must, I think, accept a humanistic view of the world in order to make our existence, our lives, and our history intelligible. And with a humanistic view of the culture and the world, we can account for the meaning and truth in the mythical, dramatic, poetic, symbolic language and rituals of religions that have enjoyed success in organizing and empowering the lives of people and historical communities.

Although the religious cultures of the world are very different in so many ways, there is something of a consensus among all the major historical religions that (1) our inner constitution and the world that generated us are such that a self-centered life focused on materialistic values is unworthy of us as human beings and even self-destructive in the long run; whereas a life in pursuit of humanistic values and the fulfillment of the more comprehensive normative requirements that impinge on us is worthwhile and meaningful and backed by the ultimate powers of the universe; (2) the ultimate causal power is divine: it consists of or constitutes the normative structure of the world and works toward the realization of what comprehensively ought to be; (3) human beings partake of the divine in that we have a normative constitution by virtue of which we are under an inner imperative to pursue higher values and to be responsive to the overriding normative requirements that impinge on us; (4) by meditating on and identifying with the divine dimension of the universe, we can strengthen and enhance the spark of the divine within ourselves; and (5) the practice of cultivating the divine within ourselves and integrating our efforts in the pursuit of higher values with the energies at work in the world for the realization of what ought to be elevates our lives, gives us inner strength, and generates life morale.[9]

With the divine understood as the causal power of higher values and God as a symbol of the divine, a devotee of most any religion should find the following meditation meaningful:

> The divine within me leads me in the paths of knowledge, wisdom, and love, and calls me in the service of the moral ought and to the pursuit of higher values. My station in life is to be an enlightened, rational, creative pulse to the divine heartbeat of the universe, working for the realization of what ought to be in my own person, in society, and in the culture.
>
> Even though I walk through the valley of death, I shall not despair, for in the inner depths of my soul there is a light that dispels the darkness and an ever-flowing fountain of faith in and hope for the values I seek.
>
> I feel the presence of the divine in green woods and fields; in a garden with spring flowers, flowering shrubs, and blossoming fruit trees; on the beach at the seashore; in the high mountains with far horizons; and under the starry sky. The beauty and the sublime in nature restore my soul.
>
> God nourishes and sustains me by preparing a table before me with my family and friends; by joining me in solidarity with all humankind with bonds of kinship, love, respect, sympathetic joy, and compas-

sion; and by anchoring me in the universe with sentiments of natural piety, reverence, and thankfulness.

I am one with God. The divine within me moves
me toward higher values; I am a member of a family,
a community, and institutions that will continue to
reach for the good; indeed, I am a part of God, the
eternal dynamic of the universe working for the realization of what ought to be.

Thanks be to God.

A RESPONSIBLE RELIGION FOR OUR TIME

Only a historical religion has the cultural richness and depth to be
effective in the lives of a community of people, and only a historical religion has the validation of lived experience under varied
conditions over a long period of time. Furthermore, for most
people, only a religion that is deeply embedded in their culture is
a live option. A religion works for people only if they can embrace
it in their hearts in a way that defines and strengthens their sense
of who they are and what they are about. The religion of another
culture is likely to seem alien and forbidding or even threatening.
However, all historical religions have acquired a lot of antiquated
and discredited baggage to which they have become hostage. A responsible religion for our time has to be one that has historical
roots in our culture, but is open to the truths of other religious
traditions; it must accept cultural freedom and promote the development and full employment of all of our knowledge-yielding
and critical powers; it must be not only intellectually, morally, and
artistically respectable and defensible, but also a leader in advancing and integrating the culture as a whole.

This opens up the question of faith and reason. I have characterized religious faith as life morale, the opposite of life despair. In
other words, religious faith is belief in the meaningfulness and worthwhileness of a life based on our inherent normative constitution

and guided by our knowledge-yielding and critical powers in pursuit of higher values. This involves the belief that the context of human existence is such that the human struggle for higher values makes sense — that human beings fit into and can trust the world that brought them forth. Religious faith is a presupposition of the human enterprise much as faith in our knowledge-yielding powers and the intelligibility of the world is a presupposition of the intellectual enterprise. Serious doubt about the meaningfulness and worthwhileness of the life struggle would result in what Leo Tolstoy called a "life arrest,"[10] just as serious skepticism about our knowledge-yielding powers and the intelligibility of the world would lead to the collapse of the intellectual enterprise.

Although the underlying faith (belief, commitment, trust) that makes the knowledge-seeking and life enterprises possible seem to transcend the jurisdiction of reason, they are not without rational support. If an enterprise works, the framework of the enterprise, including its presuppositions, gains support. Consider the knowledge-seeking enterprise. Intellectual inquiry about a subject is carried on within a body of commitments and beliefs that are not at issue in the inquiry. Some of this body of taken-for-granted commitments and beliefs may be called into question and confirmed or discredited by straightforward investigative methods. But if we probe and question deep enough, we will come to commitments and beliefs that cannot be questioned without putting all of our investigative methods in question as well. In other words, if we dig deep enough in our body of commitments and beliefs, we will come upon commitments and beliefs that will turn our spade. When this happens, we are at the bedrock of the intellectual enterprise; we are at our intellectual foundations. Some may say that our foundational commitments and beliefs are a matter of faith, without rational justification, because we cannot ground them in something even more basic. I have no quarrel with saying that our foundational framework of thought is a matter of faith so long as this is not taken to mean that it is arbitrary or lacks a rational defense. The foundational commitments and beliefs that turn our investigative spade have no alternatives, and thus are necessary within the intellectual enterprise. If there is knowledge of anything, then they have their justification and need no other.

The framework of the life enterprise is much the same. In living a life, we proceed with a whole body of commitments and beliefs, including values, goals, and principles of life criticism. As in the knowledge enterprise, many of these can be questioned and justified or rejected in straightforward ways while the life enterprise goes on. If we continue this process into the depths of the body of commitments and beliefs with which we live our lives, we will, as in the case of the knowledge enterprise, come upon commitments and beliefs that break our spade; that is, we will come upon commitments and beliefs that are so basic that, if they are put in question, the whole justificatory process and the life enterprise itself will collapse. Call this life framework a matter of faith if you like, but do not imply that it is arbitrary, without rational defense. There is no alternative and the life enterprise itself warrants it.

Our basic religious faith that life is meaningful and worthwhile, that the context of our existence is such that the human enterprise makes sense, is, as we said, one of our foundational beliefs. It is not surprising that it is embraced by all historical religions, for it is embraced by all engaged in the life enterprise. Genuine skepticism or nihilism stops life, for it paralyzes the heart. There are intellectual atheists but their hearts contradict them. There are no real atheists (those who reject the fundamental articles of faith of the life enterprise) in the thick of life. We find them mostly in clinics, psychiatric wards, or somewhere withdrawn from life, paralyzed with depression. Some may keep going for a time by concentrating on immediate concerns, but sooner or later, if they live long enough, there will be self-transcending moments when they will realize that something within them demands more of themselves and that their peculiar nature requires a universe that would make their existence intelligible and a life lived by their inner constitution meaningful. They may reject this or that way of conceptualizing or symbolizing the ultimate nature of the universe, but they do not reject that somehow the universe is a context that makes sense of our existence and of our struggle to live by our own normative constitution.

Every religion that gains an enduring purchase on the human heart offers a framework for life that is based on and makes sense of the fundamental truths about ourselves and the world that are presupposed by and revealed in lived experience. This philosophy of life is usually presented in storied, dramatic, poetic, or other symbolic forms that will engage the imagination and structure the deep emotions and aspirations of the human heart at all levels of sophistication. But the particular ways in which various religions give body to, and seek to strengthen, the basic religious faith that is necessary for the life enterprise do not have the same standing as the basic beliefs themselves. They are culture relative and historically conditioned. Unfortunately, the cultural forms in which the basic religious faith is expressed are often taken to be the substance of the religion. This is the evil of literalism in religion. When the cultural forms of a religion become antiquated or the literal interpretation of them is undermined by reflective thought or cognitive developments in other sectors of the culture, there is nothing of substance left in the religion for the literal minded.

A responsible religion in our time must distinguish between its substance and its historically evolved cultural forms. Perhaps there are those who can grasp the substance of the religion only by taking its cultural forms literally. Both St. Paul and St. Augustine spoke of babes in spirit who have to be fed only milk because they are unable to digest adult food. But religion in a society that educates its people must be presented in a form that will be acceptable to critically minded educated people. For them religion must humanize the ultimate mysteries and integrate our lives and our values in the world in a way that is intellectually and aesthetically palatable as well as life-enhancing and empowering, for otherwise they will cast it aside as vulgar wishful illusions.

Two of the most important tasks of religious institutions in our culture, in conjunction with the humanities, are, first, to develop and to promote a philosophy of culture with a unified humanistic vision of humankind and the world; and second, to teach authentic religious and artistic ways of comprehending and understanding reality along with religious and artistic modes of expression and communication. Only with success in these undertakings will a religion be able to fulfill its mission to open the hearts of people to the divine and to develop and to nurture their spirituality without falling into the evils of arrogance and absolutism.

Whatever a responsible religion promises must be possible within the framework of a defensible humanistic metaphysics, coherent with all that we know in the culture, and it must be life-enhancing and have positive support within reflected lived experience. On this basis, it seems clear that a responsible religion can no longer claim to possess an absolute truth handed down from some superhuman authority that is beyond human criticism and reconstruction, claim to be the only true religion, or promise absolute human fulfillment with everything made right in the end. We have to accept that life involves real risks and losses for all of us, but we are warranted in believing that human beings, attuned to and working with the divine, can turn whatever happens to some good.

The heaven we seek is a world in which all that ought to be is fully realized. Heaven has been considered the realm of the eternal, for it is understood as a realm in which everything has come to completion and fulfillment. In a perfect world, the dynamics of change would be over, and without change there would be no time. Thus, heaven is said to be beyond history, beyond time.

If heaven is the perfection of being, it cannot be a place where, or a state in which, the righteous continue to live beyond death, for living is a temporal matter. Perhaps eternal life, in the sense of a heavenly life, should be thought of as the quality and joy of a life lived from within a self-transcending perspective with faith in and in pursuit of higher values. In like manner, hell may be thought of as the quality and waste of a degrading, perverting, or self-destructive life in pursuit of false values from a narrow or self-centered perspective that gives one an illusory view of reality.

Living in the midst of time, we tend to think of only what exists in the fleeting present as real. Of course the present for us is not an instantaneous present, but the varying presents of our lived experiences and actions. Some people live in a much longer present than others, embracing a longer past and a longer future in the life they are living. Indeed, for some people their present is even longer than their lifetime; they may be engaged in joint endeavors with people who lived before them and with generations to come. For others, their present may be only a matter of hours or days. Of course all of us will remain a causal factor after death in ways that may affect our identity and the life we have lived, even the past before we were born. When we transcend our present, whatever its expanse, and see reality as embracing the whole of the past and the future, we see our lives as an eternal moment in the fulfillment of being. The idea of an everlasting life is a temporal image of an eternal life; it affirms the meaningfulness of life in relation to the ultimate context of human existence.

We do not need to believe that everything will be made right and good for those who love the good and live under the constraints and requirements of the eternal perspective. What we are justified in believing is that living in pursuit of higher values in light of the eternal is life-enhancing and fulfilling. Neither do we need to believe that a life in pursuit of false values from within a narrow, self-centered perspective will end in a state of absolute and final horror. It is enough to know that such a life perverts and degrades oneself, puts oneself in alliance with destructive forces, and denies oneself the higher values within human reach.

The arts in any culture, as previously observed, interpret the human condition and lived experience within the structure of the prevailing world view and the identities and social forms generated in and supported by the culture. Their role is to show life as it is or could be lived and the verdicts of lived experience on the human condition as it is or could be culturally and socially defined. But they can be a powerful ally of religion and the religious life; indeed, they are the language of religion.

The essential function of religion is as important, or even more so, than it has ever been. Although we have made great progress toward satisfying our materialistic needs through an economy based on science and technology, we were never more confused and disoriented with regard to the fundamentals of the human enterprise. One of the greatest challenges to our civilization is the development of responsible religious institutions, along with a supporting humanistic culture, that will teach and promote a sensible and effective framework for a meaningful life that is undergirded by a sound intellectual vision of humankind and the world. We need a religious culture that will help us understand ourselves and the world in a way that underwrites our human identity and the norms that define how we should live and run our institutions — a religious culture that will empower and guide us from within in our individual and collective struggle for higher values. Such a culture is as essential for the moral and civic enterprises as science and technology are for the economic enterprise.

10

TOWARD A
HUMANISTIC
REVOLUTION

The culture itself is perhaps our most important modern discovery. Progress through the advancement of the culture is perhaps the most important idea of the last five hundred years. The Enlightenment was characterized by faith in the free exercise of the educated knowledge-yielding and creative powers of the human mind to correct and to advance the culture in all its dimensions, and faith that a free and progressive culture would greatly enhance our ability to organize and direct our lives and our societies as well as to conquer nature and to harness its power for a better and richer world for all.

This faith in the unleashed powers of the human mind and spirit gave rise to three revolutions: one in the humanistic culture, especially in ethical, social, and political thought, that led to the restructuring of our lives and political institutions; one in the sciences and technology that enabled us to harness the powers of nature and put them to work for human purposes; and one in economic institutions that left individuals free to pursue their economic advantage in whatever ways they could devise, with minimal regulation or protection by government.

Few will doubt that progress has been made in human values in many respects. We think that our belief in, and concern for, human rights, equality, social justice, freedom, tolerance, and the like constitute moral progress in comparison with authoritarian, aristocratic, racist, sexist cultures of the past. No one can doubt that progress has been made in science and technology and that human understanding of, and power over nature have been greatly advanced and that the material conditions of the lives of most have been greatly improved. Yet many think, as I argued in chapter 1, that ours is a cut-flower civilization, with its humanistic dimension cut loose from its grounding and rational self-corrective methods.

Faith in progress through freedom and democracy, science and technology, and the free-enterprise system is still alive in many quarters; indeed, there seems to be a revival of faith in freedom and democracy and the free enterprise system in many places where it had been eclipsed for generations, even emergence where it had never existed before. Still there is cause for concern. "Clearly," Robert Nisbet, a political sociologist and cultural critic, says, "the idea of progress can breathe only with the greatest difficulty, if at all, in a civilization as bedeviled as our own Western civilization at the present time by irrationalism and solipsism."[1] When the identity of the twentieth century is finally fixed by future historians, Nisbet claims, the abandonment of faith in progress will be seen as one of its chief attributes.[2]

WHY THE DECLINE OF FAITH IN PROGRESS?

There are many causes for the decline of faith in progress in Western societies. I will mention only three.

First, there are increasing doubts about the materialistic values in terms of which we organize our lives and our society. Material poverty and powerlessness are the only hell we know, for wealth and power are the only heaven we recognize. Our society supports education and research primarily because they are seen as necessary means for economic growth and military power. In the business world, economic necessity reigns like military necessity in war. Many regard the economic sphere as a moral-free zone in which only legal restraints can temper the pursuit of self-gain. In the drive for political power, politicians seem to recognize no moral restraints on what will be politically effective. And, in the international sphere, it is openly acknowledged that nations act only to protect or to advance their national interests, acknowledging no limits but their own resources and the power of their adversaries.

Some deceive themselves with the myth that the capitalist free-market system, democratic political institutions, and the balance of power in international affairs take the moral burden off the shoulders of individuals, corporations, and governments; that all agents, for the most part, are left free to act in their own self-interest, without having to bother about moral matters.

As our economic, political, and legal systems relieve individuals and corporate agents of moral responsibilities, moral character deteriorates. When morality is not required for success as defined by the culture, the people tend to become amoral; self-interest becomes not only the driving force in their lives but the governing principle as well. The system perverts human beings and undermines the higher values of civilization.

With morally weak people in pursuit of happiness in a morally inferior sense, civic humanism declines, social bonds loosen, the self contracts, and life without the lift and pull of the universal and the transcendent becomes empty and meaningless. Many find success as defined in our culture unfulfilling and not worth the struggle. And private lives based on, and governed by, wants and preferences and contractual relationships grow stale and wearisome. Life demands more, but increasingly our culture offers less of what really counts in life. As this truth sinks in, progress as defined in our culture begins to lose its appeal.[3]

Second, fear for our identity and for the culture that supports the human spirit is part of the reason for the decline of faith in progress. "To be modern," Marshall Berman says, "is to experience personal and social life as a maelstrom, to find one's world and oneself in perpetual disintegration and renewal, trouble and anguish, ambiguity and contradiction: to be part of a universe in which all that is solid melts into air."[4]

The reordering of cultural values that gave rise to the reformation in science and faith in progress through science and technology involved, as we observed in chapter 1, the elimination of value, meaning, and other humanistic concepts from the descriptive/explanatory conceptual system of science. And with the success of science and technology in the struggle for economic wealth and military power, the scientific way of thought progressively became widely accepted as the way of knowledge and the scientific framework of thought came to define our modern world view.

But as we bring human beings and social and cultural phenomena under the scientific conceptual system and place ourselves in the world as it is defined by scientific categories, we find ourselves and the whole humanistic dimension of the culture highly problematic. Indeed, the humanistic conceptual system in terms of which our normative self-concept and moral values are formed is undermined. As Ernest Gellner says, "A moral style and tradition is indeed [still] adopted and imposed, by the normal methods of shared expectations, education, and social pressures and so forth. But there is a difference. It is no longer continuous with, possessing the same status as, the best cognitive and productive equipment of the society. On the contrary there is a deep fissure between the two. . . . When serious issues are at stake — such as the production of wealth, or the maintenance of health — we want real knowledge [scientific knowledge]. . . . Culture remains rich and human and is even, in various ways, more luxuriant than it used to be; but it is no longer all of a piece with the serious and effective convictions of society."[5] "Thus the price of real knowledge," Gellner concludes, "is that our identities, freedom, norms, are no longer underwritten by the vision and comprehension of things. On the contrary we are doomed to suffer from the tension between cognition and identity."[6]

The results of the divorce of our descriptive/explanatory and humanistic conceptual systems in the search for the kind of knowledge that would give us power in the manipulation and control of things have been devastating. Among them are insolvable philosophical perplexities about the humanistic conceptual system, disenchantment of the world, a severe human identity crisis; tendencies toward moral confusion, anomie, alienation, loss of inner strength, collapse of authority, social atomization, reduction of human relationships to contractual arrangements, and politics by bargained agreements among interest groups; and, in reaction, the rise of conservatism, anti-intellectualism, irrational ideologies, authoritarianism, and increasing dependence on coercive power. There is little wonder that many people are questioning whether the society we seek with its wealth and power is a fool's paradise.[7]

Third, concern about the extent to which we may be destroying the environment and disturbing the universe is another factor in the decline of faith in progress as defined in our culture. At the present rate of growth, there will be more than sixteen billion people on this planet before the end of the next century. Even at the present level of production and consumption, we can hardly imagine what that will do to the environment. But the industrialized countries are committed to a policy of endless economic growth; and the other nations aspire and struggle to catch up and to keep up with the present industrialized countries. What if we should succeed in all of this? And what if we should have a nuclear war among major powers? I leave to the reader's imagination what the consequences would be for future generations and for the whole ecological system. The human race has become a cancer in the ecological system.

The environmental issue is not just a practical problem that calls for a technological solution. Of course, we need to find ways of meeting our materialistic needs without destroying the life-support system of the planet, science and technology will be an essential part of the solution. But the problem challenges us in a more profound way, for it is a moral problem.

At the personal level, a moral problem is one that puts the agent into question. How one responds to a moral problem reflects on one as a person. A morally wrong act is a basis for judging the agent as morally defective in some way. The environmental problem is a moral problem also; it puts into question the character of our civilization — the organizing and governing values and ways of thought of our way of life.

Although there are humanistic subcultures and legacies of the past with which many of us are involved, we have a culture that, in its mainstream, generates spiritually impoverished people, a social structure that makes for morally weak individuals, and an economic and military system and a world order that threaten human survival. There is no wonder that faith in progress, which has been the driving force of modern Western civilization and the worldwide modernization process, is waning, at least in the Western societies that gave it birth.

WHAT SHOULD WE DO?

We need to rethink the fundamentals of our culture and to restructure our society. The big questions are these: How can we change the course of a civilization that is five hundred years in the making? How can we shift our priorities from materialistic values to humanistic values? How can we shift from endless economic growth to human growth? How can we shift from economic and military necessity to moral necessity? How can we develop a culture and the social institutions that would make for human growth and nourishment of the human spirit? And how can we build a world order based on justice and international law rather than national interest and balance of power?

For those whose minds are tuned to immediate practical problems for which a solution is expected before the end of the year or by the next election, these questions lack all meaning. For many the very idea that something could be wrong in the foundations of our civilization is unthinkable. Yet, there are widespread complaints about the pervasive materialism, the deterioration of morals, the disintegration of the family, the injustice of our institutions, and the impairment of the environment.

Most of the revolutions with which we are familiar in modern times were quite different from what we are proposing. With the democratic revolutions of the eighteenth and nineteenth centuries, intellectuals developed a counter culture that a rising economic class used to overthrow the old feudalistic order and the culture and world view that legitimized it. In similar manner, communist revolutions in this century were based on a counter culture developed by the intelligentsia and used by revolutionaries to arouse and to unite victims of Western imperialism and exploited economic classes to overthrow the established system and its supporting culture. In recent revolutions within and against communists societies, the appeal was to the historic culture of the Western democracies and their market economies. In the present situation in the Western democracies, we do not have a viable counter culture. Neither do we have a rising or an exploited economic class to be united and motivated by a counter culture. The upper, middle, and lower classes share the same materialistic values. And there is not a widely recognized tyranny or economic collapse. So how is the fundamental change I am talking about possible? It would be easy to say that it is impossible and do nothing. But I do not believe that anyone can understand the problems in our civilization and what is at stake and then let go of them.

In a sense, we already have a counter culture — the humanistic framework of values and thought in which we all are inescapably involved. And there is the wisdom of our religious and civic traditions. The problem is that materialistic values are dominant and our mainstream intellectual life has undermined, weakened, and often perverted the humanistic culture. The situation calls for cultural criticism and consciousness raising about the basic problems we face; the intellectual validation and development of a strong humanistic culture; the restructuring of our lives and institutions in a way that gives priority to humanistic values and embodies a humanistic culture; and the establishment of a world order based on the ethics of peace rather than the logic of power.

CULTURAL CRITICISM

AND CONSCIOUSNESS RAISING

At this point, there are two lively lines of cultural criticism developing. The best known and most popular is the environmental movement.[8] But few seem to appreciate the full significance of it for our way of life. Most think the environmental problem can be managed with relatively minor cost and inconvenience, and that, in any case, economic growth and military power must be given priority. But the pending environmental crisis, as we just observed, calls into question the fundamental values and dominant ways of thought of modern Western civilization.

The other line of criticism that is developing focuses on the culture itself. There is a widespread feeling that something is wrong with the value dimension of our culture, not only with morality and the values by which people live, but also with the way in which we think about values in general. There is also a growing awareness that there is a human identity crisis as we bring ourselves and the whole human phenomenon under the scientific conceptual system and place ourselves in the world as defined in scientific categories. "A spreading emotional malaise," according to Daniel Goleman, "can be read in numbers showing a jump in depression around the world, and in the reminders of a surging tide of aggression — teens with guns in school, freeway mishaps ending in shootings, disgruntled ex-employees massacring former fellow employees."[9] This unease about our moral and spiritual climate is what fundamentalist religion and conservatism in general feed on in their politics of meaning. In a growing body of cultural studies,[10] there is considerable agreement that our modern culture is individually and socially destructive and needs some kind of correction. But there is no consensus about what the correction should be. Many conclude that liberal individualism must be sacrificed for some form of communitarianism; that value judgments and our human identity must be grounded in a traditional religion or the moral traditions and classics of Western civilization. There is little inclination toward examining and reconstructing the conditions that generated the widespread value subjectivism and crisis of meaning in the first place, for that would put our dominant culture into question, and the society as well, including our economic system.

The troubles in modern Western civilization are deep and systemic. We are beyond the point where partial cultural criticism and piecemeal solutions can solve even the limited problems. Nothing short of total cultural criticism and reconstruction is realistic. And this would lead to radical social transformation. Anything else addresses only symptoms of the deep malady in the modern Western mind and heart. We must reexamine the organizing and governing values and ways of thought in our way of life.

Graduate/research universities are our dominant cultural and educational institutions. The business of universities is not just education, as important as that is. They have a special responsibility for the culture. Their faculties are not just the custodians and transmitters of the culture; it is their responsibility to examine the culture critically, to correct it, to integrate it, and to advance it. Although specialists in each area of the culture have the responsibility to develop their respective disciplines, the entire faculty, regardless of discipline, has the responsibility as a community of scholars and cultural critics to examine critically how the several disciplines bear on one another, how they can be fitted together to form a coherent whole and provide a unified view of humankind and the world, and how they are related to life and society. But some disciplines take the culture itself as their subject matter. This is true of the humanities. Philosophy is perhaps the most ambitious discipline, for it takes the whole culture and the world for its subject matter. But in this age of specialization the intellectual community is failing in its responsibility to criticize, to integrate, and to reconstruct the culture. The humanities, which bear the heaviest responsibility in this regard, are the greatest culprits. They are more victims of the culture than masters of it.

Here, of course, is an intriguing problem. "How could it be other wise?" the cultural relativist exclaims. Our subjectivism and relativism are, I contend, a consequence of our modern puritanical assumptions and theories about the knowledge-yielding powers of the human mind. A solid case can be made, I believe, for the claim that we can transcend our provincialism, become to some degree masters of our culture, and achieve a measure of objectivity through internal cultural criticism and correction in light of the total range of human experience and the knowledge-yielding and critical powers of the human mind. The humanities especially have been crippled, even perverted and distorted, under the influence of the dominant patterns of thought and paradigms of intelligibility in our scientific and technological age. They must be rehabilitated and reconstructed in terms of their own indigenous categories and methods of inquiry if they are to perform their full cultural mission.

To help break out of our present culture-bound situation and overcome the fissure in modern Western civilization between the humanistic culture of selfhood and the search for meaning on one hand and the scientific/technological culture in the pursuit of wealth and power on the other, we need several well-funded research centers of philosophy and cultural criticism to lead the way. They should be dedicated to total cultural criticism with the focus on how the various sectors of the culture (common sense, morality, social and political thought, the arts, religion, and the sciences) and the culture as a whole are grounded in experience and reveal or obscure the metaphysical structure of selfhood and the world. Among the topics that should be studied are the nature of philosophy and its role in cultural criticism and reconstruction; philosophy of the humanities and their proper functions in the culture and in education; the social character, the structure of feeling, and the cultural mind of modern Western civilization; value materialism and its impact on our intellectual life and culture; the subjectivistic and relativistic turn in modern Western culture; the semantic and knowledge-yielding powers of the human mind; humanism versus naturalism; humanistic interpretations of science; realistic humanism versus subjectivistic humanism; moral realism; humanistic metaphysics; and philosophy of religion.

The primary mission of these centers should be to search for ways in which the culture could be integrated with a unified vision of humankind and the world that would do justice to our human identity, nurture the human spirit, and generate and sustain a society committed to human growth and meaningful lives for all. (See appendix B for a suggested "mission and issues" charter for such centers.) But the contradictions in the foundations of our culture are not just a matter for philosophers to work out among themselves; a genuine solution on humanistic terms would involve a profound cultural and social transformation. Assuming the credibility of some version of realistic humanism with its vision of humankind and the world, the centers should explore and promote ways of working toward a genuine humanistic culture and society. This, of course, is a daunting task for it would involve shifting our priorities from materialistic to humanistic values as well as transforming the framework of thought that defines our dominant intellectual life.

The virtue of such centers would be that they could search out and bring together people who share a common concern, a somewhat common working perspective, and a common mission. But they must not be doctrinaire; they must be constituted by people who are prepared to examine the culture openly and critically and to consider ways of correcting and advancing it. And they must be prepared to submit their own ideas and proposals to severe critical examination by themselves and others. There should be no effort to change the culture but by critical investigation, open rational debate of the issues, and education.

These centers would have to find ways to engage intellectuals in academic disciplines, especially the humanities and social sciences, in thinking these matters through as they pertain to their own disciplines in ways that would be fruitful in their work. The centers should work also with public intellectuals, opinion-makers, and institutional decision-makers in rethinking their values and ways of thought. They should experiment with ways of humanistic education and cultural criticism, ways of making the resources of philosophy and the humanities in general available to the wider society, and ways of promoting a widespread critical dialogue about the present state of our culture and society and possibilities for the future.

No great social revolution can take place peacefully without a widely shared deep cultural change that offers a new intellectual vision of humankind and the world. The objective of the research centers would be for the ideas and concerns they generated to spread into universities, the schools, among the intelligentsia in general, and to institutional leaders through various educational and consciousness-raising programs and publications. If we could succeed in changing the dominant values and ways of thought of a significant segment of culturally influential people, they would become alienated in our materialistic society and become a powerful force for reconstruction of the social order in terms of the new culture.

Once our intellectual life takes a humanistic turn, or even the humanistic perspective and framework of thought gain respectability in intellectual and educational circles, responsible religious institutions, along with the environmental movement and other concerned groups, could be powerful allies in promoting the humanistic cultural revolution we seek. Indeed, they have intellectual resources to contribute as well as the capacity to reach the minds and hearts of the people.

Our modern way of life seems to be such that if it continues on its course it will be a total disaster, but what we have known as the modern age may be coming to a close. We may be at the dawn of a new era. The late twentieth century may be comparable in many ways, as Barbara Tuchman contends,[11] to the late fourteenth century in Europe. That was a time when Christian feudalism was coming to an end and there were already turnings, the beginning of a new civilization. Surely this is a unique time in human affairs. Perhaps the five-hundred-year modern age spent itself in the seventy-five-year war of the twentieth century, which finally seems to be over. A new beginning is possible, indeed imperative. Such a historic opportunity imposes a tremendous responsibility on all of us.

Philosophers, as we observed at the end of chapter 1, played a powerful role in the early modern period in discrediting and dismantling Christian feudalism and in defining and defending the emerging moral and intellectual vision of modern Western civilization. At the present juncture in our history, philosophers, although they cannot do it alone, may play a significant role in criticizing modern Western civilization and in helping to generate a new moral and intellectual vision that will underwrite a humanistic culture that will support the human spirit, generate a society fit for human beings, and make for human growth and well-being. Such a cultural transformation is our best hope and the greatest challenge of our time.

A SUMMARY CASE

FOR REALISTIC

HUMANISM*

Medieval philosophers were ridiculed for talking about how many angels could stand on the head of a pin. But the point of the discussion was that, since (according to their doctrine) angels were immaterial substances, it made no sense to say that one, ten, or a hundred could stand in any given area of space regardless of its size. These philosophers began with a view about the categorial nature of angels. But we can turn the matter around. We can discover (or confirm a view about) the categorial nature of any given subject matter by considering what it makes sense to say and does not make sense to say about it.

Consider emotive experience. We like some things and dislike others. We feel good and we feel bad. We get hungry and thirsty. At times we are lonely. Some things frightened us. We may be embarrassed, feel ashamed or guilty. We may be happy or wretched. We may live with high life morale or with despair. We may want a particular thing. We may feel that we ought to do something that we dislike doing or that we ought not to do something that we like doing. And so forth. What is the basic character of these modes of experience?

One may say "I liked your book; it is good." What is the relationship between the two sentences? The first sentence, of course, reports how one experienced the book. The second, I suggest, expresses (puts into words) the semantic (intentional) structure of the experience. We may say that the sentence is "synonymous" with the experience. To like the book is to experience it as good. "I feel good," by its very structure, shows that feeling has a semantic content. To feel good, I suggest, is to feel that one (or something with which one identifies) is in good condition and doing well. To be hungry is to feel a bodily lack and that one needs food. To be lonely is to feel a personal lack and that one needs companionship. To feel guilty is to feel that something that one has done (or not done) has injured one as a person. To desire something is to feel that one needs it or at least that it is something it would be good to have. To be happy is to feel that one's life is right for one and that one is living well. In short, emotive experiences are expressible in value sentences. They have their identity and unity in terms of a structure of meaning much as the linguistic acts that express them.

Furthermore, it makes sense to talk about emotive experiences having logical structures and relationships. In fact, we may say that an emotive experience has the logical form of the sentence that is the most appropriate expression of it. And emotive experiences may be said to be consistent or inconsistent with one another or with assumptions or beliefs that one has. Feelings and desires often are premises from which we reason.

One more point. It makes sense to say that feelings and desires are illusory or correct, rational or irrational, and so forth. One may feel good falsely; that is, one may feel that one is in good bodily condition when one is in fact ill. One may have an illusory pain; that is, one may have a pain in one location (feel that something is wrong there) when the trouble is elsewhere. Intoxicants may make one feel better than one is or experience situations or other people more favorably (or unfavorably) than they warrant. Feelings and desires may or may not be responsive to reasons. If they are, we say that they are rational; if not, we say that they are irrational. A person who is terrified by any ordinary house cat, for example, has an irrational fear, for it is not responsive to evidence that such animals are harmless.

In sum, because it makes sense to speak of emotive experiences as expressible in language, as having logical form and logical relationships, as illusory, hallucinatory, or as correct or incorrect, as rational or irrational, we may conclude that they are knowledge-yielding modes of experience that provide a window on the world. We need value language to report what we discover in this manner.

Value sentences have three basic syntactical forms: predicative (e.g., "The dinner was good"), normative (e.g., "A human being ought to be kind," or "There ought to be someone who would help him"), and imperative (e.g., "John, bolt the door," or "Let's go to the office"). For the most part, philosophers have considered the predicative type as basic, but a better case can be made for the claim that the normative sentence is fundamental. I suggest that to say that a thing is good is to say that it is more or less the way it ought to be. Regardless of the properties that it may possess, an object is neither good nor bad unless there is a way that it ought to be. In other words, a predicative value sentence may be analyzed in terms of a normative sentence and a nonvalue predicative sentence. An imperative sentence is, I suggest, a stripped down normative sentence. We can ask "Why?" of an imperative sentence with the same force that we ask it of the correlative normative sentence. The "Why?" asks for validating reasons in each case. The major difference between an imperative sentence and its correlative normative sentence, for our purposes, is that the latter states that there are validating reasons and the former only assumes that there are such reasons without saying it.

The normative sentence, "The carpet ought to be rose," is incomplete as it stands. The more appropriate form is something like "The color scheme of the room being what it is, the carpet ought to be rose," or the conditional "If the color scheme of the room is such and such, then the carpet ought to be rose." Here the other colors of the room consist of facts that are the validating reasons for choosing a rose-colored carpet. We may take a sentence of the form "If a thing has a given feature or complex of features, then it (or perhaps something else) ought to have some other feature" to be a basic sentence, not a compound one, with "ought" part of the connective, not part of the consequent. The "If . . . , then . . . ought . . ." indicates, I suggest, a real structure in the subject matter, namely, normative requiredness. What the sentence says is that the factual situation located by the antecedent of the conditional normatively requires that enjoined in the consequent.

This realistic interpretation of normative sentences, made possible by the epistemic interpretation of emotive experience, means that at least some subject matters have inherent normative structures or constitutions. Consider the human embryo. It is clear that it has a factual constitution. A report of what we can discover about the human embryo by sensory observation consists of only factual predicative statements and causal statements about antecedent, elemental, or subsequent factual conditions. Yet it is difficult to avoid thinking of an embryo as having an inherent normative structure. We talk about what it is in terms of what it ought to become, and if it fails to become what it ought to become, we say that something went wrong, and we need an explanation of why it did not become what it ought to have become. The form of a mature human being is not existentially in a human embryo, but it is normatively in it from conception. This is part of its real constitution. When we say that a human being is a rational animal, we are not saying that all human beings are in fact rational in their thought and behavior; we are saying that a human being is the kind of being who by one's nature ought to be rational in one's mature state, and if one is not, something will have gone awry or one is at fault in some way.

The language of meaning is more like value language than it is like purely factual language. We speak of the development of an embryo as a process with an end normatively (but not yet existentially) in it—that which it ought to become and what it will be at maturity if nothing goes wrong. Any process that may be spoken of meaningfully as completed, thwarted, or aborted has an inherent normative structure. In a somewhat similar way, we may speak of some subject matters as having something semantically but not existentially in them. For example, we may talk about some event's being *in* the newspaper. This is clearly a different meaning of "in" than in the sentence, "There were thirty-two pages *in* the newspaper today." The latter is the existential use. We may call the former the "semantic" use. We have the same distinction in the use of "on," "of," and some other prepositions. We can talk about what is *on* one's head and what is *on* one's mind, and we can talk about what a part is *of* (e.g., the leg of the table), and we can talk about what an experience or idea is *of.* Whatever has an inherent semantic content or object is constituted by an inherent structure of meaning. Indeed, personal states and acts have their identity and unity in terms of their inherent structures of meaning, which constitute their subjective dimension.

This is an ontological story about meaning and subjectivity that stands or falls according to whether there is an acceptable epistemological story that shows how it is possible for us to talk about and to have knowledge of inherent structures of meaning in some events or states, which are not accessible to the kind of sensory observation on which modern science depends. It is obvious that we have self-knowledge of some of our own subjective and overt states and acts in that we can remember and reflect on them and correctly avow them. I have self-knowledge of some of my own somatic sensations, experiences of the environment, desires and intentions, worries, thoughts, speech acts, and other overt behavior. And I can reflect on all such states and acts of which I have self-knowledge. But we have another equally primary and even earlier access to inherent structures of meaning, namely, perceptual understanding of the expressions and behavior of others. Hearing what someone says or "reading" what someone does is not simply auditory or visual perception. It involves grasping the internal semantic structure of the linguistic or other overt act, for speech and other overt acts have their identity and unity in terms of their internal semantic dimension. Perceptual understanding of the subjectivity and behavior of others cannot be based on or derived from self-knowledge and reflection. Infants obviously are able to sense the feelings and attitudes of others and to understand some of their behavior before they can be said to have much self-knowledge and certainly before they can reflect on their own subjectivity and overt acts. In fact, perceptual understanding of others seems to be temporally prior in human beings to sensory perception of physical objects. Children seem to begin with humanistically categorized sensory perception. They have to learn to perceive purely physical things (purely factually constituted things). Indeed, it seems that the race did not acquire this capacity until relatively late, not until humanistic categories were stripped from descriptive/explanatory language in the modern period.

Realistic humanism, as previously observed, is based on twin foundations: a realistic interpretation of value language that is validated by the knowledge-yielding character of emotive experience; and a realistic interpretation of the language of meaning that is justified by the epistemic nature of reflection on one's own subjectivity and perceptual understanding of others.

appendix B

A Suggested "Mission and Issues Charter"

for a University Center for

Philosophy and Cultural Criticism

There are contradictions deep in the foundations of our modern culture. On the one hand, we have a humanistic culture, the product of centuries of reflected experience; it is generated by our total experiential involvement with reality in living our lives and participating in society, under a governing concern for moral, social, political, aesthetic, and religious values. On the other hand, we have our modern scientific/technological culture, which is developed from our sensory encounter with reality, under the governing concern with mastering our environment in pursuit of wealth and power. The cultural contradictions occasioned by these two culture-generating approaches to reality have engaged philosophers and other cultural critics ever since the seventeenth century. Various intellectual strategies have been employed in trying to relieve the tensions and achieve a coherent, integrated culture with a unified vision of humankind and the world, but with the success of science and technology in our quest for wealth and power, no solution on humanistic terms has been able to overcome the tide of materialism and the modern scientific world view. Philosophers, for the most part, persist in trying to validate the scientific framework of thought and to find an interpretation or explanation of other sectors of the culture that would be consistent with or not challenge the naturalistic presuppositions of empirical science.

Yet, some claim that any philosophical interpretation or explanation of the culture on naturalistic terms (i.e., the categories of scientific thought) would undermine morality and religion and do violence to our human identity and the social order; indeed, some claim that it would undermine science itself and the whole human enterprise, for human selfhood, lived experience, and all our activities presuppose humanistic categories and ways of thought. In fact, it seems that, in our modern culture, we have a human identity crisis, the meaning of life is problematic, and the moral values and norms by which we live and organize society have gone soft and lost their power. Some contend that in spite of, or even because of, our success in the quest for wealth and power and the kind of knowledge that is useful in the pursuit of these goals, we have a cut-flower civilization that will neither nourish the human spirit nor sustain itself. Nietzsche spoke of "the death of God" and C. S. Lewis of "the abolition of man."

If a naturalistic solution (a solution in terms of the categories of scientific thought) to the deep philosophical problems in our culture were possible, such a solution would reinforce our culture much as it is, with the humanities and the whole humanistic dimension of the culture undermined and weakened. On the other hand, a humanistic solution would be a mere intellectual exercise unless it were taken to heart in a way that redefined the goals of the human enterprise and thus changed our approach to reality and transformed the culture and society accordingly.

The primary mission of the University Center is to search for and to promote an integrated culture with a unified vision of humankind and the world that will do justice to our human identity, nurture the human spirit, and generate and sustain a society committed to human growth and meaningful lives for all. In pursuit of this goal, the Center is dedicated to sustained, rigorous philosophical cultural criticism, with the focus on the foundations of the humanities, the commonsense of lived experience, morality, the arts, and religion. The presumption is that such an integrated culture and a unified world view can be achieved only by re-solving the deep philosophical problems in our culture by giving full play to the categories of humanistic thought as more basic and in-clusive than the naturalistic categories of modern science. But the Center is committed to facing honestly all difficulties for and rea-soned challenges to this position. It is committed to following wherever sound philosophical reasoning leads, so long as the con-clusions reached do justice to all sectors of the culture and human experience and make for ongoing cultural and social development that supports human growth and well-being.

The solution to the deep philosophical contradictions involved in the clash of our humanistic culture grounded in selfhood and lived experience and our materialistic/scientific culture is not just a matter for philosophers to work out among themselves; a genuine solution on humanistic terms would involve a profound cultural and social transformation. Assuming the credibility of some ver-sion of philosophical humanism with its vision of humankind and the world, the Center will explore ways of working toward a genuine humanistic culture and society. This, of course, is a daunting task, for it would involve shifting our priorities from materialistic to hu-manistic values as well as transforming the framework of thought that defines our dominant intellectual life. Perhaps modern Western civilization, five hundred years in the making, weary with intractable problems and the crisis of meaning, is ripe for a humanistic turn.

The specific issues that will be explored in the Center must be defined and redefined as the work of the Center progresses. But here are some central issues that merit serious consideration:

1. What is the role of philosophy in cultural criticism? Can phi-losophy bring critical intelligence into the development or re-construction of the culture in its foundational values and ways of thought? And, if so, how?

2. How has science as a paradigm of knowledge influenced or per-verted our conception and practice of philosophy?

3. How do the various sectors of the culture (common sense, morality, social and political thought, the arts, religion, the

humanities, the sciences, etc.) and the culture as a whole reveal or obscure the metaphysical (i.e., the fundamental, categorial) structure of their subject matter or the world as a whole? By what methods can philosophy discover the basic (categorial or metaphysical) nature of any given subject matter or establish a philosophical world view?

4. What is the nature of presuppositions? By what methods does philosophy explore and test our assumptions and theories about the presuppositions in the culture and try to achieve a coherent and correct account of them? Does philosophy have a role in the culture other than working for a coherent interpretation of the presuppositions present in the culture? Are there unavoidable or necessary presuppositions in human experience, thought, and action? If so, what kinds of unavoidable presuppositions do we find in the culture? If there are conflicts between the presuppositions of two sectors of the culture such as modern science and humanistic thought, which, if any, are unavoidable? Is it a part of the role of philosophy to judge and to try to correct the presuppositions in any sector of the culture if they are found to be inconsistent with the presuppositions of another sector of the culture or with unavoidable presuppositions of the culture? For example, what if the presuppositions of science are found to be inconsistent with the presuppositions of morality or religion? In such a case, must philosophy restrict itself to working for a correct account of what the presuppositions actually are but leave them as they are? Or does philosophy have a role in reconstructing the presuppositions for consistency and coherence in a way that changes the culture? If so, how does it judge which presuppositions have priority or are unavoidable and which must be reconstructed or sacrificed for the sake of coherence?

5. Why did science, beginning in the seventeenth century, eliminate value and other humanistic concepts from its descriptive/explanatory conceptual system? How was it connected with the rise of modern value materialism (the priority of materialistic vlaues)? How did it change the metaphysical world

view presupposed in science? How has it impacted on our cultural vision of humankind and the world? What has been its impact on our self-concept and life attitudes, morality, social and political thought, education, and religion? What has been the response of philosophy to this change in the categories of scientific thought? What strategies have philosophers employed to relieve the tension between the categorial presuppositions of the humanistic dimension of the culture and modern science, especially with regard to the presuppositions of our self-concept, rational thought and action, morality, politics. and religion? Have any of our naturalist, idealist, constructivist, pragmatist, subjectivist, relativist, or nihilist theories proved successful?

6. Given the long history of failures in our efforts to come to terms with or to overcome the fissure in the foundations of the culture that was occasioned by the rise of modern value materialism and our scientific/technological culture, and assuming that the troublesome presuppositions of modern science are not unavoidable, what is the possibility of reconstructing or reinterpreting the presuppositions of modern science in a way that would make room for a realist interpretation of the culture, including a realist interpretation of morality and religion? In other words, what is the possibility of validating a metaphysics that recognizes basic structures of value (or normativity) and inherent structures of meaning as well as factuality, with all of these involved in the causal dynamics of the universe? This would have to be underwritten by a theory of the semantic and knowledge-yielding powers of the human mind that would make it possible. Furthermore, for such a philosophical position to take hold in the culture and overcome the fissure between humanistic and scientific thought, the culture itself, not just our philosophical theories, would have to change accordingly. This, of course, is a tall order, but what is at issue makes the undertaking imperative.

7. Does any mode of experience have a semantic outreach to items, features, and structures in the world so that it can fund language and symbols with semantic ties to the world? If so, what

structures and powers must experience have to make this possible? What structures and powers must a mode of experience have and what conditions must it meet in order to be data-gathering or knowledge-yielding? What modes of experience, if any, can semantically ground language to items, features, and structures in the world? What modes of experience are data-gathering or knowledge-yielding? In particular, how does sensory experience fund the language of science with meaning and yield knowledge about the physical world? In what mode or modes of experience is value language grounded? Do these modes of experience have the requisite structures to ground value language semantically to features or structures in the world? Are they knowledge-yielding? If so, is value experience of or about unique features or structures of reality that are categorially different from what we know through other modes of experience? In other words, can we translate what we say in value language into non-value language without loss of meaning? Is objective moral knowledge possible? If so, how? What are the metaphysical presuppositions of objective moral knowledge? What are the implications of moral knowledge for the metaphysics of selfhood? Is there a logical incompatibility between the presuppositions of morality and behavioral science? If so, how should the problem be dealt with? How is the language of meaning, subjectivity, selfhood, and social reality grounded? In terms of what modes of experience, if any, do we know behavior and other subject matters with inherent structures of meaning? Is any naturalistic theory of meaning and the mental adequate? What kind of theory of knowledge and what kind of philosophical world view is required to make sense of the whole human phenomenon? How does naturalism undermine religion? How would a humanistic turn in the culture affect the role of religion in the culture? What would be a responsible religion in a constructive post-modern humanistic culture? How would a genuine humanistic culture transform our social institutions?

8. Assuming that the deep problems in the foundations of modern Western culture can be resolved only on humanistic terms, how can we work toward reconstructing the culture and the society along humanistic lines? How can we engage intellectuals in other academic disciplines, especially in the humanities and the social sciences, in thinking these matters through as they pertain to their own disciplines in a way that would be fruitful in their work? How can we engage public intellectuals, opinion-makers, and institutional decision-makers in rethinking their values and ways of thought? How can we humanize the culture and practice of education at all levels? How can we cooperate with or engage religious institutions, civic organizations, and other concerned groups in cultural criticism and consciousness raising? Can we through such a broad educational and dialogical program generate an effective cultural and social ferment that will bring about the humanistic transformation we seek?

9. If these issues do not seem to be appropriately formulated for those working in the Center, how should they be reformulated and addressed to achieve the objective of a culture and society that would do justice to our humanity and meet our deep humanistic as well as our materialistic needs? Are there other problems or obstacles in the foundations of the culture that threaten to misorient the human enterprise, derange the cultural mind, deform society, thwart human growth, or destroy life morale? If so, how can philosophy address these problems and work to correct them both intellectually and in the fabric of the culture and the society?

notes

1. CULTURE AND THE HUMAN ENTERPRISE

1. One might conclude that this way of thinking would justify ascribing a higher value and priority to the cultural society than to human beings as individuals on the ground that the universe comes to fuller self-knowledge in the cultural community than in individual human beings. But whatever we make of this way of extending the concept of humanistic needs or normative requirements to the universe itself in order to render the human phenomenon intelligible, two things seem solid. First, the fundamental imperatives that human beings are under are the rational and moral imperatives inherent in their normative constitution as knower-agents. And second, a cultural society is to be judged by the kind of human beings and the quality of life that it generates and supports. The normative constitution and needs of human beings are the ground of our judgment on a cultural society; and the human phenomenon is the basis of any humanistic beliefs about the ultimate constitution of the universe. To reverse the priority between human beings and the cultural society on the basis of a humanistic cosmic theory would be to reject a primary reality on the basis of a theory constructed to explain it.

2. HUMAN BEINGS AND SOCIETY

1. See Plato's dialogue "Protagoras," 320–23.

2. A key question for morality is whether one's self-concept or concept of a human being in general is such that it is correct or incorrect. It is not very popular in our modern cultural climate to think of normative concepts as part of our descriptive language or to talk about the correctness or incorrectness of concepts of any kind, but, as I have already indicated, I have argued for both theses in other works. See my *Ethical Naturalism and the Modern World-View* (Chapel Hill: University of North Carolina Press, 1960; Westport, Conn.: Greenwood Press, 1973, 1985); *Philosophy and the Modern Mind* (Chapel Hill: University of North Carolina Press, 1975; Lanham, Md.: University Press of America, 1985); *The Metaphysics of Self and World* (Philadelphia: Temple University Press, 1991); and *Religion and Cultural Freedom* (Philadelphia: Temple University Press, 1993).

In spite of all our efforts to eliminate normative and predicative value concepts from our descriptive/explanatory language, we seem compelled to recognize that an organism, for example, has a normative structure involved in its internal causal dynamics. We talk about an organism's being well-formed or deformed, mature or immature, healthy or sick, and the like. These value predications presuppose that there is a form the organism ought to have or ought to come to have and a way the organism and its organs ought to act. Furthermore, we seem compelled to acknowledge that the inner causal processes of the organism work for the realization and maintenance of the form the organism ought to have and keep the organism operating the way in which it ought to perform. Value realism underwrites these commonsense convictions.

It seems compelling to think of the knower-agent, as well as an organism, as having an inherent normative structure. As a thinking self, one is, as we have already observed, under an inherent imperative to be consistent and correct in one's perceptual takings and beliefs, and, as a rational agent, one is under an inherent imperative to define and to live a life of one's own that would be meaningful and worthy of one as a human being and as the individual one is. The latter imperative defines the office of personhood; it constitutes one's primary responsibility as a person; it is presupposed in life criticism, just as the fundamental logical imperative is presupposed in logical criticism.

The point is that one's concept of oneself as human being is correct or incorrect according to whether it embraces the imperatives that are inherent in the normative structure of one's selfhood as a human being with relatively mature and normal powers. If one goes wrong in forming one's self-concept as a human being, the error will systematically pervert not only one's moral judgments, but also one's identity and life as well.

It even makes sense to talk about the correctness or incorrectness of the normative idea one forms of oneself as an individual. One can certainly form a wrong idea of the individual one ought to be, and one can discover the wrongness of such an idea. This does not mean that there is only one correct idea of what an individual ought to be. For example, there may be several equally good vocational options for some, while for others there may be only one right vocation in the circumstances of their existence.

There are not, however, several equally valid normative concepts of oneself as a human being. No normative concept of oneself as a human being is correct unless it includes the basic imperative to stand justified in experience, thought, and action under rational and moral criticism.

3. The argument against value subjectivism, as already indicated, turns on the epistemic character of nonindifferent (or value) experience. The case against the relativity of basic conceptual systems turns on the claim that the fundamental categories of human thought are presupposed in the constitutional principles, the inherent normative structure, of the human mind. This, however, does not commit us to a subjectivistic view of the categories, for a case can be made for the thesis that the basic structure of the human mind reflects the basic structure of the world. And the argument against the relativity of concepts of natural kinds depends on a teleological view of nature. If there are ends normatively in natural kinds of things (ends that, if realized, would be the fulfillment of their inner dynamism), then the concept of natural kinds in terms of what is being realized in specimens of them is either correct or incorrect.

3. CHARACTER

1. See Robert Bellah, Richard Madsen, William M. Sullivan, Ann Swindler, and Steven M. Tipton, *Habits of the Heart* (Berkeley: University of California Press, 1985); and *The Good Society* (New York: Alfred A. Knopf, 1991); Alasdair MacIntyre, *After Virtue* (Notre Dame, Ind.: University of Notre Dame Press, 1981); and Amitai Etzioni, *The Spirit of Community* (New York: Crown, 1993).

2. See John D. Barrow and Frank J. Tipler, *The Anthropic Cosmological Principle* (New York: Oxford University Press, 1986).

3. See Robert Bellah et al., *Habits of the Heart* (Berkeley: University of California Press, 1985).

4. THE PRIMACY OF FAMILY AND COMMUNITY

1. The most advanced nation in an epoch, Hegel says, has "an absolute right of being the vehicle of this present stage in the world mind's development" and, in contrast, "the minds of other nations are without rights, and they, along with those whose hour has struck already, count no longer in world history. . . . [This] justifies civilized nations in regarding and treating as barbarians those who lag behind them in institutions which are the essential moments of the state. . . . The civilized nation is conscious that the rights of barbarians are unequal to its own and treats their autonomy as only a formality." Hegel's *Philosophy of Right*, trans. by T. M. Knox (New York: Oxford University Press, 1952), para. 347–51.

2. See Charles Taylor, *Hegel* (New York: Cambridge University Press, 1975), pp. 389–93.

3. Robert Bellah, Richard Madsen, William M. Sullivan, Ann Swindler, and Steven M. Tipton, *The Good Society* (New York: Alfred A. Knopf, 1991); Amitai Etzioni, *The Spirit of Community* (New York: Crown, 1993); Alasdair MacIntyre, *After Virtue* (Notre Dame, Ind.: University of Notre Dame Press, 1981); and F. A. Hayek, "Law, Legislation and Liberty," vol. 2, in *The Mirage of Social Justice* (London: Routeledge and Kegan Paul, 1976).

6. HUMANIZING THE ECONOMIC ENTERPRISE

1. Karl Polanyi, *The Great Transformation* (Boston: Beacon Press, 1957; copyright 1944 by Karl Polanyi).

2. Lewis Mumford, *The Transformations of Man* (New York: Harper and Row, 1972), p. 104.

3. See Robert Heilbroner, *21st Century Capitalism* (New York: W. W. Norton, 1993), pp. 46–48.

4. See Joseph A. Schumpeter, *Capitalism, Socialism, and Democracy* (New York: Harper and Brothers, 1942).

5. See John Maynard Keynes, *The General Theory of Employment, Interest, and Money* (New York: Harcourt, Brace, 1936).

6. See Robert Heilbroner, *21st Century Capitalism* (New York: W. W. Norton, 1993), pp. 54–55.

7. Adam Smith, *Wealth of Nations* (New York: Modern Library, 1937), p. 734.

9. RELIGION AND THE ARTS

1. John Dewey, *A Common Faith* (New Haven, Conn.: Yale University Press, 1934), pp. 15–14.

2. John Dewey, *Art as Experience* (New York: G. P. Putnam's Sons: A Perigee Book, 1980 [1934]), p. 195.

3. George Steiner, *George Steiner: A Reader* (New York Oxford University Press, 1984), p. 8.

4. Ibid., p. 8.

5. See Raymond Williams, *The Long Revolution* (New York: Harper and Row,, 1966), pp. 47–48.

6. W. T. Stace, "Man Against Darkness," *Atlantic Monthly,* vol. 182 (September 1948), p. 58.

7. William Shakespeare, *Macbeth,* 5.5.17.

8. See "Jesus Travels to India," by Dr. Aziz Ahmad Chowdhrary, *The Review of Religion* (European Edition), vol. 80, no. 8 (August 1985): pp. 6–14. A monthly magazine devoted to the dissemination of the teaching of Islam.

9. See E. M. Adams, *Religion and Cultural Freedom* (Philadelphia: Temple University Press, 1993), p. 171.

10. See Leo Tolstoy, *My Confession,* trans. Leo Wiener (London: J. M. Dent and Sons, 1905).

10. TOWARD A HUMANISTIC REVOLUTION

1. Robert Nisbet, *History of the Idea of Progress* (New York: Basic Books, 1980), p. 383.

2. Ibid., p. 317.

3. Much of this paragraph is repeated from E. M. Adams, *Religion and Cultural Freedom* (Philadelphia: Temple University Press, 1993), p. 178.

4. Marshall Berman, *All That Is Solid Melts Into Air* (New York: Simon Schuster, 1982), p. 345.

5. Ernest Gellner, *Legitimation of Belief* (Cambridge: Cambridge University Press, 1974), p. 194–95.

6. Ibid., p. 207.

7. Most of this paragraph is repeated from my *The Metaphysics of Self and World* (Philadelphia: Temple University Press, 1991), p. 10.

8. George Sessions, ed., *Deep Ecology for the 21st Century,* (Boston and London: Shambhala, 1995).

9. Daniel Goleman, *Emotional Intelligence* (New York: Bantam Books, 1995), p. x.

10. See especially Roberto Unger, *Knowledge and Politics* (New York: Free Press, 1975); Daniel Bell, *The Cultural Contradictions of Capitalism* (New York: Basic Books, 1976); Christopher Lasch, *The Culture of Narcissism* (New York: W. W. Norton, 1978) and *The Minimal Self* (New York: W. W. Norton, 1984); Alasdair MacIntyre, *After Virtue* (Notre Dame, Inc.: University of Notre Dame Press, 1981); Robert Bellah, Richard Madsen, William M. Sullivan, Ann Swindler, and Steven M. Tipton, *Habits of the Heart* (Berkeley: University of California Press, 1985) and *The Good Society* (New York: Alfred A. Knopf, 1991); Michael Lerner, *The Politics of Meaning* (Reading, Mass.: Addison-Wesley, 1996); and I will add my own *Ethical Naturalism and the Modern World-View* (Chapel Hill: University of North Carolina Press, 1960; Westport, Conn.:

Greenwood Press, 1973, 1985), *Philosophy and the Modern Mind* (Chapel Hill: University of North Carolina Press, 1975; Lanham, Md.: University Press of America, 1985), *The Metaphysics of Self and World* (Philadelphia: Temple University Press, 1991), and *Religion and Cultural Freedom* (Philadelphia: Temple University Press, 1993).

11. Barbara Tuchman, *A Distant Mirror* (New York: Ballatine Books, 1978).

APPENDIX A

* For a fuller account, see my *Ethical Naturalism and the Modern World-View,* 1960, 1973, 1985; *Philosophy and the Modern Mind: A Philosophical Critique of Modern Western Civilization,* 1975, 1985; and *The Metaphysics of Self and World: Toward a Humanistic Philosophy,* 1991.

index

NOTE ON

SUPPORTING CENTER

This series is published under the auspices of the Center for Process Studies, a research organization affiliated with the Claremont School of Theology and Claremont University Center and Graduate School. It was founded in 1973 by John B. Cobb, Jr., founding director, and David Ray Griffin, executive director; Mary Elizabeth Moore and Marjorie Suchocki are now also co-directors. It encourages research and reflection on the process philosophy of Alfred North Whitehead, Charles Hartshorne, and related thinkers, and on the application and testing of this viewpoint in all areas of thought and practice. This center sponsors conferences, welcomes visiting scholars to use its library, and publishes a scholarly journal, *Process Studies,* and a newsletter, *Process Perspectives.* Located at 1325 North College, Claremont, California 91711, it gratefully accepts (tax-deductible) contributions to support its work.